RECOGNITION OF
WHITEBOARD *NOTES*

Online, Offline and Combination

SERIES IN MACHINE PERCEPTION AND ARTIFICIAL INTELLIGENCE*

Editors: **H. Bunke** (Univ. Bern, Switzerland)
P. S. P. Wang (Northeastern Univ., USA)

*For the complete list of titles in this series, please write to the Publisher.

Series in Machine Perception and Artificial Intelligence – Vol. 71

RECOGNITION OF WHITEBOARD *NOTES*

Online, Offline and Combination

Marcus Liwicki
DFKI GmbH, Germany

Horst Bunke
University of Bern, Switzerland

World Scientific

NEW JERSEY • LONDON • SINGAPORE • BEIJING • SHANGHAI • HONG KONG • TAIPEI • CHENNAI

Published by

World Scientific Publishing Co. Pte. Ltd.

5 Toh Tuck Link, Singapore 596224

USA office: 27 Warren Street, Suite 401-402, Hackensack, NJ 07601

UK office: 57 Shelton Street, Covent Garden, London WC2H 9HE

British Library Cataloguing-in-Publication Data
A catalogue record for this book is available from the British Library.

Series in Machine Perception and Artificial Intelligence — Vol. 71
RECOGNITION OF WHITEBOARD NOTES
Online, Offline and Combination

ISBN-13 978-981-281-453-1
ISBN-10 981-281-453-1

Printed in Singapore.

Marcus Liwicki dedicates this book to Nicole
Horst Bunke dedicates this book to Helga

Preface

This book addresses the issue of processing online handwritten notes acquired from an electronic whiteboard. Notes written on a whiteboard is a new modality in handwriting recognition research that has received relatively little attention in the past. The main motivation for this book is smart meeting room applications, where not only speech and video data of a meeting are recorded, but also notes written on a whiteboard are captured. The aim of a smart meeting room is to automate standard tasks usually performed by humans in a meeting. In order to allow for retrieval of the meeting data by means of a browser, semantic information needs to be extracted from the raw sensory data.

The main achievements of this book can be summarized as follows. A new online handwritten database has been compiled, and four handwriting recognition systems have been developed. These are an offline and an online recognition system, a system combining offline and online data, and a writer-dependent recognition system. The online recognition system includes novel preprocessing and normalization strategies which have been developed especially for whiteboard notes. A novel classification strategy based on bidirectional long short-term memory networks has been applied for the first time in the field of handwriting recognition. In the combination experiments both the offline and online system were integrated into a single recognizer. To the best of the authors' knowledge these are the first experiments in the field of online sentence recognition combining systems based on offline and online features. Furthermore, external recognition systems were included in the combination experiments. The experimental results on the test set show a highly significant improvement of the recognition performance over the individual systems. The optimal combination achieved a word level accuracy of more than 86 %, implying a relative error reduction of about 26 %, compared to the best individual classifier.

The first author would like to thank many colleagues of the Institute of Computer Science and Applied Mathematics at the University of Bern, Switzerland, who have made inestimable contributions to this work. Roman Bertolami, Dr. Simon Günther, Christoph Hofer, Dr. Christophe Irniger, Vivian Kilchherr, Dr. Michel Neuhaus, Mathias Scherz, Barbara Spillmann, Dr. Tamás Varga, and Dr. Mathias Zimmermann – thank you very much. Special thanks go to Dr. Alex Graves and Dr. Andreas Schlapbach for their contributions to Sections 2.2 and 2.3, respectively, and other parts of this book. Thanks to Gemma for proofreading the manuscript. Furthermore, the authors owe many thanks to persons of other institutions for useful discussions and contributions. These are Samy Bengio, Maël Guillemot, Stefan Knerr, Johnny Mariéthoz, Darren More, Jay Pittman, Jonas Richiardi, Markus Schenkel, Pierre Wellner, and all volunteers who took the time for participating in the recordings for the IAM-OnDB. Part of the work described in this book is based on the first authors's PhD thesis. Many thanks are due to Prof. Hanspeter Bieri for chairing the PhD defence and to Prof. Ching Y. Suen for being an external reviewer. Additional thanks go to Joachim Schenk, who re-implemented the HMM-based system and validated the recognition results. Last but not least the first author thanks his parents who supported him in the beginning of his stay in Switzerland. Finally, special thanks to Nicole who accompanies him in the ups and downs of life.

Furthermore, the authors would like to acknowledge partial funding by the Swiss National Science Foundation NCCR program *Interactive Multimodal Information Management IM2* in the individual project *Visual/Video Processing*.

Marcus Liwicki and Horst Bunke
May 2008

Contents

List of Figures

List of Tables

Chapter 1

Introduction

In our everyday life we benefit from intelligent machines that accomplish many operations for us. Sometimes we are not even aware of how many intelligent devices aid us in performing common tasks, such as driving a car, buying goods with a credit card, booking a trip at a travel agency, or writing a document in an advanced text editor. It is a challenge to artificial intelligence to improve such systems to make life more comfortable.

One specific research area in artificial intelligence is the field of natural language processing (NLP). NLP aims to automate generation and understanding of natural human languages, i.e., to convert information from computer databases into human language and vice versa. The automated transcription of written or spoken data into a machine readable format is closely related to this field. This is an essential step to understand human language. The research community focuses on speech recognition, machine printed text recognition, and handwritten text recognition. Assuming Roman script, the latter sub-field can be further divided into isolated character recognition, cursive word recognition, and cursive word sequence recognition. While there already exist mature solutions for isolated character recognition, cursive word sequence recognition is the most complex task in the field of handwriting recognition of Roman script.

This book considers a relatively new task, the recognition of text written on a whiteboard. As people stand, rather than sit, during writing and the arm does not rest on a table, handwriting rendered on a whiteboard is different from handwriting produced with a pen on a writing tablet. It has been observed that the baseline of handwritten text usually cannot be interpolated with a simple polynomial up to degree 2. Furthermore, the size and width of the characters often tend to become smaller as the writer moves to the right.

Fig. 1.1   Picture of the IDIAP Smart Meeting Room with the whiteboard to the left of
the presentation screen

This chapter first describes the motivation of the work described in this
book and embeds the topic into the context of smart meeting room research
in Section 1.1. Second, in Section 1.2 a detailed overview of related research
in handwriting recognition is presented including recent work and studies.
Next, Section 1.3 states issues that need to be considered when comparing
the results of different recognition systems with each other. Other topics in
the area of handwriting are outlined in Section 1.4. Following, Section 1.5
describes the contributions of this book, and finally, Section 1.6 outlines
the remaining chapters.

1.1   Motivation

The main motivation of this book is to develop smart meeting room applications [McCowan *et al.* (2005); Moore (2002); Reiter and Rigoll (2004);
Waibel *et al.* (2003)] which are described in Section 1.1.1. Handwriting
recognition of whiteboard notes can also be applied to recorded lectures.
For example, the E-Chalk system [Friedland *et al.* (2004); Rojas *et al.*

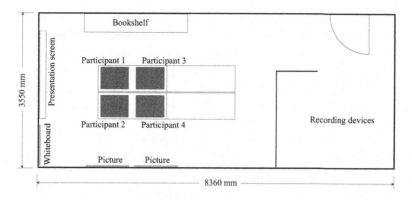

Fig. 1.2   Schematic overview of the IDIAP Smart Meeting Room (top view)

(2001)] is a platform independent recording system for lectures involving an electronic whiteboard. While recognition systems for specific data, such as mathematical formulas [Tapia and Rojas (2003)] or symbols [Liwicki and Knipping (2005)], already exist, a recognition system for unconstrained handwriting is still an open issue.[1]

Throughout this book linguistic knowledge is supplied to the recognition system in forms of a lexicon and a statistical language model. This is mainly motivated by the observation that humans also have a higher reading performance if they know the language. A detailed description and an example are given in Section 1.1.2.

1.1.1   *Smart Meeting Rooms*

In smart meeting room applications not only speech and video data of a meeting are recorded, but also notes written on a whiteboard are captured. The aim of a smart meeting room is to automate standard tasks usually performed by humans in a meeting. These tasks include, for instance, note taking and extracting important issues of a meeting. To accomplish these tasks, a smart meeting room is equipped with synchronized recording interfaces for audio, video, and handwritten notes. Figure 1.1 shows an example picture of a smart meeting room.

The challenges in smart meeting room research are manifold. In order

---

[1]The authors are aware that there exist commercial software for whiteboards, such as the whiteboard system from SMART© Technologies. However, these systems are often based on the Microsoft© HWR, which is also used in this book (see Chapter 6.

to allow indexing and browsing of the recorded data [Wellner *et al.* (2004)], speech [Morgan *et al.* (2001)], handwriting [Liwicki and Bunke (2005a)], and video recognition systems [Fasel and Luettin (2003)] need to be developed. Another task is the segmentation of the meeting into meeting events. This task can be addressed by using single specialized recognizers for the individual input modalities [Reiter and Rigoll (2004)] or by using the primitive features extracted from the data streams [McCowan *et al.* (2005)]. Further tasks are the extraction of non-lexical information such as prosody, voice quality variation, and laughter. To authenticate the meeting participants and to assign utterances and handwritten notes to their authors, identification and verification systems have been developed. They are based on speech [Mariéthoz and Bengio (2002)] and video interfaces [Grudin (2000); Sanderson and Paliwal (2003)] or on a combination of both [Czyz *et al.* (2003)].

The handwriting recognition system presented in this book has been developed for the IDIAP Smart Meeting Room [Moore (2002)]. This meeting room is able to record meetings with up to four participants. It is equipped with multiple cameras, microphones, electronic pens for note-taking, a projector, and an electronic whiteboard. A schematic overview of this meeting room is presented in Fig. 1.2. Note that the picture in Fig. 1.1 shows the same meeting room. The camera is located in the lower right corner of the schema, facing the whiteboard and the presentation screen on the left hand side.

The whiteboard shown in Figs. 1.1 and 1.2 is equipped with the eBeam[2] system, which acquires text written on the whiteboard in electronic format. A normal pen in a special casing is used to write on the board. The casing sends infrared signals to a triangular receiver attached in one of the corners of the whiteboard. The acquisition system outputs a sequence of (x, y)-coordinates representing the location of the pen-tip together with a time stamp for each location. An illustration of the data acquisition process is shown in Fig. 1.3.

1.1.2 *Human Performance*

If a human person is asked to transcribe a handwritten text, a high recognition performance is expected. Often the human recognition performance is seen as an upper bound on any automatic transcription system. The goal of the automated recognition is to process the data with the same or

---

[2]eBeam© system by Luidia©, Inc. – www.e-Beam.com

Fig. 1.3 Recording session with the data acquisition device positioned in the upper left corner of the whiteboard

nearly the same accuracy as humans [Bunke (2003); Plamondon and Srihari (2000); Vinciarelli (2002)].

However, a high performance is only achieved by the human person if he or she is familiar with the underlying language of the handwriting. To demonstrate this effect, an example text written by the same writer is presented in Figs. 1.4 and 1.5. The example is taken from "The Feynman Lectures" [Feynman *et al.* (1977)] available in English and in Hungarian. If the reader is not familiar with Hungarian the word recognition rate will drop to about 30 % in the second text, while it will be nearly perfect for the first text. Note that the # symbol in the transcription denotes that the writer has crossed out a word.

This example shows that the quality of the transcription is highly dependent on the linguistic background and the capability of understanding the text. It also follows that the recognition accuracy would be poor if only a character by character recognition is performed. Therefore it is wise to utilize linguistic knowledge in automatic transcription systems to improve the recognition performance. Generally speaking, the task specific knowledge has a significant impact on the resulting recognition performance.

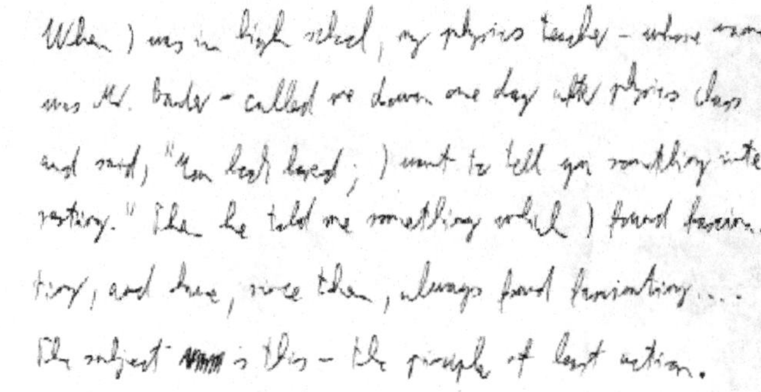

Fig. 1.4   Handwritten English text (transcription below)

When I was in high school, my physics teacher - whose name
was Mr. Bader - called me down one day after physics class
and said, "You look bored; I want to tell you something interesting."
Then he told me something which I found fascinating,
and have, since then, always found fascinating....
The subject # is this - the principle of least action.

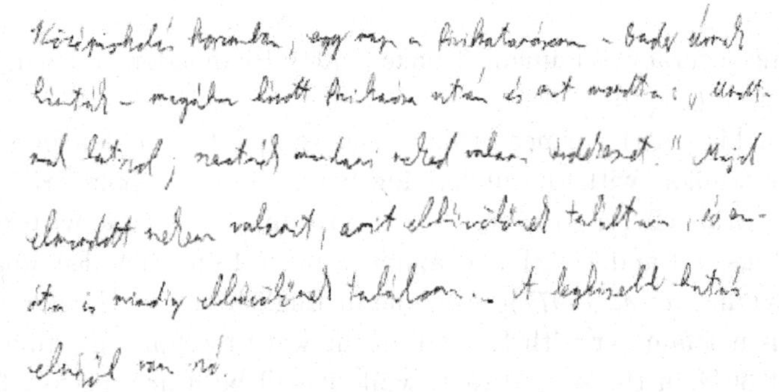

Fig. 1.5   Handwritten Hungarian text written by the same writer as in Figure 1.4
(transcription below)

Középiskolás koromban, egy nap a fizikatanárom - Bader úrnak hivták
- magához hívott fizikaóra után és azt mondta: "Unottnak látszol; sz-
eretnék mondani neked valami érdekeset." Majd elmondott valamit, amit
elbûvõlõnek találtam, és azóta is mindig elbûvõlõnek találom ... A legkisebb
hatás elvérõl van szó.

1.2 Handwriting Recognition

Handwriting recognition is the transcription of handwritten data into a digital format. It is a classical pattern recognition problem. The task lies in assigning a pattern to one class out of a set of classes [Duda *et al.* (2001)], for example, assigning a handwritten sample to a specific character. As stated above, the goal of the automated recognition is to process the data with the same or nearly the same accuracy as humans. Although automated handwriting recognition has been a research topic for more than forty years [Bunke (2003); Plamondon and Srihari (2000); Vinciarelli (2002)], there are still many open challenges in this field, especially in the domain of unconstrained handwritten text line recognition.

The handwritten data may be present in online or offline format. In the case of online recognition, a time ordered sequence of coordinates, representing the pen movement, is available. This may be produced by any electronic sensing device, such as a mouse, an electronic pen on a tablet, or a camera recording gestures. In the case of offline recognition, only the image of the text is present, which usually is scanned or photographed from paper.

In this section an overview of offline and online handwriting recognition and its applications is presented. First, Section 1.2.1 describes the main units for recognition systems. Next, in Section 1.2.2 related work for the offline case is given and discussed. Finally, the online case is treated in Section 1.2.3.

1.2.1 *Recognition System Overview*

A recognition system for unconstrained Roman script is usually divided into consecutive units which iteratively process the handwritten input data to finally obtain the transcription. The main units are illustrated in Fig. 1.6 and summarized in this section. Certainly, there are differences between offline and online processing, but the principles are the same. Only the methodology for performing the individual steps differs.

The first unit is preprocessing, where the input is raw handwritten data and the output usually consists of extracted text lines. The amount of effort that need to be invested into the preprocessing depends on the given data. If the data have been acquired from a system that does not produce any noise and only single words have been recorded, there is nothing to do in this step. But usually the data contains noise which need to be removed

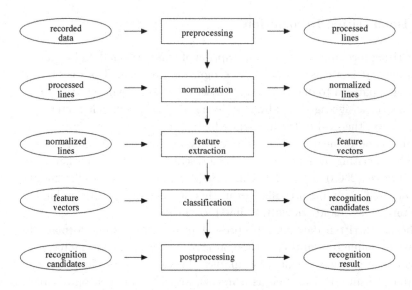

Fig. 1.6   Recognition system overview

to improve the quality of the handwriting. Another preprocessing step is the extraction of the handwritten text lines [Kavallieratou *et al.* (2002); Li *et al.* (2006); Liwicki *et al.* (2007b); Manmatha and Rothfeder (2005); Yu and Jain (1996)], which may also include the separation of text and graphics [Rossignol *et al.* (2004); Shilman *et al.* (2003); Wenyin (2003)]. Depending on the recognition system, the preprocessing may also include word extraction [Kavallieratou *et al.* (2002); Kim *et al.* (2002); Liwicki *et al.* (2006a); Mahadevan and Srihari (1996); Varga and Bunke (2005)] and even character segmentation [Kavallieratou *et al.* (2002); Tappert *et al.* (1990)].

However, the task of character segmentation is especially difficult if considered separately. This is because a word often can not be correctly segmented before it has been recognized, and can not be recognized without previously segmenting it into characters. This phenomenon is known as Sayre's paradox [Sayre (1973)].

After preprocessing, the recorded data need to be normalized. This is a very important part of handwriting recognition systems, because the writing styles of the writers differ with respect to skew, slant, height, and width of the characters. In the literature there is no standard way of normalizing the data, but many systems use similar techniques. First, the text line is corrected in regard to its skew, i.e., it is rotated, so that the baseline is

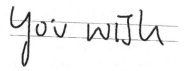

Fig. 1.7   Baseline and corpus line of a part of an example text line

parallel to the x-axis. Then, slant correction is performed so that the slant becomes upright. The next important step is the computation of the baseline and the corpus line (see Fig. 1.7). These two lines divide the text into three areas: the upper area, which mainly contains the ascenders of the letters; the middle area, where the corpus of the letters is present; and the lower area with the descenders of some letters. These three areas are normalized to predefined heights. Often, some additional normalization steps are performed, depending on the domain. In offline recognition, thinning and binarization may be applied. In online recognition the delayed strokes, e.g., the crossing of a "t" or the dot of an "i", are usually removed, and equidistant resampling is applied.

In general, normalization can be seen as a special preprocessing step, i.e., the data are processed before the recognition takes place. Because of this reason the normalization is sometimes not treated separately from the preprocessing in the literature. Depending on the point of view even the following step, feature extraction, may be seen as a preprocessing operation for the classifier.

Feature extraction is essential for any handwriting recognition system, for any classifier needs numeric data as input. However, no standard method for computing the features exists in the literature. One common method in offline recognition of handwritten text lines is the use of a sliding window moving in the writing direction over the text [Marti and Bunke (2001c)]. Features are extracted at every window position, resulting in a sequence of feature vectors. In the case of online recognition the points are already available in a time-ordered sequence, which makes it easier to get a sequence of feature vectors in writing order. If there is a fixed size of the input pattern, such as in character or word recognition, one feature vector of a fixed size can be extracted [Bunke (2003); Suen *et al.* (2000)] for each pattern.

After feature extraction, the same methods can be used for offline and online recognition. The next unit is the classification of the input features.

If there is a fixed length feature vector, neural networks [Lee (1996); Oh and Suen (2002)], support vector machines [Bahlmann *et al.* (2002)], nearest neighbor classifiers [Liu and Nakagawa (2001)], and other techniques can be applied. For sequences of feature vectors, *hidden Markov models* (HMMs) [Bunke *et al.* (1995)], *time delay neural networks* (TDNNs) [Jäger *et al.* (2001)], or hybrid approaches [Brakensiek *et al.* (1999); Caillault *et al.* (2005b); Marukatat *et al.* (2001); Rigoll *et al.* (1998); Schenkel *et al.* (1995)] can be used for classification. The output is a single recognition result or a list of alternative candidates. This list usually includes a probability for each output candidate.

The last recognition step illustrated in Fig. 1.6 is the postprocessing. This step is only possible if additional knowledge about the domain is available. For example, in the case of word recognition, the output sequence of characters can be assigned to the most similar word in the dictionary. In the case of word sequence recognition, statistical language models can be applied.

1.2.2 *Offline Handwriting Recognition*

In offline handwriting recognition the data which are to be transcribed have usually been scanned and stored as an image. A large variety of problems have been considered in research, and also some commercial systems have been developed. For example, there exist systems for postal address reading [Srihari (2000)] as well as for bank check [Impedovo *et al.* (1997)] and forms processing [Gopisetty *et al.* (1996); Ye *et al.* (2001)]. These systems take advantage of prior knowledge, working in narrow domains with limited vocabularies, where task specific knowledge and constraints are available.

In this section recent studies in offline handwriting recognition are described. Many systems have been developed in the last few decades, and one could think that the problem of offline handwriting recognition should already be solved. However, there is an increasing interest in the research community, as, in fact, many issues are unsolved in this field. This section focuses on some aspects only; for a complete overview of early work in this domain see [Bunke (2003); Plamondon and Srihari (2000); Steinherz *et al.* (1999); Suen *et al.* (2000); Vinciarelli (2002)].

One research direction in recent years is the combination of multiple classifiers. A study combining twelve different classifiers and evaluating several combination schemes has been published in [K. Sirlantzis and Hoque (2001)]. An in-depth investigation of different ensemble methods based on modifications of the training set has been performed in [Günter and Bunke (2004b)], where an improved recognition rate has been achieved for sufficiently large training sets. In [Bertolami and Bunke (2005)] multiple classifier system techniques have been used for the first time to unconstrained handwritten text line recognition. A new language model based approach has been used to automatically generate classifiers, and the ROVER [Fiscus (1997)] scheme for combination has been applied to handwritten word sequence recognition.

Many studies focus on improving existing classifiers. New algorithms have been published for each stage of the general recognition system depicted in Fig. 1.6. In the preprocessing stage some recent works concentrate on image enhancement [Shi and Govindaraju (2004)]. For normalization, a nonuniform slant correction method has been proposed in [Taira *et al.* (2004)]. A novel 2D approach for feature extraction and for classification has been introduced in [Chevalier *et al.* (2005)]. There are many other approaches for recognition which have been published recently [Brakensiek *et al.* (1999); Choisy and Belaïd (2000); Rigoll *et al.* (1998)]. Consequently there is a wide spectrum of classifiers available.

A specific topic is automated word spotting, where a given word need to be found in handwritten documents. This is useful to search in a large number of handwritten manuscripts for which the transcription is not available. Several new approaches have been proposed in recent years [Ball *et al.* (2006); Rath and Manmatha (2003)]. Related to this topic is the problem of mapping a given transcription to handwritten text [Huang and Srihari (2006); Zimmermann and Bunke (2002a)], which is also useful for historical document indexing if the transcription, e.g., a published book based on the manuscript, is available but not linked to the handwriting.

An emerging research topic is document image analysis for digital libraries. Recently, the first workshop on this topic was held [Baird and Govindaraju (2004)]. The workshop was devoted to new technologies that help integrating scanned and encoded documents into digital libraries, so that ideally everything that can be done with encoded documents is also possible for scanned documents. An essential part of preprocessing is document layout analysis [Kennard and Barrett (2006); Srihari and Kim (1997); Srihari and Shi (2004)], where the structure of a document is investigated and the text is located. Another contribution to this workshop is a systematic approach of recognizing words in historical documents [Lavrenko *et al.* (2004)], where a fixed-length feature vector is extracted for each word and the recognition is performed with hidden Markov models (HMMs). The topic of text alignment also plays an important role for digital libraries [Kornfield *et al.* (2004)].

1.2.3 *Online Handwriting Recognition*

In online handwriting recognition the data to be transcribed are acquired with an electronic interface, such as a mouse or an electronic pen on a tablet. Thus a time ordered sequence of points representing the location of the tip of the pen is available. In some cases, even the pressure, the tilt, and the angle of the pen are known for each point. During the last two decades a significant growth of activities in online handwriting recognition research has occurred. For the task of isolated character and digit recognition, high recognition rates have been reported. In this field highly accurate commercial systems have also become available, such as recognizers running on PDAs. However, in the case of general word or sentence recognition, where no constraints are given and the lexicon is large, the state of the art is still limited and recognition rates are rather low. While this section gives an overview of important milestones and recent work, complete surveys are available in [Tappert *et al.* (1990); Plamondon and Srihari (2000)].

In the field of online isolated character recognition much research has been done [Tappert *et al.* (1990)]. A writer-dependent method for symbol recognition has been proposed in [Wilfong *et al.* (1996)], where the user defines arbitrary symbols that are to be recognized. This method assumes that the user always writes a given symbol in the same stroke order and direction. Motivated by the domain of speech recognition, HMMs have also been applied to isolated character recognition. In [Hu *et al.* (2000)], for example, a writer-independent approach has been proposed. It was evaluated on the UNIPEN database [Guyon *et al.* (1994)], which also served as a test bed in the following references of this paragraph. A hybrid technique called *cluster generative statistical dynamic time warping* (CSDTW) has been introduced in [Bahlmann and Burkhardt (2004)]. CSDTW combines dynamic time warping with HMMs. It embeds clustering and statistical sequence modeling in a single feature space. Recently, in [Bahlmann *et al.* (2002)] an approach based on *support vector machines* with a novel Gaussian dynamic time warping kernel has been proposed, which gives similar accuracies as the HMM-based approach. Depending on the number of characters in the test set, the error rates range from 3 % (digits) to about 10 % (lower case characters).

Compared to cursive handwritten word and sentence recognition, the task of isolated character recognition is considered to be rather simple. In spite of Sayre's paradox, many segmentation-based approaches have been developed. Common approaches for character segmentation are based on unsupervised learning and data-driven knowledge-based methods [Plamondon and Srihari (2000)]. Other strategies first segment the text into basic strokes rather than characters. These methods are usually based on special techniques, such as splitting a word at the minima of the velocity, at the minima of the y-coordinates, or at the location of maximum curvature. For example, an approach which first segments the data at the points of the minima of the y-coordinates and then applies self-organizing maps has been presented in [Schomaker (1993)]. Another approach [Kavallieratou et al. (2002)] uses the minima of the vertical histogram for an initial estimation of the character boundaries and then applies various heuristics to improve the segmentation.

To avoid the problem of segmenting words into characters, some systems have been developed which use the words directly as target recognition symbols. One of these systems is described in [Wilfong et al. (1996)], where only a small set of 32 words was used for testing. Despite the small vocabulary, a rather high error rate of 4.5 % for writer-dependent recognition was reported. One of the main reasons is that the order of writing strokes differs even when the same writer is writing a word. For larger vocabularies the expected error is even higher. Another drawback of using the words as targets is that each word must be present in the training set, which makes the acquisition of a database unfeasible for large vocabularies. The conclusion is that it is better to model characters individually.

A widely accepted technology to overcome the problem of segmenting a word into its constituent characters is the use of HMMs [Hu et al. (1996)]. The idea of using HMMs is motivated by previous experiences in speech recognition [Rabiner (1989)]. Each character is represented by one single HMM. The models are then concatenated resulting in models for complete words from a given dictionary. Early work addressing the use of HMMs for online word recognition has been presented in [Bercu and Lorette (1993); Starner et al. (1994); Hu et al. (1996)]. The approach of [Hu et al. (2000)] proposes an advanced writer-independent HMM-based system. It combines point oriented and stroke oriented features to obtain an improved accuracy.

Recurrent neural networks (RNNs) are powerful sequence learners that are, in principle, capable of approximating any sequence-to-sequence mapping to any arbitrary precision [Haykin (1994)]. One of their main advantages is the ability to access contextual information, an important asset for handwriting recognition. This is particularly true for state-of-the-art RNN architectures, such as *bidirectional long short-term memory* (BLSTM) [Graves and Schmidhuber (2005)]. Nevertheless, there have been only few previous applications of RNNs to handwriting recognition [Bourbakis (1995)], and these have used neural networks to classify individual characters only.

To combine the advantages of neural networks and HMMs, hybrid approaches have been developed. Hybrid systems use HMMs to model long-range dependencies in the data and neural networks to provide localized classifications. Hybrid approaches which use RNNs combined with HMMs have been proposed in [Senior and Robinson (1998); Rigoll *et al.* (1998); Schenk and Rigoll (2006)]. There exist also a number of hybrid approaches based on other forms of neural networks. Classical neural networks have been used for state modeling in [Marukatat *et al.* (2001)]. Time delay neural networks combined with HMMs have been applied to online word recognition in [Schenkel *et al.* (1995)]. The application of a similar hybrid approach as in [Schenkel *et al.* (1995)] has been proposed in [Jäger *et al.* (2001)] on an advanced feature set. This application has further been improved with pruning techniques, enabling it to be used in real-time with large dictionaries. A more detailed analysis of TDNN/HMM systems is given in [Caillault *et al.* (2005a)].

Another important issue in the field of online handwriting recognition is the extraction of handwritten text. In [Shilman *et al.* (2003)] a system for extracting text from documents written on a tablet PC has been presented. This system uses the time stamps to derive an initial guess about the text line locations, and groups the lines and blocks afterwards. Then a set of local and global features is extracted and classified using a decision tree. A similar task is the detection of modes, e.g., drawings, text, and gestures, in an interactive pen-based system. A system that distinguishes between three modes (*drawing, text,* and *gesture*) has been presented in [Rossignol *et al.* (2004)].

Recently, approaches for combining online and offline handwritten data have been proposed. The combination of online and offline Japanese characters has been studied in [Velek *et al.* (2003)]. For isolated digits a combination has been investigated in [Vinciarelli and Perrone (2003)]. Both approaches show a significant increase in recognition performance. Hence, combining online and offline recognizers for handwritten text lines is a promising idea, which is also investigated in this book.

1.3 Comparability of Recognition Results

In the field of handwriting recognition a large number of studies have been published. The reported recognition results range from values lower than 50 % up to nearly 100 %. Sometimes even a perfect recognition rate has been achieved in specific environments. However, it is nearly impossible to identify a universally best recognition system. In general, a single recognition system which performs best for all tasks cannot exist, for each level of generalization causes a loss of knowledge in specific domains. For example, if a postal address in a specific country needs to be recognized, the system can take advantage of the knowledge of possible city and zip code relations to improve the accuracy. Of course, it may be possible to apply an initial preprocessing step recognizing the specific domain first, but all preprocessing steps produce errors, which limits the possible overall recognition accuracy.

In short, three problem areas in comparing results from different systems with one another exist: the considered recognition task, which defines the overall difficulty of the problem; the data set, which usually differs from other data sets in quality and quantity of the data; and the amount of data used for training and testing. In the remainder of this section a detailed description of the three problems is provided.

The performance of a system crucially depends on the considered task. For example, in the case of isolated digit recognition the performance is usually higher than in unconstrained handwritten text line recognition. When comparing recognition results, one must be aware of the following aspects:

- *number of classes*: With an increasing number of classes the task becomes more difficult. In character recognition, for example, it is assumed that recognizing ten different digits produces higher classification results than recognizing all the 25×2 letters of the Latin alphabet.
- *input (isolated vs. sequence)*: The task becomes easier if the boundaries of the characters are known, in which case a recognition system for isolated characters can be applied instead of a word recognizer.
- *vocabulary size*: As a rule of thumb, a higher performance can be expected for smaller vocabulary sizes under the constraint that the vocabulary covers all data in the test set.

- *number of writers*: The most difficult task is writer-independent recognition, i.e., when there is no training data available of the writers represented in the test set. For writer-dependent recognition it must be considered whether there is one recognition system for only one writer or for a number of writers.
- *language model*: Recognition systems can gain additional information from statistical language models. One can expect higher recognition rates from systems utilizing a language model.

These elementary facts are well known in the research community. However, there are many publications which do not clearly state all of the relevant details and therefore make it difficult to use them as a reference.

The second important issue is the data set used for evaluating the system. If the database is not publicly available, it is impossible to make a direct comparison of the results. Therefore it is important that existing databases for training and testing are shared in the research community. There are some databases which are publicly available. The UNIPEN database [Guyon *et al.* (1994)] is a large online handwriting database. It contains mostly isolated characters, single words, and a few sentences on several topics. Another online word database is IRONOFF [Viard-Gaudin *et al.* (1999)]. It additionally contains the scanned images of the handwritten words. For the task of offline handwriting recognition there are also databases available, including CEDAR [Hull (1994)], created for postal address recognition, NIST [Wilkinson *et al.* (1992)], containing image samples of hand printed characters, CENPARMI [Lee (1996)], consisting of handwritten numerals, and the IAM-DB [Marti and Bunke (2002)], a large collection of unconstrained handwritten sentences. All these databases vary in the amount of data, the quality of the raw data, the quality of the transcription, and also in the range of possible applications. Therefore it should be considered which database, or which part of a database, is to be used to train and test a system when comparing performance results.

Even if the same data have been used and the same recognition task has been conducted, there may be differences in the difficulty of the task. Usually the training and test data are randomly selected from the database causing different recognition results. Another possible difference is the amount of data used for training and testing. Common experience is that the larger the training set is, the better the recognizer performs. An example of problematic comparability between several systems is the UNIPEN database. Many results have been reported on this database, but in most cases the data have been manually preprocessed and manually selected, which makes a comparison of the results difficult [Vuurpijl *et al.* (2004)].

Because of all these problems, it is useful to define benchmark tasks where all recognition conditions are described as precisely as possible. The data should be divided at least into a training and a test set, and possibly a validation set for validating training parameters. Both the recognition classes and the dictionary need to be listed.

1.4   Related Topics

In the field of document analysis there are several other topics related to handwriting recognition. This section addresses some of them.

The first important topic is writer identification and verification based on online and offline data, including signature verification. The task of writer identification is to assign a handwritten text sample to one specific writer out of a given set of writers, while the task of writer verification is to determine whether a given handwritten sample or a signature stems from a claimed writer or is a forgery. Surveys in this domain are given in [Gupta and McCabe (1997); Leclerc and Plamondon (1994); Plamondon and Lorette (1989); Plamondon and Srihari (2000)]. In recent works, various approaches based on dynamic time warping, neural networks, hidden Markov models, and Gaussian mixture models have been investigated [Feng and Wah (2003); Liwicki *et al.* (2006b); Richiardi and Drygajlo (2003)]. It is evident that writer identification can help the process of handwriting recognition, for if the writer is known, a writer-specific recognizer can be applied for recognition. A higher recognition accuracy can be expected from such a specific recognizer.

Another related topic is the recognition of hand-sketched figures. It has been a research topic for more than 20 years [Murase and Wakahara (1986)], and a number of systems using sketched inputs for various types of applications have been developed. The DENIM application [Lin *et al.* (2000)], for example, allows users to build web pages by drawing, SketchySPICE [Hong and Landay (2000)] is a simple-circuit CAD tool, Tahuti [Hammond and Davis (2002)] is used for creating UML diagrams by sketches, and AS-SIST [Alvarado and Davis (2006)] is a sketch-based CAD tool. A recognition system for hand-drawn diagrams that uses conditional random fields has been proposed in [Szummer and Qi (2004)]. For the E-Chalk system mentioned above, applications for the animation of algorithms [Esponda

Argüero (2004)], the simulation of biological and pulse-coded neural networks [Knipping (2005); Krupina (2005)], and the simulation of logic circuits [Liwicki and Knipping (2005)] have been realized.

A population of individuals can often be partitioned into sub-categories based on various criteria. Dividing a population into sub-categories is an interesting research topic for numerous reasons, for example, if one is only interested in one specific sub-category, or if specifically processing each sub-category leads to improved results. Especially the classification of gender from handwriting has been a research topic for many decades [Broom *et al.* (1929); Newhall (1926); Tenwolde (1934)]. Some automatic systems have been proposed in [Cha and Srihari (2001)], [Bandi and Srihari (2005)], and [Liwicki *et al.* (2007c)].

1.5   Contribution

The main contribution of this book is the development of recognition systems for online handwritten text written on a whiteboard. This is a novel task in the research community. A similar task has been considered in [Fink *et al.* (2001); Munich and Perona (1996)]. However, in [Fink *et al.* (2001); Munich and Perona (1996)] a video camera was employed to capture the handwriting, whereas the eBeam© interface based on infrared sensing is used in this book. This system is easier to use than a video camera and is less vulnerable to artifacts arising from poor lighting conditions, self-occlusion and low image resolution.

To be more specific, in the context of the research described in this book, a novel online handwritten database has been compiled, and four individual handwriting recognition systems have been developed. The four systems consist of an offline and an online recognition system, a system combining offline and online data, and a writer-dependent recognition system. A short summary of the contributions is provided in this section.

During the work described in this book the IAM Online Handwriting Database (IAM-OnDB) has been compiled [Liwicki and Bunke (2005b)]. This database is a large publicly available collection of online handwritten English text acquired from a whiteboard. In addition to the recorded data and its transcription, some information about the writers, which could be useful for future work, is stored in the IAM-OnDB. Two benchmark tasks have been defined for this database for comparison issues.

Moreover, an offline recognition system for handwritten text has been developed [Liwicki and Bunke (2005a)] which includes the optimization of several training parameters as well as the integration of a statistical language model. This system has been further investigated with respect to the influence of different training sets, and the size of the training data [Liwicki and Bunke (2007c)].

Next, a new online recognition system has been introduced [Liwicki and Bunke (2006)]. This system includes novel preprocessing and normalization strategies which have been developed especially for whiteboard notes. A recently introduced classification strategy based on bidirectional long short-term memory networks has been applied for the first time in the field of handwriting recognition [Liwicki *et al.* (2007a)].

A combination of online and offline approaches for handwriting recognition is investigated in this book as well [Liwicki and Bunke (2007a)]. In some initial experiments three HMM-based recognition systems have been combined. In a broader experimental study, more recognition systems have been included in the combination, involving external recognizers from Microsoft© and Vision Objects©.

Another main contribution of this book is the generation of writer-dependent recognition systems [Liwicki and Bunke (2008)]. For that purpose a writer identification system, which has been developed for offline writer identification, has been adapted to online features [Liwicki *et al.* (2006b); Schlapbach *et al.* (2008)]. Furthermore, the writer identification system has been used to investigate the problem of automatic handwriting classification [Liwicki *et al.* (2007c)].

1.6 Outline

The structure of this book is as follows. Chapter 2 reviews general methods used throughout this book. These methods are not a novel contribution, but their main ideas are important to understand the work described in the other chapters.

In Chapter 3 the main resources that have been used for training and testing the recognizers are introduced. One database, namely the IAM Online Handwriting Database, has been specifically compiled for the research described in this book. Thus this database is explained in more detail. Further resources for post-processing are also described in Chapter 3.

The offline recognition approach is introduced in Chapter 4. Various experiments with this recognition system and extended versions are reported.

The first results may be seen as baseline results for the experiments described in the remainder of this book.

Chapter 5 is devoted to the online recognition system. The description includes preprocessing, enhanced normalization for whiteboard notes, and feature extraction techniques. The results of various experiments on these features are discussed. The chapter also reports on feature selection experiments using the proposed feature set.

The combination of online and offline classifiers for handwritten text lines is investigated in Chapter 6. First, the focus is on combination and voting strategies. Next, experiments with several classifiers and combinations schemes are reported.

An approach based on writer-dependent recognition is introduced in Chapter 7. For this purpose, a writer identification system for handwritten whiteboard notes is proposed. Experiments based on an adaptation of the online recognizer are then reported. Furthermore, Chapter 7 also describes the handwriting classification experiments.

Finally, Chapter 8 provides the main conclusions of this book, shortly summarizes the results, and gives an outlook on future research.

Chapter 2

Classification Methods

Various methods from the field of pattern recognition have been used in the research described in this book. The purpose of this chapter is to summarize the main ideas of these methods, and to give an impression of how the algorithms work.

This chapter is organized as follows. First, hidden Markov models, which have been used in most of the experiments, are described in Section 2.1. Second, a short summary of neural networks and a detailed description of a novel classification system based on recurrent neural networks is provided in Section 2.2. Next, Section 2.3 gives a brief overview of Gaussian mixture models, which have been used for writer identification in the writer-dependent experiments. Finally, an introduction to statistical language models is given in Section 2.4.

2.1 Hidden Markov Models

Hidden Markov models (HMMs) are statistical models for sequence analysis. They were first used in the field of speech recognition and have been successfully adopted to handwriting recognition later. This section gives an introduction to HMMs. For a detailed description of HMMs and their application to speech recognition see [Rabiner (1989)].

The outline of this section is as follows. First, Section 2.1.1 gives the standard definition of HMMs. The methods for training and testing the models are described in Section 2.1.2. Finally, Section 2.1.3 lists important parameters which must be considered when applying HMMs to a pattern recognition task.

2.1.1   *Definition*

A hidden Markov model (HMM) λ is characterized by a five-tuple $\lambda = (S, V, A, B, \pi)$, where

(1) $S = \{S_1, \ldots, S_N\}$ is a set of hidden states. A state at a given time t is denoted as q_t.

(2) $V = \{v_1, \ldots, v_M\}$ is a set of distinct observation symbols per state. It is also called the *alphabet*.

(3) $A = \{a_{ij}|1 \leq i, j \leq N\}$ is the probability distribution of the state transitions represented as a matrix, where

$$a_{ij} = p(q_{t+1} = S_j | q_t = S_i) \tag{2.1}$$

is the probability that state S_j follows after state S_i. If a state cannot be reached from another state in a single step, the corresponding matrix element a_{ij} is set to zero.

(4) $B = \{b_j(k)|1 \leq j \leq N, 1 \leq k \leq M\}$ is the observation symbol probability distribution for the states, where

$$b_j(k) = p(v_k \text{ at } t | q_t = S_j) \tag{2.2}$$

is the probability that the observation symbol v_k is produced when the model is in state S_j.

(5) $\pi = \{\pi_i|1 \leq i \leq N\}$ is the initial state distribution where

$$\pi_i = p(q_1 = S_i) \tag{2.3}$$

is the probability that state S_i is an initial state.

Note that the transition probability matrix A and the observation probability matrix B are constant over time, i.e., a_{ij} and $b_j(k)$ do not depend on t. Only matrices A and B that correspond to valid probability distributions are considered. Often the compact notation $\lambda = (A, B, \pi)$ is used, because the number of states and observations can be derived from these three parameters.

An HMM can be used to generate an observation sequence X of length T. The observation sequence $X = x_1, \ldots, x_T$ (where $x_t \in V, 1 \leq t \leq T$) can be generated by a state sequence $Q = q_1, \ldots, q_T$ (where $q_t \in S, 1 \leq t \leq T$) of the HMM λ.

An HMM can be represented by a graph where the nodes are the states S_i and the edges are the state transition probabilities a_{ij}. A second set of nodes may be used for the observation symbols which are connected to the states by edges representing the observation probabilities $b_j(k)$. If any of

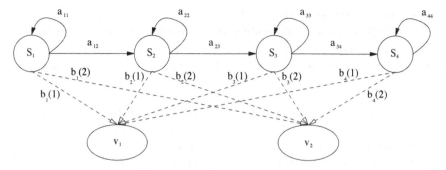

Fig. 2.1   Illustration of a hidden Markov model with four states and two observation symbols

the probabilities $a_{ij}, b_j(k)$ is zero, the corresponding edge can be removed. An illustration of an HMM represented by a graph is given in Fig. 2.1. This HMM consists of four states S_1, S_2, S_3, S_4 and produces two observations v_1, v_2. Note that in this example some state transition probabilities are set to zero, and the corresponding edges have been removed.

There exist a number of distinct types of HMMs defined by the structure of the state transition matrix A. The general case, where all matrix elements a_{ij} are greater than zero, is called *ergodic model*. In such a model, each state can be reached from every other state. Other types of HMMs are more suitable for applications in speech and handwriting processing. The *left-right model*, for example, has the property that the state index increases, or remains the same, with each forward movement of time, i.e., $a_{ij} = 0$ if $j < i$ and $\pi_1 = 1$. Thus it can easily model signals whose properties change over time, such as speech signals. A special type of left-right model is the *linear model*, where only state transitions from a state to itself and to the next state are allowed, i.e., $a_{ij} = 0$ if $i < j - 1$. The example shown in Fig. 2.1 is actually a linear model.

2.1.2   *Training and Testing*

For HMMs to be applicable to real-world tasks, three problems of interest need to be solved [Rabiner (1989)]. These problems are:

(1) Given an observation sequence $X = x_1, \ldots, x_T$ and a model $\lambda = (A, B, \pi)$, how can the probability of the observation sequence $p(X|\lambda)$, given the model λ, be computed in an efficient way?

(2) Given an observation sequence $X = x_1, \ldots, x_T$ and a model $\lambda = (A, B, \pi)$, how can a corresponding state sequence $Q = q_1, \ldots, q_T$ be chosen, which is optimal in some meaningful sense?

(3) How can the model parameters $\lambda = (A, B, \pi)$ be adjusted to maximize $p(X|\lambda)$?

For the solution of the first problem, there exists an efficient procedure that is based on induction. The algorithm is called *forward-backward algorithm*. It uses a forward variable $\alpha_t(i)$ which stores the probability of the partial observation sequence until time t and state S_i at time t, given the model λ:

$$\alpha_t(i) = p(x_1, \ldots, x_t, q_t = S_i|\lambda), 1 \le i \le N, 1 \le t \le T \qquad (2.4)$$

These values can be calculated inductively, starting at $t = 1$. The sum of all $\alpha_T(i)$ gives the desired probability $p(X|\lambda)$.

Using this forward calculation of the forward-backward algorithm, the first problem is already solved. However, for solving the other two problems, the backward calculation is also needed. Here, a backward variable $\beta_t(i)$ is used for storing temporal results:

$$\beta_t(i) = p(x_{t+1}, \ldots, x_T|q_t = S_i, \lambda), 1 \le i \le N, 1 \le t \le T \qquad (2.5)$$

Again the values can be calculated inductively, this time, however, starting at $t = T$.

For the second problem there are several possible definitions of an optimal state sequence. A suitable criterion is to find the single best valid state sequence, i.e., a state sequence which is possible according to λ and produces the output sequence X with highest probability among all other possible state sequences. With a modification of the forward calculation an efficient way of finding the best state sequence can be formulated. This dynamic programming-based method is called the *Viterbi algorithm* [Forney (1973)]. It is commonly used for finding the producing model in HMM-based speech and handwriting recognition.

The third problem is certainly the most difficult one. There exists no efficient optimal way of solving this problem. However, a suboptimal method does exist that iteratively maximizes $p(X|\lambda)$ by re-estimating, i.e., updating and improving, the model parameters of λ. This method is called *Baum–Welch algorithm* [Dempster *et al.* (1977)].

All methods described until now rely on the assumption that a discrete observation alphabet V is given. If the observations consist of continuous signal values it is advantageous to use HMMs with continuous observation

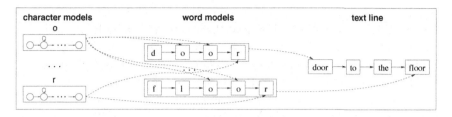

Fig. 2.2 Concatenated HMM for text line recogniton

densities. The methods described above can be adapted to the continuous case under certain restrictions on the probability density function. In most cases, Gaussian distributions are used because they fulfill the given restrictions and they are suitable for a variety of applications.

2.1.3 *Design Parameters*

In this section some design parameters which are important for HMM-based classification are described, and possible strategies for finding the best choice, especially in the field of handwriting recognition, are listed.

For any recognition task, it first must be decided which type of HMM is chosen. For handwriting recognition a linear topology is a common choice because handwriting is produced from left to right. Another issue is observation representation. In hybrid methods, discrete HMMs are often chosen for the second stage, because the first stage quantizes the signals. However, if only HMMs are used for the classification, continuous HMMs are preferred. The third essential design parameter is the number of models to be trained. If the alphabet is not too large, one HMM can be trained for each character or digit. Otherwise, the characters can be split into graphemes, which are shared among several characters, and one HMM can be trained for each grapheme.

In the application of handwritten word recognition there exist two strategies for choosing the HMMs. Under the first strategy one HMM is trained for each word in the dictionary. This strategy fails if there is a large number of words in the dictionary, because in this case there is not a sufficiently large amount of training data for each HMM. To overcome this problem, in the second strategy, one HMM is trained for each character that appears in the target lexicon. Then the character HMMs are concatenated according to each of the words in the dictionary. This also results in one (large) HMM for each dictionary word, but for training only samples for each character are needed, because the same HMMs are used for each occurrence of a letter in all the words. Furthermore, by taking additional language model information into account (see Section 2.4), word HMMs can be concatenated to HMMs for whole text lines. Figure 2.2 illustrates the process of concatenating the character HMMs in the first stage and then using the word HMMs for the concatenation in the second stage. Theoretically the number of HMMs in one text line is infinite, because the number of words can be increased without any limitation. This would result in an infinitive set of possible concatenations which is computationally impossible to handle. To overcome this problem, a token passing algorithm [Young *et al.* (1989)] is used during decoding of the text lines. Additionally a pruning parameter can be set to ignore all hypotheses with a low likelihood during decoding. This is useful to speed up the decoding process, but can also lead to a lower recognition rate because the correct alternative can get rejected at an early decoding stage.

Another design parameter which needs to be set is the number of states for each HMM. In the case of handwriting recognition it was shown that the recognition rate can be improved by allowing each character to have an individual number of states. There are several methods for optimizing the number of states, of which the Bakis method [Bakis (1976)] produced the best results in the handwriting recognition system of [Zimmermann and Bunke (2002b)]. The Bakis method sets the number of states for each character HMM to the average number of observation vectors multiplied with a constant f, which needs to be determined experimentally. Finding the optimal value of f can be done by measuring the recognition rate on a separate validation set.

It has been pointed out in [Günter and Bunke (2004a)] that the number of Gaussian mixtures and training iterations have an effect on the recognition results as well. Three strategies for jointly optimizing the number of Gaussian mixtures and training iterations are proposed. Under the strategy that obtained the best performance in [Günter and Bunke (2004a)] the number of Gaussian components is incremented stepwise by one. In each step, the optimal number of training iterations is found by testing the performance on a separate validation set. For the next step the best performing system is chosen. It has been observed that the optimal number of Gaussian components increases with an increasing amount of data since more variations are encountered.

2.1.4 *Adaptation*

HMM adaptation is a method to adjust the model parameters θ of a given background model λ to the parameters θ_{ad} of the adaptation set of observations X. The background model is usually trained on a large set of writers, while the adaptation set consists of a small amount of data, e.g., data from one specific writer only.

The aim is to find the vector θ_{ad} which maximizes the *posterior* distribution $p(\theta_{ad}|O)$:

$$\theta_{ad} = \underset{\theta}{\operatorname{argmax}}\, p(\theta|X) \tag{2.6}$$

Using Bayes theorem, $p(\theta|X)$ can be written as follows:

$$p(\theta|X) = \frac{p(X|\theta)p(\theta)}{p(X)} \tag{2.7}$$

where $p(X|\theta)$ is the likelihood of the HMM with parameter set θ, and $p(\theta)$ is the *prior* distribution of the parameters. When $p(\theta) = c$, i.e., when the prior distribution does not give any information about how likely θ is, *Maximum Likelihood Linear Regression* (MLLR) [Leggeter and Woodland (1995)] can be performed. If the prior distribution is informative, i.e., $p(\theta)$ is not a constant, the adapted parameters can be found by solving the equation:

$$\frac{\partial}{\partial \theta} p(X|\theta)p(\theta) = 0 \tag{2.8}$$

The aim of solving this equation is to minimize the Bayes risk over the adaptation set. This minimization can be done with *Maximum a Posteriori* (MAP) estimation, which is also called *Bayesian Adaptation*. As described in [Vinciarelli and Bengio (2002)], it is possible to adapt only the Gaussian means μ_{jm} (where m refers to the actual state and j is the index of the considered mixture in state m) of the parameters θ of each HMM. The use of conjugate priors then results in a simple adaptation formula:

$$\hat{\mu}_{jm} = \frac{N_{jm}}{N_{jm} + \tau}\bar{\mu}_{jm} + \frac{\tau}{N_{jm} + \tau}\mu_{jm} \tag{2.9}$$

where $\hat{\mu}_{jm}$ is the new mean and $\bar{\mu}_{jm}$ the old mean of the adaptation data, μ_{jm} is the mean of the background model, and N_{jm} is the sum of the probabilities of each observation in the adaptation set being emitted by the corresponding Gaussian. After each iteration the values of $\hat{\mu}_{jm}$ are used in the Gaussian mixtures, which leads to new values of $\bar{\mu}_{jm}$ and N_{jm} in Eq. (2.9). This procedure is repeated until the change in the parameters falls below a predefined threshold. The parameter τ weights the influence of the background model on the adaptation data. A large value of τ corresponds to more influence of the background model.

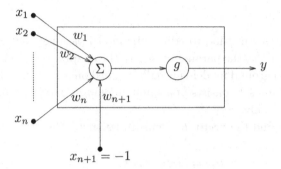

Fig. 2.3   Illustration of a perceptron

2.2   Neural Networks

Neural networks are a popular modeling technique in pattern recognition. They are inspired by the human central nervous system. Only the concepts that are important for the handwriting recognition task considered in this book are presented here. Especially the recently introduced bidirectional long short-term memory network combined with connectionist temporal classification is described in more detail, as it has been applied to the field of handwriting recognition for the first time in the context of the research described in this book. For an overview of general neural networks see [Haykin (1994); Rojas (1996)].

This section is structured as follows. First, a brief introduction to perceptron and multilayer perceptron networks is given in Section 2.2.1, followed by a short summary about recurrent neural networks in Section 2.2.2. Next, Section 2.2.3 is devoted to long short-term memories, and the idea of bidirectional neural networks is presented in Section 2.2.4. Finally, Section 2.2.5 focuses on connectionist temporal classification including a detailed description of the mathematical background. Note that Sections 2.2.2–2.2.5 closely follow the description given in [Graves *et al.* (2008)].

2.2.1   *Multilayer Perceptron Networks*

The basic unit of classic neural networks is the perceptron. The concept of a perceptron is motivated by neurons and their axons, dendrites, and synapses. A perceptron uses an input weight vector $x = (x_1, \ldots, x_n)$ and a vector $w = (w_1, \ldots, w_n)$. The output of a perceptron is calculated by an

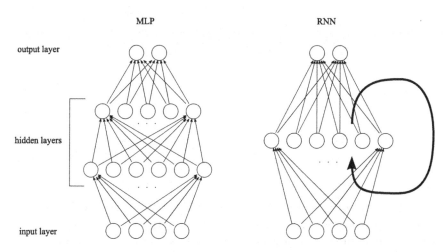

Fig. 2.4   Schematic illustration of the difference between a multilayer perceptron network and a recurrent neural network

activation function g:

$$y = g(\langle x, w \rangle) \tag{2.10}$$

where $\langle \cdot, \cdot \rangle$ is the standard dot product of two vectors.

The activation function g may be defined by a hard threshold, a linear threshold function, or a more complex function. Note that function g is also called *squashing function*. Often the sigmoid function $g(x) = 1/(1 + \exp(-x))$ is used, because it is differentiable and has the simple first derivative $g' = g(1 - g)$. To overcome the problem that this equation only holds for the threshold 0, an additional input $x_{n+1} = -1$ is added, such that its weight w_{n+1} becomes the actual threshold. This additional input is called *bias*. Figure 2.3 shows a common illustration of a general neuron with bias w_{n+1}.

Perceptrons are able to find a linear separating hyperplane between two classes if such a hyperplane exists. The corresponding algorithm is the *perceptron learning algorithm*. However, there are many cases where a single perceptron is not sufficient, i.e., where the classes are not linearly separable. An example of such a function, which is not linearly separable, is the XOR function.

To overcome the limitation of a single perceptron, *multilayer feedforward neural networks*, usually known as *multilayer perceptrons* (MLP), have been introduced. Such a network consists of several perceptron layers,

Fig. 2.5   Importance of context in handwriting recognition

where the outputs of the perceptrons of each layer are connected to the inputs of the perceptrons of the next layer. If all outputs of one layer are connected to all inputs of the next layer, the MLP is called a *fully connected* MLP. In Fig. 2.4 a schematic illustration of an MLP is given on the left hand side.

If the activation function is differentiable, the *backpropagation* algorithm can be used to train the MLP. To classify an unknown test sample, the network output can be calculated by feeding the feature vector of the test sample into the input layer of the network. For more details about neural networks and the algorithms mentioned in this section, see [Haykin (1994); Rojas (1996)].

2.2.2   *Recurrent Neural Networks*

If a hidden layer of a neural network contains recurrently connected network units, the network is called *recurrent neural network* (RNN).

The difference between RNNs and MLPs is illustrated in Fig. 2.4. One benefit of the recurrent connections is that a "memory" of previous inputs remains in the network's internal state, allowing it to make use of contextual information that would be difficult to access with MLPs or other non-sequential algorithms. Context is important for many sequence learning tasks, including handwriting recognition, as illustrated in Fig. 2.5. In this figure the word "defence" is clearly legible. However the letter "n" in isolation is ambiguous, i.e., it may be easily misclassified as a the letter "u", for example. Another important advantage of recurrency is that the rate of change of the internal state can be finely modulated by the recurrent weights, which builds in robustness to localized stretching and compression of the input data.

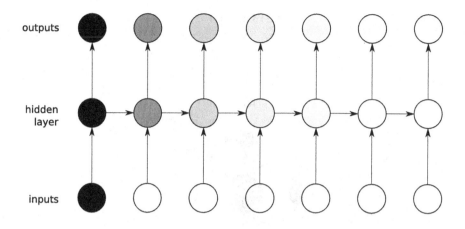

outputs

hidden
layer

inputs

Fig. 2.6   Illustration of the vanishing gradient problem on a single hidden node

2.2.3   *Long Short-Term Memory*

As mentioned above, an important benefit of RNNs is their ability to use
contextual information. Unfortunately, the range of context that standard
RNN architectures can access is limited. The problem is that the influence
of a given input on the hidden layer, and therefore on the network output, either decays or grows exponentially as it cycles around the network's
recurrent connections, and is repeatedly scaled by the connection weights.
In practice this shortcoming (referred to as the *vanishing gradient problem*
in the literature [Hochreiter *et al.* (2001); Bengio *et al.* (1994)]) makes it
hard for an RNN to learn to bridge gaps of more than about 10 time steps
between relevant input and target events [Hochreiter *et al.* (2001)]. The
vanishing gradient problem is illustrated schematically in Fig. 2.6. The diagram shows a recurrent network unrolled in time (increasing from left to
right), with a single input, a single output, and a single hidden node. The
shading of the units corresponds to the derivative of their activations with
respect to the first input (where black is high and white is low).

   Long short-term memory (LSTM) [Hochreiter and Schmidhuber (1997);
Gers *et al.* (2002)] is an RNN architecture specifically designed to address
the vanishing gradient problem. An LSTM hidden layer consists of multiple
recurrently connected subnets, known as memory blocks. Each block contains a set of internal units, known as cells, whose activation is controlled
by three multiplicative units: the input gate, forget gate, and output gate.

   Figure 2.7 provides a detailed illustration of an LSTM memory block

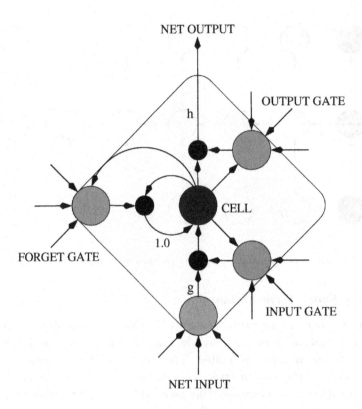

Fig. 2.7   LSTM memory block with one cell

with a single cell (CEC). The cell has a recurrent connection with fixed weight 1. The three gates collect activations from the rest of the network, and control the cell via multiplicative units illustrated by small circles. The activations of the input and output gates scale the input and output of the cell. The activations of the forget gate scale the recurrent connection of the cell. The cell input and output squashing functions (g and h) are applied at the indicated places. The internal connections from the cell to the gates are called "peephole weights".

The gates allow the cells to store and access information over long periods of time, thereby avoiding the vanishing gradient problem. For example, as long as the input gate remains closed (i.e., has an activation close to 0), the activation of the cell is not overwritten by new inputs arriving in the network. Similarly, the cell activation is only available to the rest of the network when the output gate is open, and the cell's recurrent connection is

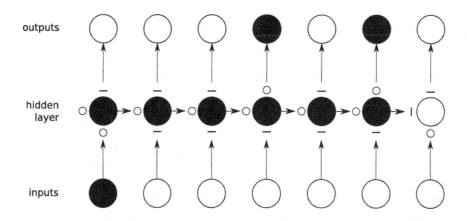

Fig. 2.8   Preservation of gradient information by using an LSTM memory block

switched on and off by the forget gate. Figure 2.8 illustrates how an LSTM block maintains gradient information over time. The diagram shows a network unrolled in time with a single hidden LSTM memory block. The input, forget, and output gate activations of the block are respectively displayed below, to the left and above the memory block. The shading of the units corresponds to the derivative of their activation with respect to the first input, where black is high and white is low. For simplicity, the gates are considered to be either entirely open ("O") or entirely closed ("—"). Note that the dependency is "carried" by the memory cell as long as the forget gate is open and the input gate is closed, and that the output dependency can be switched on and off by the output gate, without affecting the hidden cell.

2.2.4   *Bidirectional Recurrent Neural Networks*

LSTM improves RNNs by increasing the range of previous context accessible to them. But for many tasks it is also useful to have access to future context. For example, in handwriting recognition, the identification of a given letter is eased by knowing the letters both to the right and left of itself.

An RNN containing two separate hidden layers, one of which processes the inputs in the forward direction, while the other processes them backwards, is called *bidirectional recurrent neural network* (BRNN). BRNNs are able to access context in both directions along the input sequence [Schuster

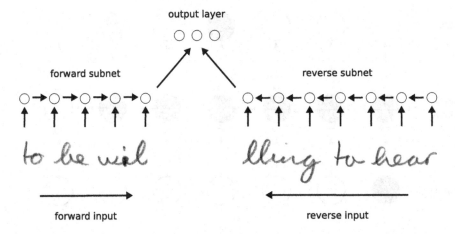

Fig. 2.9   Illustration of a BRNN

and Paliwal (1997); Baldi *et al.* (1999)]. Both hidden layers are connected to the output layer, which therefore has access to all past and future context of every point in the sequence.

The application of a BRNN to handwriting recognition is illustrated in Fig. 2.9, where the handwritten phrase "to be willing to hear" is processed. The output layer receives previous context for the first "l" in "willing" from the forward hidden layer, and future context from the reverse hidden layer. BRNNs have outperformed standard RNNs in several sequence learning tasks, notably protein structure prediction [Baldi *et al.* (2001)] and speech processing [Schuster and Paliwal (1997); Fukada *et al.* (1999)].

A BRNN containing hidden layers with LSTM cells is called *bidirectional LSTM* (BLSTM). It thereby maximizes the amount of context available to the network. Bidirectional LSTM has previously outperformed other neural network architectures, including standard LSTM and BRNNs, on phoneme classification [Graves and Schmidhuber (2005)] and hybrid speech recognition [Graves *et al.* (2005)].

2.2.5   *Connectionist Temporal Classification*

Until recently, the only way to apply RNNs to sequence labeling tasks was to pre-segment the input sequences and then provide the networks with separate classification targets for every segment. This limited their applicability in domains such as cursive handwriting recognition, where segmentation is

targets

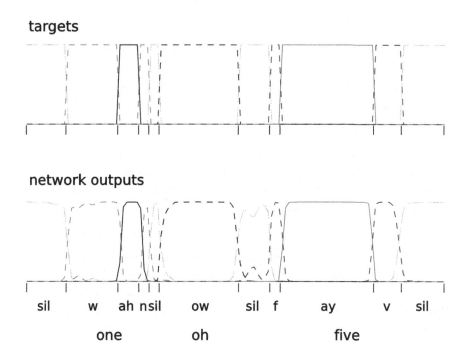

network outputs

| sil | w | ah nsil | ow | sil f | ay | v | sil |

| one | oh | five |

Fig. 2.10   Phoneme classification with an RNN using a standard objective function

difficult to perform. Moreover, because the outputs of a standard RNN are
a series of independent, local classifications, some form of post processing
is required to transform them into the desired label sequence. Figure 2.10
shows an RNN with a standard classification objective function applied to
speech recognition. The network outputs correspond to the probabilities of
observing different phonemes at each time step. Note that the targets, i.e.,
the phonemes to be recognized, are pre-segmented.

One way of circumventing these problems is to combine RNNs with
HMMs in the so-called *hybrid approach* [Bengio (1999); Bourlard and Morgan (1994); Robinson (1994)]. Hybrid systems use HMMs to model the
long-range sequential structure of the data, and neural nets to provide
localized classifications. However, as well as inheriting the drawbacks of
HMMs, hybrid systems do not exploit the full potential of RNNs for sequence modeling.

2.2.5.1   *Model Structure*

Connectionist temporal classification (CTC) [Graves *et al.* (2006)] is an RNN output layer specifically designed for sequence labeling tasks. It does not require the data to be pre-segmented and directly outputs probability distribution over label sequences. CTC has been shown to outperform RNN-HMM hybrids in speech recognition tasks [Graves *et al.* (2006); Fernández *et al.* (2007); Graves *et al.* (2005)].

A CTC output layer contains as many units as there are labels in the task, plus an additional "blank" or "no label" unit. The output activations are normalized using the *softmax* function [Bridle (1990)], so that they sum up to 1 and each one lies in the range $(0, 1)$:

$$y_k^t = \frac{\exp\left(u_k^t\right)}{\sum_{k'} \exp\left(u_{k'}^t\right)},\qquad(2.11)$$

where u_k^t is the unsquashed activation of output unit k at time t, and y_k^t is the activation of the same unit after the softmax function is applied.

The above activations are interpreted as the conditional probabilities $p(l, t|\mathbf{x})$ of observing the label (or blank) with index l at each point in the input sequence $\mathbf{x}$:

$$p(l, t|\mathbf{x}) = y_l^t\qquad(2.12)$$

The conditional probability $p(\pi|\mathbf{x})$ of observing a particular *path* π through the lattice of label observations is then found by multiplying together the label and blank probabilities at every time step:

$$p(\pi|\mathbf{x}) = \prod_{t=1}^{T} p(\pi_t, t|\mathbf{x})\qquad(2.13)$$

where π_t is the label observed at time step t along path π. Implicit in the above equation is the assumption that the network outputs are conditionally independent at different times, given the internal state of the network. This is ensured by requiring that no feedback connections exist from the output layer to itself or the network.

Paths are mapped onto label sequences $\mathbf{l} \in \mathbf{L}^{\leq T}$, where $\mathbf{L}^{\leq T}$ denotes the set of all strings on the alphabet L of length $\leq T$, by an operator $\mathcal{B}$ that first removes the repeated labels, then the blanks. For example, both $\mathcal{B}(a, -, a, b, -)$ and $\mathcal{B}(-, a, a, -, -, a, b, b)$ yield the labeling (a,a,b). Since the paths are mutually exclusive, the conditional probability of a given labeling $\mathbf{l} \in \mathbf{L}^{\leq T}$ is the sum of the probabilities of all the paths corresponding to it:

$$p(\mathbf{l}|\mathbf{x}) = \sum_{\pi \in \mathcal{B}^{-1}(\mathbf{l})} p(\pi|\mathbf{x})\qquad(2.14)$$

2.2.5.2 *Training*

The step of Eq. (2.14) allows CTC to train with unsegmented data. The intuition is that, because it is not known where the labels within a particular sequence will be observed, a sum is computed over all the places where they could be observed, so that the sequence remains unchanged. In general, a large number of paths will correspond to the same label sequence, therefore a naive calculation of the above sum is unfeasible. However, it can be efficiently evaluated using a graph-based algorithm, similar to the forward-backward algorithm for HMMs.

To allow for blanks in the output paths, modified label sequences l' are considered, with blanks added to the beginning and the end of l, and inserted between every pair of consecutive labels. The length of l' is therefore $2|l| + 1$. In calculating the probabilities of prefixes of l' all transitions between blank and non-blank labels are allowed as well as those between any pair of distinct non-blank labels.

An illustration of how the CTC forward backward algorithm works is given in Fig. 2.11. Black circles represent labels, and white circles represent blanks. Arrows signify allowed transitions. Forward variables are updated in the direction of the arrows, and backward variables are updated against them.

For a labeling l, the forward variable $\alpha_t(s)$ is defined as the summed probability of all *path beginnings* reaching index s of l' at time t, i.e.,

$$\alpha_t(s) = P(\pi_{1:t} : \mathcal{B}(\pi_{1:t}) = l_{1:s/2}, \pi_t = l'_s | \mathbf{x})$$

$$= \sum_{\substack{\pi: \\ \mathcal{B}(\pi_{1:t})=l_{1:s/2}}} \prod_{t'=1}^{t} y_{\pi_{t'}}^{t'}, \qquad (2.15)$$

where, for some sequence $\mathbf{s}$, $\mathbf{s}_{a:b}$ is the subsequence $(\mathbf{s}_a, \mathbf{s}_{a+1}, \dots, \mathbf{s}_{b-1}, \mathbf{s}_b)$. Note that index s of l' corresponds to index $s/2$ (rounded down) of the original label sequence l. As shown later, $\alpha_t(s)$ can be calculated recursively from $\alpha_{t-1}(s)$ and $\alpha_{t-1}(s-1)$.

Allowing all paths to start with either a blank (b) or the first symbol in l (l_1), the following rules for initialization are derived:

$$\alpha_1(1) = y_b^1$$
$$\alpha_1(2) = y_{l_1}^1$$
$$\alpha_1(s) = 0, \ \forall s > 2$$

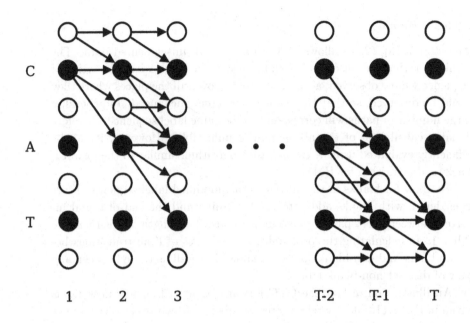

Fig. 2.11   CTC forward backward algorithm

and recursion:

$$\alpha_t(s) = \begin{cases} \big(\alpha_{t-1}(s) + \alpha_{t-1}(s-1)\big)y^t_{\mathbf{l}'_s} & \text{if } \mathbf{l}'_s = b \text{ or } \mathbf{l}'_{s-2} = \mathbf{l}'_s \\ \big(\alpha_{t-1}(s) + \alpha_{t-1}(s-1) + \alpha_{t-1}(s-2)\big)y^t_{\mathbf{l}'_s} & \text{otherwise} \end{cases}$$

Note however that $\alpha_t(s) = 0 \ \forall s < |\mathbf{l}'| - 2(T-t) - 1$, because these variables correspond to states for which there are not enough time steps left to complete the sequence (the unconnected circles in the top right of Fig. 2.11).

The backward variables $\beta_t(s)$ are defined as the summed probability of all *path endings* that would complete the labeling $\mathbf{l}$ if the path beginning had reached index s of $\mathbf{l}'$ at time t:

$$\beta_t(s) = P\left(\pi_{t+1:T} : \mathcal{B}(\pi_{t:T}) = \mathbf{l}_{s/2:|\mathbf{l}|}, \pi_t = \mathbf{l}'_s | \mathbf{x}\right)$$

$$= \sum_{\substack{\pi: \\ \mathcal{B}(\pi_{t:T}) = \mathbf{l}_{s/2:|\mathbf{l}|}}} \prod_{t'=t+1}^{T} y^{t'}_{\pi_{t'}} \tag{2.16}$$

The rules for initialization and recursion of the backward variables are as follows:

$$\beta_T(|\mathbf{l}'|) = y_b^T$$
$$\beta_T(|\mathbf{l}'| - 1) = y_{\mathbf{l}_{|\mathbf{l}|}}^T$$
$$\beta_T(s) = 0, \ \forall s < |\mathbf{l}'| - 1$$

$$\beta_t(s) = \begin{cases} \left(\beta_{t+1}(s) + \beta_{t+1}(s+1)\right)y_{\mathbf{l}'_s}^t & \text{if } \mathbf{l}'_s = b \text{ or } \mathbf{l}'_{s+2} = \mathbf{l}'_s \\ \left(\beta_{t+1}(s) + \beta_{t+1}(s+1) + \beta_{t+1}(s+2)\right)y_{\mathbf{l}'_s}^t & \text{otherwise} \end{cases}$$

Note that $\beta_t(s) = 0 \ \forall s > 2t$ (the unconnected circles in the bottom left of figure 2.11).

The label sequence probability is given by the sum of the products of the forward and backward variables at any time step:

$$p(\mathbf{l}|\mathbf{x}) = \sum_{s=1}^{|\mathbf{l}'|} \alpha_t(s)\beta_t(s). \tag{2.17}$$

The CTC objective function is defined as the negative log probability of the network correctly labeling the entire training set. Let S be a training set, consisting of pairs of input and target sequences $(\mathbf{x}, \mathbf{z})$, where the length of sequence $\mathbf{z}$ is less than or equal to the length of the input sequence $\mathbf{x}$. Then the objective function can be expressed as:

$$O^{CTC} = - \sum_{(\mathbf{x},\mathbf{z}) \in S} ln\left(p(\mathbf{z}|\mathbf{x})\right). \tag{2.18}$$

The network can be trained with gradient descent by first differentiating O^{CTC} with respect to the outputs, then using backpropagation through time [Williams and Zipser (1990)] to find the derivatives with respect to the network weights.

Noting that the same label (or blank) may be repeated several times for a single labeling $\mathbf{l}$, the set of positions where label k occurs are defined as $lab(\mathbf{l}, k) = \{s : \mathbf{l}'_s = k\}$, which may be empty. Then $\mathbf{l}$ is set to $\mathbf{l} = \mathbf{z}$ and Eq. (2.17) is differentiated with respect to the network outputs to obtain:

$$-\frac{\partial ln\left(p(\mathbf{z}|\mathbf{x})\right)}{\partial u_k^t} = y_k^t - \frac{1}{p(\mathbf{z}|\mathbf{x})} \sum_{s \in lab(\mathbf{z},k)} \alpha_t(s)\beta_t(s), \tag{2.19}$$

where u_k^t and y_k^t are respectively the *unnormalized* and *normalized* outputs of the softmax layer.

2.2.5.3   *Testing*

Once the network is trained, it could ideally be used to transcribe a previously unseen input sequence **x** by selecting the label sequence l* corresponding to the most probable path:

$$\mathbf{l}^* = \mathcal{B}\left(\arg\max_{\pi} p(\pi|\mathbf{x})\right) \tag{2.20}$$

Using the terminology of HMMs, the task of finding this labeling is referred to as *decoding*. Unfortunately, no tractable decoding algorithm is known that is guaranteed to give optimal results. However a simple and effective approximation is given by assuming that the most probable path corresponds to the most probable labeling:

$$\mathbf{l}^* \approx \mathcal{B}\left(\arg\max_{\pi} p(\pi|\mathbf{x})\right) \tag{2.21}$$

This is trivial to compute, since the most probable path is just the concatenation of the most active outputs at every time step.

2.2.5.4   *Including a Language Model*

For some tasks it is desirable to constrain the output labelings according to a language model (see Section 2.4). For example, in continuous speech and handwriting recognition, the final transcriptions are usually required to form sequences of dictionary words. In addition it is common practice to use a language model to weight the probabilities of particular sequences of words.

These constraints are expressed by altering the label sequence probabilities in Eq. (2.20) to be conditioned on some probabilistic grammar G, as well as the input sequence **x**:

$$\mathbf{l}^* = \arg\max_{\mathbf{l}} p(\mathbf{l}|\mathbf{x}, G) \tag{2.22}$$

Note that absolute requirements, for example that l contains only dictionary words, can be incorporated by setting the probability of all sequences that fail to meet them to 0.

At first sight, conditioning on G seems to contradict a basic assumption of CTC: that the labels are conditionally independent given the input sequences (see Eq. (2.13)). Since the network attempts to model the probability of the whole labeling at once, there is nothing to stop it from learning inter-label transitions direct from the data, which would then be skewed by the external grammar. However, CTC networks are typically only able to learn local relationships such as commonly occurring pairs or triples of labels. Therefore as long as G focuses on long range label interactions (such as the probability of one word following another when the outputs are letters) it does not interfere with the dependencies modeled by CTC.

Applying the basic rules of probability, it follows that:

$$p(\mathbf{l}|\mathbf{x}, G) = \frac{p(\mathbf{l}|\mathbf{x})p(\mathbf{l}|G)p(\mathbf{x})}{p(\mathbf{x}|G)p(\mathbf{l})} \qquad (2.23)$$

where the fact that $\mathbf{x}$ is conditionally independent of G given $\mathbf{l}$ is used. If $\mathbf{x}$ is assumed to be independent of G, Eq. (2.23) reduces to:

$$p(\mathbf{l}|\mathbf{x}, G) = \frac{p(\mathbf{l}|\mathbf{x})p(\mathbf{l}|G)}{p(\mathbf{l})} \qquad (2.24)$$

Note that this assumption is in general false, since both the input sequences and the grammar depend on the underlying generator of the data, for example the language being spoken. However it is a reasonable first approximation, and is particularly justifiable in cases where the grammar is created using data other than that from which $\mathbf{x}$ was drawn (as is common practice in speech and handwriting recognition, where separate textual corpora are used to generate language models).

If it is further assumed that, prior to any knowledge about the input or the grammar, all label sequences are equally probable, Eq. (2.22) reduces to:

$$\mathbf{l}^* = \arg \max_{\mathbf{l}} p(\mathbf{l}|\mathbf{x})p(\mathbf{l}|G) \qquad (2.25)$$

Note that, since the number of possible label sequences is finite (because both L and $|\mathbf{l}|$ are finite), assigning equal prior probabilities does not lead to an improper prior.

2.2.5.5 *CTC Token Passing Algorithm*

The following algorithm is based on the *token passing algorithm* for HMMs [Young *et al.* (1989)], that finds an approximate solution to Eq. (2.25).

Let G consist of a dictionary D containing W words, and a set of W^2 bigrams $p(w|\hat{w})$ (see Section 2.4) that define the probability of making a transition from word $\hat{w}$ to word w. The probability of any label sequence that does not form a sequence of dictionary words is 0.

For each word w, the modified word w' is defined as w with blanks added at the beginning and end and between each pair of labels. Therefore $|w'| = 2|w| + 1$. Furthermore, a token $tok = (score, history)$ is defined as a pair consisting of a real valued score and a history of previously visited words. Each token corresponds to a particular path through the network outputs, and the token score is the log probability of that path. A state s of w' is then defined as an index into the sequence of labels and blanks $(1 \leq s \leq |w'|)$. The basic idea of the token passing algorithm is to pass along the highest scoring tokens at every word state, then maximize over these to find the highest scoring tokens at the next state. The transition probabilities are used when a token is passed from the last state in one word to the first state in another. The output word sequence is then given by the history of the highest scoring end-of-word token at the final time step.

At every time step t of the length T output sequence, each state s of each modified word w' holds a single token $tok(w, s, t)$. This is the highest scoring token reaching that state at that time. In addition the *input token* $tok(w, 0, t)$ is defined to be the highest scoring token arriving at word w at time t, and the *output token* $tok(w, -1, t)$ is defined to be the highest scoring token leaving word w at time t. Pseudocode is provided in Algorithm 2.1.

The CTC token passing algorithm has a worst case complexity of $O(TW^2)$, since line 2.2.5.5 requires a potential search through all W words. However, because the output tokens $tok(w, -1, T)$ are sorted in order of score, the search can be terminated when a token is reached whose score is less than the current best score with the transition included. The typical complexity is therefore considerably lower, with a lower bound of $O(TWlogW)$ to account for the sort. If no bigrams are used, lines 2.2.5.5-2.2.5.5 can be replaced by a simple search for the highest scoring output token, and the complexity reduces to $O(TW)$.

Note that this is the same as the complexity of HMM decoding, if the search through bigrams is exhaustive. Much work has gone into developing more efficient decoding techniques [Lamere *et al.* (2003)], typically by pruning improbable branches from the tree of labelings. Such methods are essential for applications where a rapid response is required. In addition, many decoders use more sophisticated language models than simple bigrams. Any HMM decoding algorithm could be applied to CTC outputs in the same way as token passing. However, this book focuses on recognition rather than decoding. Therefore a rather basic algorithm is used.

Algorithm 2.1 CTC Token Passing Algorithm

1: **Initialization:**
2: **for** all words $w \in D$ **do**
3:    $tok(w, 1, 1) = (ln(y_b^1), (w))$
4:    $tok(w, 2, 1) = (ln(y_{w_2'}^1), (w))$
5:    **if** $|w| = 1$ **then**
6:       $tok(w, -1, 1) = tok(w, 2, 1)$
7:    **else**
8:       $tok(w, -1, 1) = (-\infty, ())$
9:    **end if**
10:   $tok(w, s, 1) = (-\infty, ())$ for all other s
11: **end for**
12:
13: **Algorithm:**
14: **for** $t = 2$ to T **do**
15:    sort output tokens $tok(w, -1, t - 1)$ by ascending score
16:    **for** all words $w \in D$ **do**
17:       $tok(w, 0, t) = \arg\max_{tok(\hat{w}, -1, t-1)} tok.score + ln\left(p(w|\hat{w})\right)$
18:       $tok(w, 0, t).score \mathrel{+}= ln\left(p(w|\hat{w})\right)$
19:       $tok(w, 0, t).history \mathrel{+}= w$
20:       **for** segment $s = 1$ to $|w'|$ **do**
21:          $P = \{tok(w, s, t - 1), tok(w, s - 1, t - 1)\}$
22:          **if** $w_s' \neq blank$ and $s > 2$ and $w_{s-2}' \neq w_s'$ **then**
23:             $P \mathrel{+}= tok(w, s - 2, t - 1)$
24:          **end if**
25:          $tok(w, s, t) = $ highest scoring token in P
26:          $tok(w, s, t).score \mathrel{+}= ln(y_{w_s'}^t)$
27:       **end for**
28:       $tok(w, -1, t) = $ highest scoring of $\{tok(w, |w'|, t), tok(w, |w'|-1, t)\}$
29:    **end for**
30: **end for**
31:
32: **Termination:**
33: find output token $tok^*(w, -1, T)$ with highest score at time T
34: output $tok^*(w, -1, T).history$

2.3   Gaussian Mixture Models

Gaussian mixture models (GMMs) are used to model statistical data, e.g., feature vectors extracted from handwritten data. They provide powerful but simple means of representing a distribution of observations, i.e., the features extracted from the text written by a person. GMMs have a mathematically simple and well understood structure, and standard algorithms for training and testing exist. They are conceptually less complex than HMMs consisting of only one state and one output distribution function. Furthermore, during training only the parameters of the output distribution function need to be estimated compared to HMMs where the state transition probabilities need to be estimated as well.

Formally, GMMs consist of a weighted sum of unimodal Gaussian densities. The models were first used in speech recognition [Reynolds (1995); Reynolds *et al.* (2000)] and have recently been introduced for signature verification [Richiardi and Drygajlo (2003)]. In the research described in this book, a writer identification system based to GMMs is applied. For further details about GMMs see [Liwicki *et al.* (2006b); Schlapbach *et al.* (2008)]. Note that this section closely follows the introduction of GMMs given in [Schlapbach *et al.* (2008)].

This section is outlined as follows. First, the definition of GMMs is given in Section 2.3.1. Next, Section 2.3.2 describes the methods for training and testing GMMs. Finally, Section 2.3.3 shows the methods for adapting a global model to the data of a single individual.

2.3.1   *Definition*

The input to a GMM is a set of feature vectors $X = \{x_1, \ldots, x_T\}$ extracted from a given pattern. The distribution of these feature vectors is modeled by a Gaussian mixture density. For a D-dimensional feature vector x_t, the mixture density is defined as:

$$p(x_t|\lambda_{\text{GMM}}) = \sum_{i=1}^{M} w_i p_i(x_t).$$ (2.26)

where the mixture weights w_i sum up to one. The mixture density is a weighted linear combination of M unimodal Gaussian densities $p_i(x_t)$, each parametrized by a $D \times 1$ mean vector μ_i and a $D \times D$ covariance matrix C_i:

$$p_i(x_t) = \frac{1}{(2\pi)^{D/2}|C_i|^{1/2}} \exp\{-\frac{1}{2}(x_t - \mu_i)'(C_i)^{-1}(x_t - \mu_i)\}.$$ (2.27)

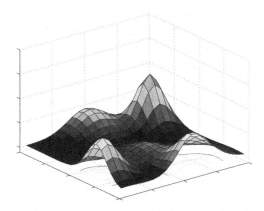

Fig. 2.12 A two-dimensional GMM consisting of a weighted sum of six unimodal Gaussian densities

The parameters of a GMM are denoted by $\lambda = (w_i, \mu_i, C_i)$ for all $i = 1, \ldots, M$. The set of parameters completely describes the model and can be used to model a person's handwriting based on feature vectors extracted from handwriting data.

Although the general model supports full covariance matrices, often only diagonal covariance matrices are used in the literature. An example of a diagonal covariance matrix in the two-dimensional case is shown in Fig. 2.12. The restriction to diagonal covariance matrices is motivated by the following observations. Theoretically, the density modeling of an M-dimensional full covariance matrix can be equally well achieved using a larger order diagonal covariance matrix. Also, diagonal covariance matrices are computationally more efficient than full covariance matrices. Furthermore, diagonal matrix GMMs outperform full matrix GMMs in various experiments [Reynolds *et al.* (2000)].

2.3.2 *Training and Testing*

A GMM is trained using the expectation-maximization (EM) algorithm [Dempster *et al.* (1977)]. The EM algorithm follows the *Maximum Likelihood (ML)* principle by iteratively refining the parameters of the GMM in order to monotonically increase the likelihood of the estimated model for the observed feature vectors x_t. The algorithm starts with the set of observations X, an initial set of M uni-modal Gaussian densities $N_i \hat{=} N(\mu_i, C_i)$, and M mixture weights w_i. Then, in the first step, for each training data point x_t the contribution of each component N_i is determined. In the second step, the component densities, i.e., the mean vector μ_i and the variance matrix C_i for each component and the weights w_i are re-estimated based on the training data. The model's parameters are updated as follows:

$$\mu_i = \frac{\sum_{t=1}^{T} P(i|x_t) * x_t}{\sum_{t=1}^{T} P(i|x_t)} \tag{2.28}$$

$$\sigma_i^2 = \frac{1}{d} \frac{\sum_{t=1}^{T} P(i|x_t) * ||x_t - \mu_i||^2}{\sum_{t=1}^{T} P(i|x_t)} \tag{2.29}$$

$$w_i = \frac{1}{T} \sum_{t=1}^{T} P(i|x_t) \tag{2.30}$$

where σ_i is the diagonal standard deviation ($\sigma_i(j) = C_i(j, j)$).

These two steps are repeated until the likelihood score of the entire data set does not change substantially or a limit on the number of iterations is reached.

The Gaussian component densities can either be initialized randomly or by using vector quantization techniques such as k-means clustering [Duda et al. (2001)]. Furthermore, variance flooring is often employed to avoid an overfitting of the variance parameter [Melin et al. (1998)]. The idea of variance flooring is to impose a lower bound on the variance parameters because a variance estimated from only few data points can be very small and might not be representative of the underlying distribution of the data [Melin et al. (1998)]. The minimal variance value is defined by:

$$\min \sigma^2 = \alpha \cdot \sigma_{global}^2 \tag{2.31}$$

where α denotes the *variance flooring factor* and the global variance σ_{global}^2 is calculated on the complete training set. The minimal variance, $\min \sigma^2$, is used to initialize the variance parameters of the model. During the EM update step, the variance parameter is set to $\min \sigma^2$ if the calculated variance is smaller than $\min \sigma^2$.

During decoding (testing), the feature vectors $x_1, \ldots, x_T$ are assumed to be independent. The log-likelihood score of a model λ for a set of feature vectors $X = \{x_1, \ldots, x_T\}$ is defined as:

$$\log p(X|\lambda) = \sum_{t=1}^{T} \log p(x_t|\lambda), \tag{2.32}$$

where $p(\mathbf{x}_t|\lambda)$ is computed according to Eq. (2.26).

2.3.3 *Adaptation*

For the problem of writer identification and verification, instead of training a GMM from scratch for each person, a *universal background model (UBM)* can be used. The basic idea is to derive a person's model by updating the trained parameters from the UBM. In the first step, all data from all persons are used to train a single, writer-independent UBM. In the second step, for each person one GMM is built by updating the parameters in the UBM via adaptation using all training data from this person.

To obtain the models for each person, a modified version of the EM algorithm is applied. This version is based on the *Maximum a Posteriori (MAP)* principle. The MAP approach provides a way of incorporating prior information in the training process, which is particularly useful for dealing with problems posed by sparse training data for which the ML approach gives inaccurate estimates [Gauvain and Lee (1994)].

Similarly to the EM algorithm, the MAP adaptation algorithm consists of two steps. The first step is identical to the expectation step of the EM algorithm, where estimates of the statistics of the individual's training data are computed for each mixture component in the UBM. Unlike the EM algorithm, however, for adaptation these new statistical estimates are combined in a second step with the old statistics from the UBM mixture parameters using a data-dependent mixture coefficient. This adaptation coefficient (called *MAP adaptation factor*) controls the adaptation process by emphasizing either the well-trained data of the UBM or the new data when estimating the parameters [Reynolds *et al.* (2000)].

2.4 Language Models

In the field of handwriting recognition of text lines, it is reasonable to integrate a language model to enhance the recognition accuracy on word sequences. One motivation of language models is the observation that a person is often able to guess a missing word when reading a given text. Hence the information of the surrounding words could be used to improve the performance of the recognizer.

Several kinds of language models exist, including n-grams, decision tree models, linguistically motivated models, exponential models, and adaptive models. This section focuses on statistical n-gram models, which have been used in this book. First, Section 2.4.1 gives a definition of n-gram language models. Next, Section 2.4.2 describes a measurement for evaluation.

Finally, Section 2.4.3 explains the integration of language models into the recognition process. For a detailed description of all types of language models see [Jelinek (1998); Rosenfeld (2000)].

2.4.1 *N-grams*

As stated above, in natural language processing the probability of a word is highly depend on the previous words. The *n-gram language models* take advantage of this observation. First, the probability of a sequence of words $w_1^k = w_1, \ldots, w_k$ is denoted by:

$$p(w_1^k) = p(w_1)p(w_2|w_1) \cdots p(w_k|w_1^{k-1}) \tag{2.33}$$

where two word sequence histories are treated as equal if they end in the same $n - 1$ words:

$$p(w_k|w_{k-n+1}^{k-1}) = p(w_k|w_1^{k-1}), k \geq n \tag{2.34}$$

Given these two equations it is easy to derive that for an n-gram language model and a vocabulary size v, there are $v^n - 1$ independent parameters (probabilities).

The estimation of the parameters by examining a given text t is called training. The concept is to count the number of occurrences of each possible word sequence. This can be done iteratively with the sequential maximum likelihood estimation, which, in general, does not lead to *consistent models* [Brown *et al.* (1992)][1]. However, if the given text t is large enough, the model will be nearly consistent.

If the vocabulary is large, it is hard to train a suitable n-gram language model. This is due to the large number of parameters to be estimated. Furthermore, not all possible word sequences that may occur are present in the training text. Thus, for training the language models on smaller resources, several methods for optimizing the training process have been proposed, such as combining classes, interpolating, or smoothing. For more details and an empirical study see [Chen and Goodman (1996)].

In some tasks just the information of which words may follow one another is needed. This is usually described by a *word pair grammar*, i.e.,

---

[1] The order-n conditional probabilities of an n-gram model form the transition matrix of an associated Markov model. The states of this Markov model are sequences of $n - 1$ morphs, and the probability of a transition from the state $w_1, w_2 \ldots, w_{n-1}$ to the state $w_2, w_3 \ldots, w_n$ is $P(w_n|w_1, w_2 \ldots, w_{n-1})$. An n-gram language model is called *consistent* if, for each string w_1^{n-1}, the probability that the model assigns to w_1^{n-1} is the steady state probability for the state w_1^{n-1} of the associated Markov model.

a simple grammar that specifies the list of words that can legally follow any given word. Extracting a word pair grammar is a much simpler task than calculating the probabilities. Throughout this book experiments using a simple word pair grammar will serve as a reference system in many experiments.

2.4.2 *Language Model Perplexity*

The perplexity is a measurement to evaluate the quality of a language model on a specific set of texts. It describes the ability of the model to predict the next word of a text line given the previous words. Given a language model M and a set of text lines $T = \{t_1, \ldots, t_n\}$, the perplexity $PP_T(M)$ is defined as:

$$PP_T(M) = 2^{H_T(M)}, \tag{2.35}$$

where $H_T(M)$ denotes the cross-entropy of M for T, which is determined by summing the text line log-probabilities of the language model $\log p_M(t_i)$ for all text lines $t_1, \ldots, t_n$:

$$H_T(M) = -\frac{1}{n} \sum_{i=1}^{n} \log p_M(t_i) \tag{2.36}$$

It follows that a smaller value of the perplexity indicates that the language model leads to better results on the considered text. Note that for training and optimizing the language model, no information of the test set should be present. Finally, the perplexity can be used to evaluate different language model training strategies.

2.4.3 *Integration into Recognition*

In this book, bigram language models have been chosen. This method approximates the previous text by the last word and models the dependency by the probability $p(w_i|w_{i-1})$, where w_i represents the considered word and w_{i-1} stands for the previous word. The probability $p(W)$ of a text line $W = (w_1, \ldots, w_n)$ can then be computed as follows:

$$p(W) = p(w_1) \left(\prod_{i=2}^{n} p(w_i|w_{i-1}) \right) \tag{2.37}$$

Including the output likelihoods of the recognizer, the most likely word sequence $\hat{W} = (w_1, \ldots, w_m)$ for a given observation sequence X is computed

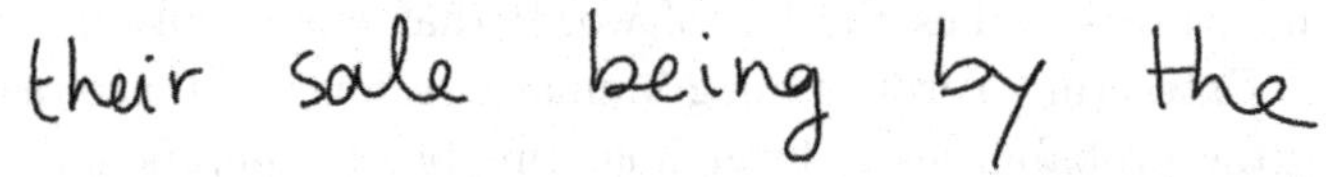

their sale being by the

GSF α	WIP β	Recognition result
0	-40	their sale being by by
0	0	their sale being by in E
15	0	their sale being long
15	20	their sale being by the
90	10	their sale being long
90	130	their sale be in a by this ,

Fig. 2.13   Influence of the parameters GSF and WIP

in the following way [Zimmermann and Bunke (2004)]:

$$\hat{W} = \operatorname*{argmax}_{W}\ \log p(X|W) + \alpha\ \log p(W) + m\ \beta \qquad (2.38)$$

According to Eq. (2.38) the model $p(X|W)$, resulting of the HMM decoding, is combined with the likelihood $p(W)$ obtained from the language model. Since the HMM system and the language model produce only approximations of probabilities, two additional parameters α and β are necessary to compensate for deficiencies and to control the integration of the language model. The parameter α is called *grammar scale factor* (GSF) and weights the influence of the language model against the optical model. The term *word insertion penalty* (WIP) is used for the parameter β which prevents the system from oversegmentation or undersegmentation. That is, the larger the value of β is, the higher is the system's tendency to split a text into many short words.

Figure 2.13 illustrates the influence of the two parameters GSF and WIP on an example text line. Multiple recognition results are produced for the handwritten text "their sale being by the". Increasing the parameter α eliminates nonsense word sequences, for example, "being by in E". Furthermore, increasing the parameter β amplifies the average number of words (including punctuation marks).

Chapter 3

Linguistic Resources and Handwriting Databases

It is a well-known fact that all handwriting recognizers, such as neural networks, support vector machines, or hidden Markov models, need to be trained. Common experience shows that the larger the size of the training set is, the better the recognizer will perform. However, the acquisition of large amounts of training data is a time consuming process with clear limitations. Therefore it is important that existing databases for training and testing are shared in the research community.

For the experiments described in this book, two different handwriting databases were used: the offline IAM-DB [Marti and Bunke (2002)], which is a large collection of unconstrained handwritten sentences, and the online IAM-OnDB [Liwicki and Bunke (2005b)], which has been compiled for research on recognition of whiteboard notes. The databases are built on a linguistic corpus, i.e., a collection of word samples from a wide range of sources. In addition to serving as the basis for handwriting databases, linguistic corpora may also be used to train statistical language models to improve the performance of the recognition system.

This chapter is structured as follows. First, Section 3.1 provides a summary of the different linguistic resources which have been used in this book. Next, Section 3.2 gives an overview of the contents and acquisition process of the offline IAM-DB. Finally, Section 3.3 describes the online IAM-OnDB, including the acquisition process and the stored data.

3.1 Linguistic Resources

In the domain of linguistics, large text corpora, i.e., collections of text, exist. These have different appearance and content. While some of them are simple word collections, others contain tags for further processing, e.g., part of speech tags [Brill (1992)]. In this section the corpora which have been used in this book are briefly described. In Section 3.1.1 major English corpora compiled in different countries are described. Section 3.1.2 is devoted to massive electronic collections. Note that the publication years of the underlying sources may be important for linguistic research, due to the changes a language undergoes during the years. In the 1960s, for example, one can expect that words such as "homepage" and "browser" did not exist, since they have been created in the context of the world wide web. Therefore the creation dates are mentioned in this section.

3.1.1 Major Corpora

Three important corpora are the Brown Corpus [Francis and Kucera (1979)], the LOB Corpus [Johansson (1986)], and the Wellington Corpus [Bauer (1993)]. These corpora have been generated in similar ways, but they are based on three different languages, i.e., American English, British English and New Zealand English.

The *Brown Corpus* of Standard American English was the first major English corpus for computer analysis. It was developed in the mid-1960s at Brown University by Henry Kucera and Nelson Francis, and consists of about 1,000,000 words of running English prose text, made up of 500 samples from randomly chosen publications of the year 1961. Each sample contains 2,000 or more words, i.e., it terminates at the first end of a sentence after 2,000 words, such that the corpus contains only complete sentences. These texts are divided into 15 categories ranging from press and popular literature to learned and scientific writing. Table 3.1 provides a detailed overview of the text categories. It is further discussed at the end of this section. The Brown Corpus has been tagged with part-of-speech markers over many years. It forms the basis for many later corpora, e.g., the LOB Corpus and the Wellington Corpus.

The *Lancaster-Oslo/Bergen Corpus* (LOB Corpus) is the result of a cooperation between the University of Lancaster, the University of Oslo, and the Norwegian Computing Center for the Humanities at Bergen. It was created in the 1970s. The LOB Corpus contains 500 English text samples, each one consisting of about 2,000 words. These texts were also published in 1961, and the sampling principles are identical to those of the Brown Corpus, although there are some differences in text selection. The LOB Corpus provides an extended version of the tags used for the tagged Brown Corpus. The aim of the LOB Corpus was to facilitate a combined

Table 3.1   Amount of text in each category for the three major corpora

Index	Text categories	Brown	LOB	Wellington
A	Press: reportage	44	44	44
B	Press: editorial	27	27	27
C	Press: reviews	17	17	17
D	Religion	17	17	17
E	Skills, trades and hobbies	36	38	38
F	Popular lore	48	44	44
G	Belles lettres, biography, essays	75	77	77
H	Miscellaneous (reports,...)	30	30	30
J	Learned and scientific writings	80	80	80
K	General fiction	29	29	a
L	Mystery and detective fiction	24	24	a
M	Science fiction	6	6	a
N	Adventure and western fiction	29	29	a
P	Romance and love story	29	29	a
R	Humor	9	9	a

[a]Note that the Wellington Corpus did not subclassify the 129 samples of fiction.

use of the two corpora. Therefore the British English material was made to match the Brown Corpus as closely as possible.

The *Wellington Corpus* of Written New Zealand English was developed in the Department of Linguistics at Victoria University of Wellington in the years 1986–1992. Unlike the LOB Corpus and the Brown Corpus, the years 1986–1990 were taken as the baseline for the Wellington Corpus. However, the distribution of texts and the amount of data is approximately the same.

The texts of the three corpora are divided into categories ranging from press and popular literature to learned and scientific writing. Thus a general representation of text types for use in research on a broad range of aspects of the language are provided by these corpora. Table 3.1 shows the categories and the number of samples of each category. It shows that there are only slight differences between the corpora.

One interesting result of computational linguistics can be observed in this distribution: Even for quite large samples, the frequency of the n-th most frequent word is roughly proportional to $1/n$. For example, "the" constitutes nearly 7 % of the Brown Corpus, and "of" more than another 3 %. About half the total vocabulary of about 50,000 words only occur once in the corpus.

It should be noted that there exist several other corpora similar to the Brown Corpus, e.g., the Macquarie's Australian Corpus of English, and the Kolhapur Corpus of Indian English texts. However, they have not been used in this book for keeping the focus on the recognition system. Integrating more linguistic corpora is left to future work.

3.1.2 *Massive Electronic Collections*

As computers have become more powerful and the processing of recorded texts becomes easier, it is possible to generate larger corpora containing significantly more data than one million words. The use of larger corpora is based on the expectation that a trained language model would be more representative and would perform better in an unknown domain. Today there exist two massive electronic collections of spoken and written English. They are described briefly in this section.

The British National Corpus (BNC) [Aston and Burnard (1998)] is a 100 million word collection of samples of written and spoken language from a wide range of sources. It was created during the years 1991–1994. The BNC has been designed to represent a wide cross-section of British English from the later part of the 20th century. Therefore nearly all of the contained data does not date back further than 1975. Only some samples in the domain of art are from 1960 onward.

The data in the BNC is divided into a written part and a spoken part. The first part contains 90 million written words. About 75 % of the written data have been chosen from informative writings. The data are roughly equally distributed over the fields of applied sciences, arts, belief and thought, commerce and finance, leisure, natural and pure science, social science, and world affairs. The remaining 25 % are imaginative, i.e., literary and creative works.

The second part is made of spoken data. This part includes a large amount of unscripted informal conversation, recorded by volunteers selected from different age, region, and social classes in a demographically balanced way, together with spoken language collected in all kinds of different contexts, ranging from formal business or government meetings to radio shows and phone-ins.

The encoding of the BNC follows the guidelines of the Text Encoding Initiative [Ide and Veronis (1995)]. It thus represents both the output from an automatic part-of-speech tagger and a variety of other structural properties of texts, e.g., headings, paragraphs, and lists. Full classification as well as contextual and bibliographic information is also included with each text. During the last decade the BNC has been improved, and errors relating to mislabeled texts and indeterminate part-of-speech codes have been manually corrected.

Modeled on the BNC, the American National Corpus (ANC) [Reppen and Ide (2004)] project was initiated in 1998 to build a large corpus for American English. The ANC follows the general design of the BNC. However, there are some differences, e.g., the ANC contains only samples from 1990 onward whereas it was 1960–1993 for the BNC. This enables the ANC to contain about 10 % of its data from recent text categories like emails, web pages, and chat room conversations.

The newest version of the ANC at the end of 2006 is the second release, which already contains about 22 million words. When completed, it will contain a core corpus of at least 100 million words, comparable across genres to the BNC. Beyond this, the corpus will include an additional component of potentially several hundreds of millions of words, chosen to provide both the broadest and largest selection of texts possible.

Also noteworthy are several other massive corpora that have been developed during the last decade to match the BNC. Nowadays many corpora with more than 100 million words are available (Polish, Czech, Hungarian, Russian, Italian, German). In addition to these word corpora, there also exist some corpora containing characters of Asian languages, e.g., the Modern Chinese Language Corpus and the Sejong Balanced Corpus.

3.2 IAM Offline Database

The IAM-DB[1] [Marti and Bunke (2002)] is a large collection of offline handwritten text lines. It is based on the LOB Corpus, which contains 500 English texts, each consisting of about 2,000 words (see Section 3.1.1). This section first focuses on the design of the database in Section 3.2.1. Second, the acquisition and processing steps are reported in Section 3.2.2. Finally, in Section 3.2.3 the handwriting recognition and writer identification benchmark tasks are described.

3.2.1 *Description*

The IAM-DB is the first database containing large amounts of general unconstrained handwritten English text. It includes over 1,500 scanned forms of texts written on normal paper by more than 650 writers. These forms

---

[1]The IAM-DB is publicly available for download at
http://www.iam.unibe.ch/~fki/iamDB

were generated from fragments of the LOB Corpus. Altogether 5,685 sentences have been written in 13,353 text lines. There are 115,515 word instances covering a vocabulary of 13,547 words.

The forms were automatically generated. First the sentences of each text fragment from the corpus have been extracted for generating LaTeX documents. These documents contain the text and the structure of the form. Each form consists of four parts (see Fig. 3.1):

(1) The title "Sentence Database" and a number assigned to the text. The first number indicates the category of the LOB Corpus the text belongs to, and the following digits identify the text number. The next three digits show with which sentence the text starts.

(2) The text the individual participant was asked to write.

(3) A blank zone providing space for copying the text with everyday handwriting.

(4) A place to put in the name of the writer.

These four parts are separated from each other by horizontal lines, which makes it easy to extract the individual parts automatically.

Unfortunately no personal information, such as sex, age, cultural and educational background of the contributing persons was collected. However, the IAM-DB covers a large variety of different text categories, writing styles, and writing instruments. Therefore it is a considerable challenge to achieve high recognition rates.

3.2.2 *Acquisition*

The writers were asked to fill in the forms using their preferred writing instrument. The filled forms were scanned with 300 dpi at a gray level resolution of 8 bit. The images were saved in a compressed TIFF-format. To make the image processing as easy as possible, the writers had to use guiding lines. However, no constraints were given for the pencil and the writers were asked to use their everyday handwriting.

The images were automatically processed as follows. First, the skew of the document was detected and the document was segmented into its four main parts. This is a relatively easy task because the four main parts are separated by long horizontal lines, which are easy to detect by horizontal projection. After finding the three horizontal lines, the part containing the handwriting was extracted.

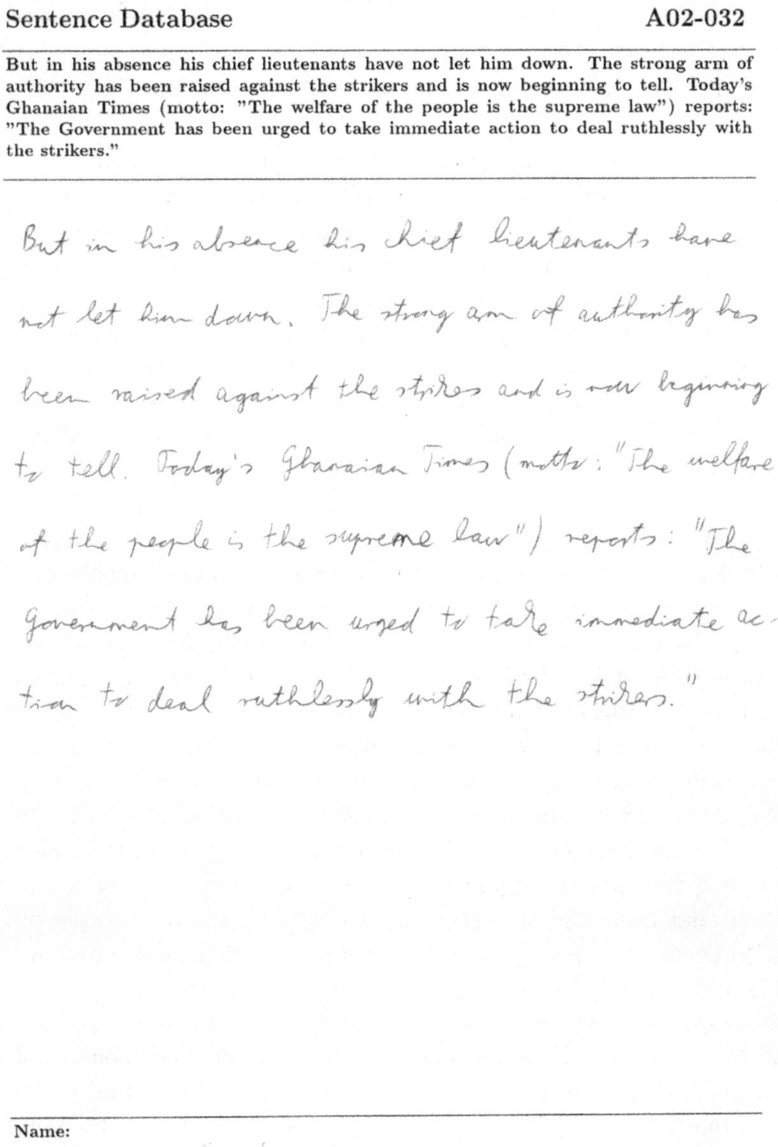

Sentence Database A02-032

But in his absence his chief lieutenants have not let him down. The strong arm of authority has been raised against the strikers and is now beginning to tell. Today's Ghanaian Times (motto: "The welfare of the people is the supreme law") reports: "The Government has been urged to take immediate action to deal ruthlessly with the strikers."

But in his absence his chief lieutenants have not let him down. The strong arm of authority has been raised against the strikes and is now beginning to tell. Today's Ghanaian Times (motto: "The welfare of the people is the supreme law") reports: "The Government has been urged to take immediate action to deal ruthlessly with the strikers."

Name:

Fig. 3.1 Scanned form of the IAM-DB

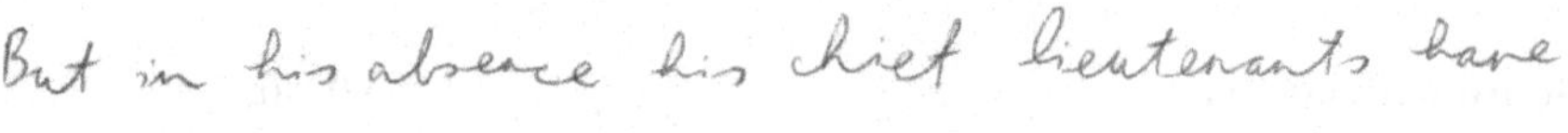

But in his absence his chief lieutenants have

Fig. 3.2   First text line from the scanned image in Fig. 3.1

The next step was cutting the text into lines. For this reason, a histogram of the horizontal black/white transitions was calculated and the text was split at the local minima. Strokes that intersect the cutting lines were assigned to the line where they have their center of gravity. This automated process results in images of the handwritten text lines (see Fig 3.2). For their transcription, the line feeds of the corresponding fragments of the LOB Corpus were manually adjusted. In some cases corrections were necessary, because the handwritten text did not correspond exactly to the printed text, for example, because the writer left out some words. These corrections were performed manually. The result of labeling is an ASCII file which contains the labels for each printed and handwritten line of text. Altogether 13,353 labeled text lines were extracted.

In addition to the labeled text lines, some lines were further segmented into words, resulting in 115,320 labeled words. The words were extracted from pages of scanned text using an automatic segmentation scheme and were verified manually. The segmentation scheme is described in [Zimmermann and Bunke (2002a)]. It consists of two steps.

In the first step an HMM based word segmentation procedure is applied on the normalized text line.[2] This is performed using a *forced alignment* technique. In the forced alignment mode, the transcription is provided to the Viterbi decoder. Hence the state sequence $Q = q_1, \ldots, q_T$ of the HMM is known, and the optimal alignment can be found by dynamic programming. Note that using this strategy bypasses Sayre's paradox, because no recognition needs to be performed. The result of the alignment procedure are the boundaries of the words in the normalized images.

As it is desired to get the segmentation of the original text line images, a second step is needed. In this second step, the connected components of each original text line are automatically assigned to the individual words resulting from the forced alignment. This is done by extracting the connected components from the original text line and filtering out small components. Next, these components are normalized individually and assigned to the word boundaries obtained by the HMMs according to their horizontal

---

[2]For more information about the normalization and feature extraction refer to Chapter 4.

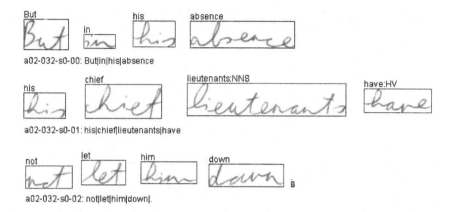

Fig. 3.3 First labeled sentence extracted from the scanned image in Fig. 3.1

positions. The word bounding box is then computed and the word can be extracted.

The automatic segmentation succeeds in more than 97 % of the words. To get the fully correct segmentation, the resulting images are inspected manually and corrections are applied whenever necessary. Finally, the labeled words are concatenated to get labeled sentences. An example of a labeled sentence is provided in Fig. 3.3.

3.2.3 *Benchmarks*

A benchmark task defines an experiment with well defined training, test, and validation sets. The motivation for defining a benchmark task is to allow researchers to compare the results of their experiments. The recognition benchmark task for the IAM-DB gives the writer IDs to be used for training, validating, and testing the recognizer. It consists of a total number of 9,862 text lines. It provides one training, one testing, and two validation sets. The text lines of all data sets are mutually exclusive, thus each writer has contributed to one set only. Detailed statistics about the sets can be found in Table 3.2. One drawback of this task is that it provides neither the set of characters to be recognized nor the vocabulary. As mentioned in Section 1.3, these parameters have an influence on the performance of the recognition systems.

Another benchmark task has been defined for writer identification. This task consists of 4,307 text lines from 100 different writers including 20,315

Table 3.2   Statistics of the four sets of the IAM-DB benchmark task

Set	#Writers	#Text lines
Training set	283	6,161
Validation set 1	46	900
Validation set 2	43	940
Test set	128	1,861

words out of 5,645 word classes. To form the training and the test sets, the text lines of five pages per writer are split up into four sets. Using the four sets, four-fold cross validation is performed. In each fold three of the sets are concatenated to form the training set, and the remaining one is used as the test set.

3.3   IAM Online Database

The IAM-OnDB is the largest database acquired from a whiteboard that is publicly available[3]. This section first describes the design of the database in Section 3.3.1. Then the acquisition procedure is reported in Section 3.3.2. Note that the first two sections closely follow [Liwicki and Bunke (2005b)], where the database has been originally introduced to the research community. Finally, Section 3.3.3 specifies the benchmark tasks, which are also publicly available.

3.3.1   *Description*

The design of the IAM-OnDB is inspired by the IAM-DB. However, while the IAM-DB is an offline database, the IAM-OnDB consists of online data acquired from a whiteboard. All texts included in the IAM-OnDB are taken from the LOB Corpus. Using a large linguistic corpus as the underlying source of text makes it possible to use language models for the experiments.

To acquire a database of handwritten sentences contained in the LOB Corpus, the texts in the corpus were split into fragments of about 50 words each. These fragments were copied onto forms on paper, and each writer was asked to write down the text of eight forms on the whiteboard. To make sure that many different word samples are obtained from each writer,

---

[3]The IAM-OnDB is publicly available for download at
http://www.iam.unibe.ch/~fki/iamOnDB

```
<Writer name="10062"
   DayOfBirth="1969-01-07"
   EducationalDegree="Master of Science"
   Gender="Female"
   NativeCountry="Germany"
   NativeLanguage="German"
   Profession="Teaching"
   WritingType="Right-handed">
 <OtherLanguage>French</OtherLanguage>
 <OtherLanguage>Italian</OtherLanguage>
 <WrittenLanguage>German</WrittenLanguage>
 <WrittenLanguage>English</WrittenLanguage>
 <WrittenLanguage>Spanish</WrittenLanguage>
</Writer>
```

Fig. 3.4   Writer information stored in the IAM-OnDB

these eight texts have been chosen from different text categories in the LOB Corpus. The resulting database consists of more than 1,700 handwritten forms from 221 writers. It contains 86,272 word instances from a 11,059 word dictionary written down in 13,049 text lines. The amount of words is comparable to the amount of words in the IAM-DB.

In addition to the recorded data and its transcription, some information about the writers, which might be useful for future work, are stored in the IAM-OnDB. These include, for each writer, the native country and language, other mastered languages, age and gender, and the writing style, i.e., right- or left-handed. The writers who contributed to the database were all volunteers. Most of them were students or staff members of the University of Bern. Both genders are about equally represented in the database, and about 10 % of the writers have left-handed writing. The additional information is stored in XML format and is thus easily accessible. An example is given in Fig. 3.4. A unique identifier has been assigned to the writer to keep his or her identity anonymous. The meaning of each attribute is easily understandable. The database distinguishes between well written languages and other spoken languages. The writer of Fig. 3.4 has good knowledge of written English. Therefore only a few spelling mistakes can be expected. To derive the age of the writer, the date of birth has been stored for each writer and the writing date has been recorded in the transcription directly after the acquisition.

Fig. 3.5   Illustration of the recording; note the data acquisition device in the upper left corner of the whiteboard

3.3.2 *Acquisition*

The eBeam© interface was used to record the handwriting of a user. It allows a user to write on a whiteboard with a normal pen in a special casing. The pen sends infrared signals to a triangular receiver mounted in one of the corners of the whiteboard. The acquisition interface outputs a sequence of (x,y)-coordinates representing the location of the tip of the pen together with a time stamp for each location. An illustration of the data acquisition process for the IAM-OnDB is shown in Fig. 3.5.

Labeling of the data is a prerequisite for recognition experiments and should be automated as much as possible for it is expensive, time consuming, and error-prone. The acquisition procedure used during during the recording of the IAM-OnDB works as follows. During the recordings an operator observes the received data with a special recording software. The software first loads the ASCII transcription of the text to be written. While the writer renders the handwritten text, the operator adjusts the line feeds during recording. He or she is also able to make corrections if the handwritten text does not correspond to the printed text. For example, if the writer leaves out some words this can be adjusted in the transcription. Fig. 3.6 shows a screen shot of the interface. The transcription produced by the operator in the lower window is saved together with the recorded

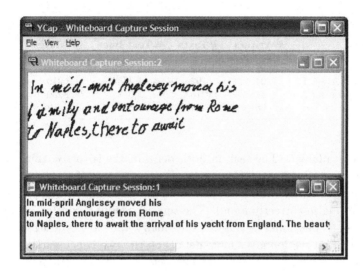

Fig. 3.6   Interface to the recording software

online data in one XML file.

The raw data stored in one XML file usually includes several consecutive lines of text. For some recognizers the data needs to be segmented into individual lines. The line segmentation process of the online data is guided by heuristic rules. If there is a pen-movement to the left and vertically down that is greater than a predefined threshold, a new line is started. There are only a few cases where a line is too short or where the writer moved back and forth across different text lines to render an i-dot. To ensure that the automatic line segmentation has been done correctly, the resulting lines are checked by the operator and corrected if necessary. Consecutive lines are highlighted in different colors on the screen to detect errors easily.

As a result of the line segmentation process, each handwritten text line is labeled with the corresponding transcription. In the IAM-OnDB there is no splitting of complete handwritten text lines into individual words provided. The main reason is that it is desired to apply segmentation-free methods for the recognition.

3.3.3   Benchmarks

Two benchmark tasks have been specified for the database, to make experiments on the IAM-OnDB comparable to one another. These benchmarks

Table 3.3   Statistics of the four sets of the IAM-OnDB benchmark tasks

Set	#Writers	#Texts	#Text lines	#Words
Training set	97	775	5,364	33,639
Validation set 1	24	192	1,438	8,219
Validation set 2	31	216	1,518	9,250
Test set	68	544	3,859	23,546

are publicly available[4]. The task in both benchmarks is to recognize the words of the test set. A word is recognized correctly only if all characters are recognized correctly (also in respect to upper case/lower case) and the boundaries are also correctly found. The sets for training and testing are identical in both benchmarks, but the vocabulary and the encoding of the letters differ. This section gives more details on the two benchmarks.

Both benchmarks are divided into four sets: one set for training; one set for validating the meta parameters of the training; a second validation set which can be used, for example, to optimize a language model; and a test set. These sets are all independent of one another. No writer appears in more than one set. Thus, a writer-independent recognition task is considered in each of the two benchmarks.

Table 3.3 shows some statistics of the four sets. Most data are used for the training set, to make sure that there is sufficient data to train a good recognition system. Since the validation of meta parameters is usually a time consuming process, the two validation sets are quite small, when compared to the other two sets. However, the variance of the handwriting is larger than the variance in the test set. This has been measured using a feature set of a writer identification system [Schlapbach *et al.* (2008)] after the sets have been randomly generated. A larger test set has been chosen to allow for more confident statements about statistical significance.

The first benchmark, called IAM-OnDB-t1, is based on a closed vocabulary, i.e., a vocabulary that contains all 11,059 words of the IAM-OnDB. It describes a set of 57 characters, including all small and capital letters, a garbage character, a character for the space, and three characters for the most frequent punctuation marks, i.e., comma, period, and quotation mark.

The second benchmark, IAM-OnDB-t2, provides a general English vocabulary containing 20,000 words. For this dictionary, the most frequent words of three corpora (LOB Corpus, Brown Corpus, Wellington Corpus)

---

[4]See benchmark tasks on http://www.iam.unibe.ch/~fki/iamondb/

have been taken. To make the dictionary independent of the test set, the sentences that occur in the IAM-OnDB have not been used to create the dictionary. The best recognition accuracy that can be achieved for this benchmark is 94.4 % because the remaining words of the test set are not present in the vocabulary. In the benchmark an enhanced set of 82 characters to be classified is given. In addition to the set of characters used in the IAM-OnDB-t1 benchmark, this set includes all other punctuation marks that appear in the IAM-OnDB. The second task is the more realistic one, because no information about the words occuring in the IAM-OnDB is present in the vocabulary.

Although the benchmark tasks for the IAM-OnDB are more restrictive than those for the IAM-DB, it does not guarantee that the results of different recognizers are perfectly comparable. For example, if an additional language model is included or if the recognizer has been trained on an additional data set, higher recognition rates can be expected.

Chapter 4

Offline Approach

A major contribution of this book is an extensive study on offline recognizers for handwritten data. Although the data output by the whiteboard sensing device are in the online format, an HMM-based offline recognizer is used. The motivation is twofold. Firstly online data can be easily converted into offline format, and secondly, there is a state-of-the-art offline recognizer available that has been developed in the context of previous work at the University of Bern [Marti and Bunke (2001c)]. Another motivation for developing an offline recognition system is its combination with the online recognizer described in the next chapter. From such a combination, an improved recognition performance can be expected [Velek *et al.* (2003); Vinciarelli and Perrone (2003)].

This chapter focuses on the offline recognizer and several experiments that have been conducted. First, Section 4.1 gives an overview of the proposed system and introduces the main steps for preprocessing the data, generating the input images for the recognizer, and recognizing the handwritten text. Next, Section 4.2 presents the main ideas for enhancing the training data. Experiments and results are described in Section 4.3. An approach based on a two-stage process that first segments the text line into individual words and than recognizes these words is investigated in Section 4.4. Finally, Section 4.5 draws some conclusions and gives an outlook on future work. Note that parts of these sections follow the presentation given in [Liwicki and Bunke (2007c)].

4.1 System Description

The system described in this section consists of six main modules (see Fig. 4.1): the online preprocessing, where noise in the raw data is reduced;

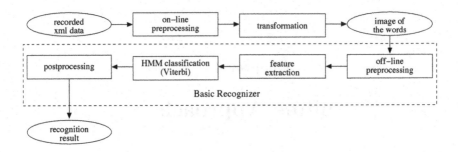

Fig. 4.1   System overview

the transformation, where the online data are transformed into offline data; the offline preprocessing, where various normalization steps take place; the feature extraction, where the normalized image is transformed into a sequence of feature vectors; the recognition, where an HMM-based classifier generates an n-best list of word sequences; and the post-processing, where a statistical language model is applied to improve the results generated by the HMM.

In the remaining of this section the individual modules applied before the recognition step are described in detail. Section 4.1.1 is devoted to the online preprocessing and Section 4.1.2 to the generation of offline data from online data. In the following, the subsequent offline preprocessing and the methods for feature extraction are summarized in Section 4.1.3. Finally, an overview of the HMM-based recognition step is given in Section 4.1.4.

4.1.1 *Online Preprocessing*

In writer-independent handwriting recognition, the preprocessing is a very important part since each writer has his or her individual writing style, which complicates recognition. The offline preprocessing steps described in [Marti and Bunke (2001c)] are supplemented with additional online preprocessing operations to reduce noise introduced by the recording interface. The recorded online data usually contain noisy points and gaps within the strokes. In Fig. 4.2 examples of both cases are shown. In the word *await* a spurious point occurs that leads to the introduction of a large artifact, i.e., two long additional strokes. Furthermore, in the first line there are many gaps within the word, caused by loss of data.

Two online preprocessing steps are applied to the data to recover from artifacts. For the first type of artifact, spurious points, the following

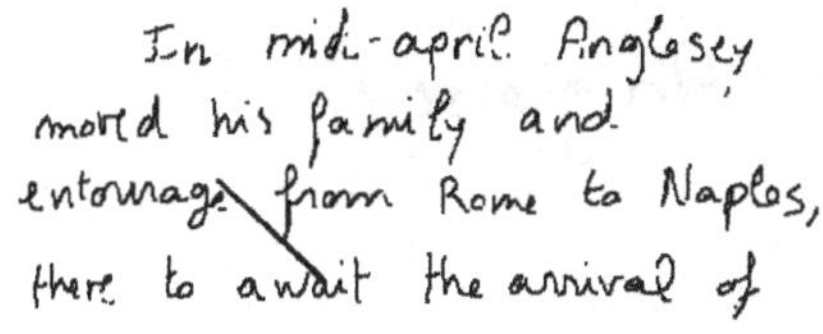

Fig. 4.2 Recorded text

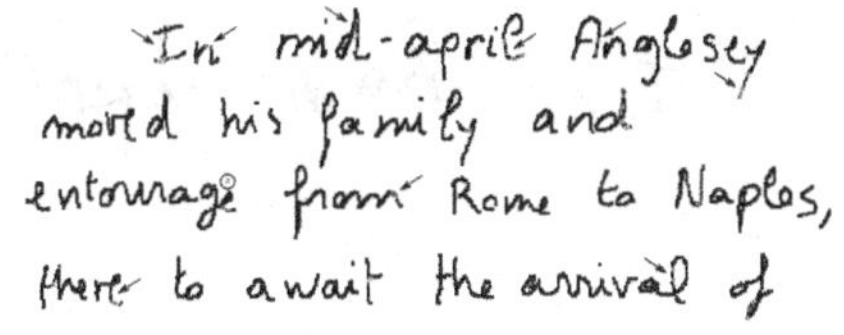

Fig. 4.3 Points where the preprocessing affects the image

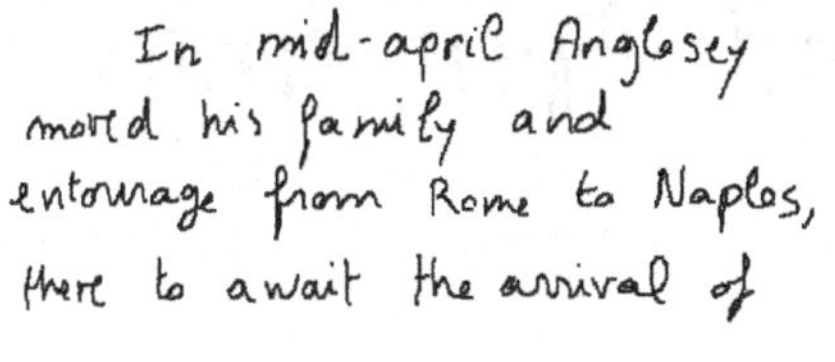

Fig. 4.4 Text after removing noise

strategy is chosen. Let $p_1, ..., p_n$ be the points of a given stroke and q_1 be the first point of the succeeding stroke, if any. If the distance between two consecutive points p_i, p_{i+1} is larger than a fixed threshold, one of the points is deleted. To decide which point must be deleted, the number of points within a small neighborhood of p_i and p_{i+1} is determined, and the point with the smaller number of neighbors is deleted.

To recover from artifacts of the second type, i.e., gaps within strokes, the distance between the timestamps of p_n and q_1 is taken into account. If it is below a fixed threshold the strokes are merged into one stroke. Note that the thresholds used for preprocessing depend on the recording environment. They can be derived from the frame-rate and the width of the pen strokes, or by scaling the average distance between succeeding timestamps in the recorded data[1]. An example of the points affected by these preprocessing steps is shown in Fig. 4.3, where the changes are marked with small arrows. The result of the preprocessing is shown in Fig. 4.4. Obviously, the handwriting is now of much better quality.

4.1.2 Online to Offline Transformation

Since the preprocessed data are still in online format, they must be transformed into an offline image, allowing them to be used as input for the offline

---

[1] In the conducted experiments, a threshold of $2 \cdot m$ was used, where m is the average value of the time intervals, or distances, respectively. This is reasonable because at $2 \cdot m$, there are distinct gaps in the histogram of all values.

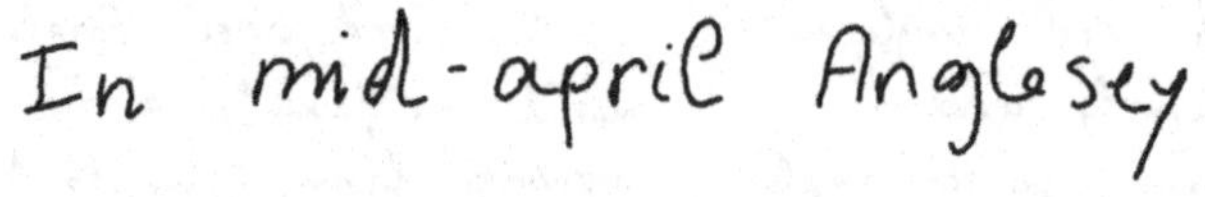

In mid-april Anglesey

Fig. 4.5   Generated gray-scale image

In mid-April Anglesey

Fig. 4.6   Image of a text line of the IAM-DB (produced by a writer different from the one in Fig 4.5)

recognizer. The recognizer was originally designed for the offline IAM-DB and optimized for gray-scale images scanned with a resolution of 300 dpi. To get good recognition results in the considered application, the images produced from the online data should be similar to these offline images. Consequently the following steps are applied to generate the images. First, all consecutive points within the same stroke are connected. This results in one line segment per stroke. Then the lines are dilated to a width of eight pixels. The center of each line is colored black with the pixels becoming lighter towards the periphery. Figure 4.5 shows an example of a generated image. Compared to Figs. 4.2 and 4.4 the handwriting looks more similar to the IAM-DB (see Fig. 4.6).

In general the realistic generation of offline data is a quite complex problem. Methods to create images that look even more similar to scanned images are proposed in [Velek *et al.* (2002)]. During the experiments reported there, the recognizer was trained and tested on computer generated images, and the best performance was achieved by using a constant thickness. However, during the experiments described in this book the recognition rate increased when this simple approach was supplemented with the generation of different gray values.

4.1.3   *Offline Preprocessing and Feature Extraction*

The basic recognizer takes, as an input unit, a complete text line, which is first normalized with respect to skew and slant. Then follows the computation of the baseline and the corpus line. The baseline corresponds to

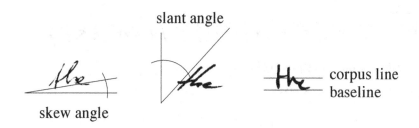

Fig. 4.7   Illustration of the offline normalization process [Marti (2000)]

the original line on which the text is written. The corpus line goes through the uppermost points of the lower case letters, e.g., "a" or "c". These lines are utilized in order to normalize the size of the text. Normalization of the baseline location means that the body of the text line (the part which is located between the baseline and the corpus line), the ascender part (located above the corpus line), and the descender part (below the baseline) are vertically scaled to a predefined size each. Writing width normalization is performed by a horizontal scaling operation. Its purpose is to scale the characters such that the scaled version has a predefined average width. An illustration of the normalization process is given in Fig. 4.7. There the input text "the" is normalized with respect to its skew and slant. On the right hand side the baseline and the corpus line are shown.

A sliding window is used to extract the feature vectors from a normalized image. Using this approach, a window of a fixed width is moved over the text from left to right. The features are then extracted at every window position. In the experiments described in this book the width of the window is fixed to one pixel, and nine geometrical features are computed at each window position. Thus an input text line is converted into a sequence of feature vectors in a 9-dimensional feature space. The nine features correspond to the following geometric quantities (the numbers in parenthesis denote the number of the feature value). The first two features represent the average gray value of the pixels in the window *(1)* and their center of gravity *(2)*. Then the second order moment in vertical direction is taken *(3)*. In addition to these global features, the locations of the uppermost and lowermost black pixel are used. Their positions *(4,5)* and their gradients *(6,7)*, determined by using the neighboring windows, are taken. The next feature is the number of black-white transitions between the uppermost and lowermost pixel in an image column *(8)*. Finally, the

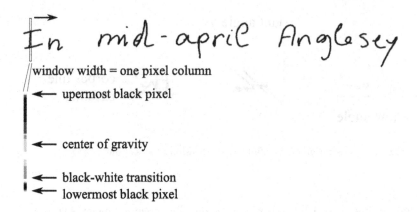

Fig. 4.8   Feature extraction with a sliding window

proportion of black pixels to the number of pixels between these two points is used *(9)*. Figure 4.8 gives an illustration of the feature extraction process.

4.1.4 *Recognition*

One HMM is built for each character in the character set, which includes all small and capital letters and some other special characters, e.g., punctuation marks. All HMMs use a linear topology, i.e., there are only two transitions per state, one to itself and one to the next state. In the emitting states, the observation probability distributions are estimated by mixtures of Gaussian components. This is equivalent to saying that continuous HMMs are used. The character models are concatenated to represent words and sequences of words. For training, the Baum–Welch algorithm is applied. In the recognition phase, the Viterbi algorithm is used to find the most probable word sequence. The output of the recognizer is a sequence of words. For a general introduction to HMMs see Section 2.1.

In the original offline recognition system described in [Marti and Bunke (2001c)], a constant number of states was defined for all characters. But in [Zimmermann and Bunke (2002b)] it was shown that the recognition rate can be improved by letting each character having an individual number of states. Optimizing the number of states of each individual character was accomplished by the Bakis method [Bakis (1976)], which sets the length of each character-HMM to a fixed fraction of the average character width found in the training set. Since the system described in this chapter creates input images that are similar to the input images used in [Zimmermann and Bunke (2002b)] (see Figs. 4.5 and 4.6), this approach has been adopted.

The number of Gaussian mixtures and training iterations also have an effect on the recognition results. The algorithm described in Section 2.1.3 is used for the recognizer of this chapter. Since the optimal number of Gaussian components increases with the amount of data, a larger optimal value can be expected on the enhanced training set. Thus a larger upper bound on the search space is taken.

Section 2.4.3 describes the inclusion of a language model in a recognition system. To find the best values for the parameters GSF and the WIP, the recognition performance is calculated on a validation set for different combinations, i.e., GSF varied from 0 to 90 and WIP from −150 to 150.

4.2 Enhancing the Training Set

The first experiments described in Section 4.3 were performed on a small subset of the IAM-OnDB. The motivation is twofold. First, many parameters need to be properly set, which requires much computational effort. Second, it is interesting to investigate the influence of enhancing the training data in several ways, for example, by using a different data set or using an enlarged training set of the same kind.

The influence of the size and the type of the training data is investigated by using data from a large existing database of offline handwritten sentences (IAM-DB) to augment the training set. This section introduces the investigated methods to enhance the database with offline data in Section 4.2.1. The use of the IAM-OnDB is described in Section 4.2.2.

4.2.1 *Enhancing the Training Set with a Different Database*

The offline images generated from the whiteboard data are similar to the images of the IAM-DB (see Section 4.1.2), so the IAM-DB can be used to enhance the small data set of whiteboard recordings. The IAM-DB includes over 1,500 scanned forms of texts written on normal paper by more than 650 writers. For the enhancement a subset containing about 18,000 words in 1,993 text lines produced by 400 different writers is taken.

Two different approaches are investigated to combine the training set with a subset of the IAM-DB. First, an HMM-recognizer trained on the IAM-DB is taken and adapted with the Maximum A Posteriori (MAP) estimation method [Gauvain and Lee (1992)]. In the second approach the HMM-recognizer is trained on the union of the selected IAM-DB subset and the whiteboard data.

Adaptation methods are normally used for writer adaptation in writer-dependent systems [Vinciarelli and Bengio (2002)], but have been successfully applied in writer-independent tasks as well [Brakensiek and Rigoll (2004)]. In this book MAP estimation is chosen for adaptation because it produced the best recognition results on adaptation sets of larger size in [Vinciarelli and Bengio (2002)]. This is due to the fact that it adapts each Gaussian component separately. The findings of [Vinciarelli and Bengio (2002)] have been validated in initial experiments, where other adaptation methods have been tested on the whiteboard data. The parameter τ weights the influence of the background model on the adaptation data (see Section 2.1.4). Whereas the parameter τ has been set empirically in [Vinciarelli and Bengio (2002)], it was optimized on a validation set in the experiments described in this chapter.

The second approach to training set enhancement is much simpler. It uses data from both the IAM-DB and the whiteboard data collection, i.e., the data of the IAM-DB and the training set of the whiteboard data, which are combined into one large training set. This set is then used to train the HMM recognition system. The validation set for optimizing the parameters is taken only from the whiteboard data. Thus, in contrast to the adaptation experiment, the training of the recognizer is optimized on the whiteboard data. This strategy consumes more time than the adaptation method because the training is performed on a larger dataset.

4.2.2   *Enhancing the Training Set with the IAM-OnDB*

In order to conduct experiments on the recognition of handwritten whiteboard data, the IAM-OnDB has been compiled (see Section 3.3). This database contains 86,272 word instances from a 11,050 word dictionary written down in 13,040 text lines by 221 writers. Analogously to mixed training on the small whiteboard data set and the IAM-DB, recognition experiments using these samples for supplementing the training set are conducted.

4.3 Experiments

In this section a large set of experiments is presented to investigate the influence of the training set size as well as the type of the training data on the recognizer's behavior. Before reporting on the experiments, several performance measures are described in Section 4.3.1 and the methodology used for testing the significance is presented in Section 4.3.2. After that, the baseline experiments and the effect of the optimization steps are reported in Section 4.3.3. Next, he training set enhancement strategies are then evaluated in Section 4.3.4. Finally, the performance of the proposed system is measured on the IAM-OnDB-t1 benchmark in Section 4.3.5.

4.3.1 *Performance Measures*

To measure the performance of handwritten text line recognizers is a complex problem. First, it must be decided on what level the performance is measured. Second, it should be decided which types of errors are taken into account. In the following, several possibilities to evaluate a recognizer are presented.

An intuitive idea is to measure the performance directly on the text line level. A text line is correctly recognized if an exact match of the recognized words and the transcription of the corresponding image can be found. This is not very often the case, especially if the recognizer is not very good. This makes it hard to directly compare several recognizers, because there are rarely significant differences between their performance on the text line level if only a few text lines are correctly recognized. However, an advantage of this performance measure is that it can be easily computed.

More elaborated methods measure the performance on the word level. The *word recognition rate* (WRR) counts the number of correctly recognized words given the transcription of the text line image. This number is then divided by the number of all words in the transcription. For the comparison of the text line hypothesis found by the recognizer with the correct transcription, a string alignment method based on dynamic programming is used. The method finds the optimal alignment by counting the number of correctly recognized words (hits $= H$), the number of deletions (D), the number of insertions (I), and the number of substitutions (S). Examples of alignments and the corresponding counts are given in Table 4.1. The

Table 4.1   Number of hits, deletions, insertions, and substitutions and the corresponding word recognition rates and word level accuracies for the target transcription "it was a good"

Alignment					H	D	I	S	N	**WRR**	**ACC**
it	was	a	good		4	0	0	0	4	100%	100%
it	was		good		3	1	0	0	4	75%	75%
it	a	a	good		3	0	0	1	4	75%	75%
it	was	a	good	a	4	0	1	0	4	100%	75%
it	a	a	good	a	3	0	1	1	4	75%	50%

WRR is defined as:

$$\text{WRR} = \frac{H}{N} \tag{4.1}$$

where N is the total number of words in the transcription. A word recognition rate of 100% is reached if all words present in the transcription are correctly recognized. However, this does not necessarily mean that a perfect recognition has been made, because additional words (insertions) may be present in the recognition result.

To overcome the above stated problem the *word level accuracy* (ACC) can be used. This performance measure also takes the insertions into account. It is defined as:

$$\text{ACC} = \frac{H - I}{N} \tag{4.2}$$

Table 4.1 shows the values of the word recognition rate and the word level accuracy in the last two columns. The values of the WRR are an upper bound on the values of ACC. Especially in row four it can bee seen that the WRR suggests a perfect transcription, while the ACC indicates that there is a wrongly inserted word.

Similarly to the recognition rate and the accuracy on the word level, the values on the character level can be used for measuring the performance. The *character recognition rate* may be useful to see how many characters of the trancsription are present in the recognition result, while the *character level accuracy* also takes inserted characters into account. The latter value gives an estimate of how many edit operations are to be done manually in a word processing interface to get the correct transcription.

4.3.2   Testing Significance

If several different methods for a pattern recognition task are available, it is desirable to compare them on an objective and scientifically sound basis. Differences in the recognition performance might be due to chance. Therefore a method is needed which measures how likely a result is caused by chance. In this book statistical significance tests are used to measure this probability.

Before a significance test can be applied, an assumption, or more formally a *null hypothesis*, must be formulated. This may be, for example, "The mean performance of method X is the same as the mean performance of method Y". Then a statistical significance test can be applied to answer the question of how well the findings fit the possibility that chance factors alone might be responsible for the outcome [Cramer and Howitt (2004)]. The probability of making a decision to reject the null hypothesis when the null hypothesis is actually true (the type I error) is then called *significance level*. The smaller the significance level, the more significant is the difference. Note that a highly significant difference does not imply that there is a large difference of the recognition results (and vice versa). This is due to the fact that the significance is also dependent on the size of the underlying test set and the variance of the results.

In this book the statistical Z-test was used in all experiments to test the null hypothesis. The variables to test are the recognition rates at the text line level. Given n text line results of two methods $X = (x_1, \ldots, x_n)$ and $Y = (y_1, \ldots, y_n)$ the Z-value is calculated as follows. First, the mean values of the results of each method are calculated:

$$\mu_X = \frac{\sum_{i=1}^{n} x_i}{n}, \qquad \mu_Y = \frac{\sum_{i=1}^{n} y_i}{n} \qquad (4.3)$$

Next, the variances and the covariance are computed.

$$\sigma_X^2 = \sum_{i=1}^{n}(x_i - \mu_X)^2, \qquad \sigma_Y^2 = \sum_{i=1}^{n}(y_i - \mu_Y)^2 \qquad (4.4)$$

$$Cov(X,Y) = \sum_{i=1}^{n}(x_i - \mu_X)(y_i - \mu_Y) \qquad (4.5)$$

Finally, the Z-value is:

$$Z = \frac{\sqrt{n} * (\mu_X - \mu_Y)}{\sqrt{\sigma_X^2 + \sigma_Y^2 - Cov(X,Y)}} \qquad (4.6)$$

This Z-value is then compared to a Z table that contains the percentage p of the area under the Gaussian distribution curve between $-\infty$ and the Z-value (see Fig. 4.9). If the Z value is enough different from the mean it is unlikely that the sample mean happened by chance, i.e., it is more likely to reject the null hypothesis. The significance level α is then calculated by $\alpha = 1 - p$. Typical significance levels are $\alpha = 5\%$ ($Z > 1.65$ as illustrated in Fig. 4.9) and $\alpha = 1\%$ ($Z > 2.33$).

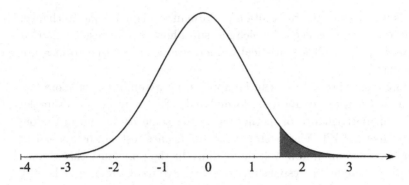

Fig. 4.9   Gaussian distribution with shaded type I error area

4.3.3   *Initial Experiments*

The amount of recorded data for the first experiments (small set) is 6,204 words in 1,258 lines from 20 different writers. Each writer wrote approximately the same number of words. The data set was randomly divided into five disjoint sets of approximately equal size (sets $s_0, \ldots, s_4$). On these sets, 5-fold cross validation was performed in the following way (folds c_0, $\ldots, c_4$). For $i = 0, \ldots, 4$, sets $s_{i\oplus2}, s_{i\oplus3}$, and $s_{i\oplus4}$ were taken for training the recognizer, set $s_{i\oplus1}$ was used as a validation set, i.e., for optimizing the parameters, and set s_i was used as a test set for measuring the system performance. Note that $\oplus$ denotes the summation *modulo* 5. Each set consists of data from four writers, and no writer appears in more than one set. Consequently, writer-independent recognition experiments were conducted. The recognition rate was measured on the word level in the experiments described in this section. The word-dictionary includes exactly those 2,337 words that occur in the union of all five sets. The language model was generated from the LOB Corpus [Johansson (1986)]. This setup differs from the setup in the IAM-OnDB-t1 benchmark. However, it was only used to optimize the basic meta parameters of the recognizer, e.g., the number of gray-levels in the online to offline transformation step. Later in this section a benchmark test is described to make the results of the offline recognizer comparable to the results in other chapters.

The basic recognizer, which has the same parameters as the offline recognizers developed in previous work at the University of Bern, served as a reference system for the initial experiments. This recognizer was trained with 32 iterations. After every 4th iteration, a splitting operation was

Table 4.2   Recognition performance of basic and optimized systems for each fold of the cross validation on the validation sets

Fold	c_0	c_1	c_2	c_3	c_4	**Average**
basic system	61.2	61.4	66.5	52.2	56.4	59.5
1st opt. sys.	64.1	62.3	66.9	52.1	59.0	60.9
2nd opt. sys.	66.8	66.9	71.2	57.1	65.8	65.6

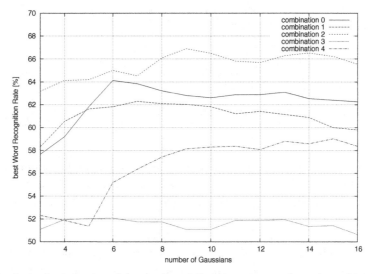

Fig. 4.10   Optimization of the number of Gaussian mixtures for each combination

applied to increase the number of Gaussian mixtures by one. Hence eight Gaussian mixtures were used. The average recognition rate of this recognizer was 59.5 % on the five validation sets and 59.6 % on the five test sets (see Tables 4.2 and 4.3). Note that there is a small difference between the recognition results even though the union of the test sets is the same. This observation can be explained by the different constellations in every fold, i.e., different sets were used for training.

An enhancement of the training procedure used for the basic recognizer is obtained if the number of Gaussian mixtures and training iterations are simultaneously optimized, as described in Section 2.1.3. This idea was implemented in the following experiments. For each number of Gaussian mixtures, the optimal number of training iterations was determined on the validation set. Figure 4.10 shows the optimal number of training iterations

Table 4.3   Recognition performance of basic and optimized systems for each fold of the cross validation on the test sets

Fold	c_0	c_1	c_2	c_3	c_4	Average
Basic system	60.0	62.7	59.8	65.1	50.3	59.6
1st opt. sys.	60.4	61.6	61.2	63.9	52.1	59.8
2nd opt. sys.	66.5	64.1	64.0	70.5	55.6	64.3

Table 4.4   Optimized values of the constants for the fold c_0

Parameter	Value
Number of Gaussian mixtures	16
GSF for language model	25
WIP	10
τ for MAP estimation	0.1

for each number of Gaussian mixtures in each combination, and a summary is given in the second line of Table 4.2. With this procedure, the average recognition rate on the validation set was increased to 60.9 %. On the test set a slight improvement from 59.6 % to 59.8 % was achieved. This indicates that eight Gaussian components for the basic recognizer is a good choice.

As described in Section 4.1.4 a bigram language model is included. By including a bigram language model instead of just using a word pair grammar, the average recognition rate was further increased up to 64.3 % on the test set. This improvement is statistically significant using a standard Z-test at a significance level of 1 %. A summary of the first experimental results on the test set is provided in Table 4.3. Note that this is the baseline experiment, where only the small whiteboard dataset was used for training. For the reader's convenience the optimal values of the parameters in the experiments are listed in Table 4.4 for the fold c_0. However, these parameters depend on the amount of training data and the quality of the language model. Therefore they were all optimized on validation sets before applying the resulting recognition system to the test set.

4.3.4   Experiments on Enhanced Training Data

A subset of the IAM-DB containing about 18,000 words in 1,993 text lines produced from 400 different writers was taken for enhancing the training data. The background model for the adaptation was trained on the data of 320 writers. For the resulting recognizer the number of Gaussian mixtures was optimized on the validation set consisting of the remaining 80 writers. The performance of this recognizer was 54.9 % on the whiteboard data (using a word pair grammar only).

In the first enhancing experiments, the recognizer was adapted with the small training sets from the recorded whiteboard data described in the previous section. To find the best value of parameter τ for the MAP estimation, the performance on the validation set of the whiteboard data was calculated for different values of τ. This optimization was done for each fold of the cross validation separately. The average recognition rate on the test sets was 64.6 % with just a simple word pair grammar. By including a bigram language model, the average performance was increased to 67.5 %. The last row in Table 4.4 shows the optimal value of τ for the example of fold c_0. The influence of the background model is small because of the large amount of adaptation data.

By training on the IAM-DB and the small whiteboard data set simultaneously, as described at the end of Section 4.2.1, the performance was even higher. The average recognition rate on the test sets was 65.3 % with using a simple word pair grammar. It increased up to 68.5 % when the statistical language model was included. For both the non-optimized and the optimized system a significant improvement of the recognition rate was achieved by the proposed methods.

To investigate the effect of an increased amount of whiteboard training data, the training set size was increased in two steps. First a larger set produced by 50 writers was used to train the recognizer (medium set). Second, the full IAM-OnDB was used for the experiments. The experimental conditions (5-fold cross validation using a training, a validation, and a test set) were always the same as for the small data set.

In the 50-writer experiments there were texts of 30 writers in addition to the small set. These texts were added to each training set s_i. The optimization parameters were validated on the same validation sets, and the performance was tested on the same test sets as in the experiments with the small set. The average recognition rate on the test sets was 60.4 % with a simple word pair grammar. It increased to 64.8 % when a statistical language model was included.

In the large experiments all data from the writers that do not appear in the test sets were used for training. The average recognition rate was 61.0 % on the test sets. By integrating a statistical language model the

Table 4.5   Overview of all enhancing experiments (WPG = word pair grammar, LM = language model)

System	Using a WPG	Including LM
Basic system	59.8	64.3
Adapted from IAM-DB	64.6	67.5
Trained on mixed data with IAM-DB	65.3	68.5
Trained on medium set of IAM-OnDB	60.4	64.8
Trained on large set of IAM-OnDB	61.0	66.4
Trained on IAM-OnDB + IAM-DB	65.5	68.6

performance was increased to 66.4 % on the test sets.

Having both IAM-DB and IAM-OnDB available leads to the idea of combining both databases into one large training set. The resulting recognition rate was 65.5 % with a simple word pair grammar and 68.6 % with a statistical language model. Obviously, this is the best recognition rate described in the experiments reported in this section. Table 4.5 gives a summary of all experiments on the enhanced set.

The enhancement with the offline IAM-DB was slightly better than using the large set of the IAM-OnDB. This may be surprising at first, but a possible explanation is that in the experiments with the IAM-DB more than 300 writers were present, while there were less than 200 in the experiments including the IAM-OnDB. The good performance of the system trained on data from the offline IAM-DB confirms the statement that the generated images of the whiteboard data are very similar to the images of the IAM-DB.

4.3.5   *Experiments on the IAM-OnDB-t1 Benchmark*

In order to make the results of the offline recognition system comparable to the results obtained by other systems, the recognizer was evaluated on the IAM-OnDB-t1 benchmark. This benchmark provides a closed vocabulary of 11,059 words. Further details on this benchmark are available in Section 3.3.3. Note that the test set differs from the test set of the previous experiments. The test set used in this experiment was larger and contains data from more writers than in the previous test sets. Lower recognition results have to be expected, because of the larger vocabulary.

Table 4.6 shows the results on the IAM-OnDB-t1 benchmark. The recognition rate of the mixed system was higher than those of the other systems. Mixing the training set with the IAM-DB increased the

Table 4.6 Results of the offline systems on the IAM-OnDB-t1 benchmark test set with a simple word pair grammar

System	Recognition rate (%)	Accuracy (%)
Adapted from IAM-DB	41.69	37.92
Trained on IAM-OnDB	61.91	43.10
Trained on IAM-OnDB + IAM-DB	67.85	61.36

recognition rate by 5.94 % to 67.85 %. This improvement is statistically significant using a standard Z-test at a significance level of 1 %. The accuracy reported in the third column takes also inserted words into account (see Section 4.3.1).

4.4 Word Extraction

In spite of Sayre's paradox, a two-stage approach was investigated in addition to the recognition systems introduced before [Liwicki *et al.* (2006a)]. Unlike the approach to handwriting recognition in the case of complete text lines, it first extracts the words and then recognizes the isolated words. From isolated word recognition, a higher performance can be expected, for this is a simpler task. However, there is an upper bound on the recognition accuracy because of the errors made at the word extraction stage. Although the two-stage approach is not used in the remainder of this book, this section reports on all results that were achieved.

This section is devoted to the word extraction system and the corresponding experiments. First, in Section 4.4.1 previous work in the domain of word extraction is summarized. Second, the preparation steps of the word extraction system are described in Section 4.4.2. Next, the proposed word extraction method is presented in Section 4.4.3, and the extraction performance of this system is reported in Section 4.4.4. Finally, the word recognition rate of the two-stage approach is compared to the single-stage approach in Section 4.4.5. Note that this section closely follows [Liwicki *et al.* (2006a)].

4.4.1 *Previous Work*

There exists some work in the field of online text segmentation, but it is mainly based on text/graphic segmentation or structure analysis [Jain *et al.* (2001); Ye *et al.* (2005)]. In [Oudot *et al.* (2004)] the segmentation task is studied explicitly. Similarly to the approach described in this section the approach in [Oudot *et al.* (2004)] is based on horizontal distance information. The system in [Oudot *et al.* (2004)] uses neural networks for classification, while the system in this section is based on recently proposed offline word segmentation [Varga and Bunke (2005)]. The method introduced in [Varga and Bunke (2005)] relies on the assumption that the size of gaps between consecutive words may vary considerably, but humans usually leave more whitespace between two consecutive words (inter-word gaps) than between two connected components that belong to the same word (intra-word-gaps) up to some predefined factor.

In this section a method for online word segmentation is proposed, which is based on the same assumption. The method first segments a line of text into a sequence of connected components where the gaps between two sequences are larger than a previously calculated threshold. Then it further splits sequences where the largest gap inside a sequence is larger than a fraction of the gaps that separate the considered sequence from other sequences.

Several performance measures for the evaluation of word segmentation algorithms exist [Kim *et al.* (2002); Mahadevan and Srihari (1996)]. These measures take different aspects into account, as the task of word segmentation can be interpreted in various ways. It can be interpreted as a word extraction task [Varga and Bunke (2005)], a gap classification task [Mahadevan and Srihari (1996)], or the task of finding inter-word gaps. In the word extraction experiments in this section the results are presented using three different measures that are based on these three interpretations.

4.4.2 Data Preparation

Some preprocessing steps are applied to the handwritten text lines for the purpose of normalization (see Section 4.1). As a first step the text lines are normalized with respect to slant and skew. Then it is assumed that words can be separated from each other by vertical cuts[2]. The upper and lower baseline are estimated for each text line, which allows us to perform height normalization. Another preprocessing step is width normalization, where the number of characters is estimated using the number of white runs[3] between the upper and the lower baseline. Finally, punctuation marks are removed from the input data using some simple heuristics. This step is

---

[2]This assumption is satisfied by more than 99 % of the data.

[3]A white run is a series of white pixels connecting two black pixels in one pixel row.

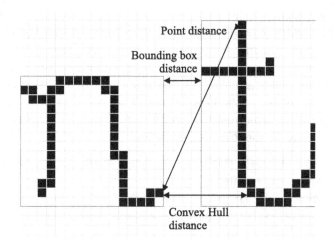

Fig. 4.11 Illustration of the distance measures on a simplified example

useful because punctuation often causes errors during the segmentation of a text line [Kim *et al.* (2002); Varga and Bunke (2005)].

A connected component, or component for short, consists of one or several horizontally overlapping strokes. In the procedure proposed in this section the distances between adjacent components need to be calculated. For these distances several gap metrics exist (see Fig. 4.11):

- *Bounding box distance*: the width of the white gap in the vertical projection of the components.
- *Convex hull distance*: the minimal white run-length between the convex hulls of both components. If the components do not overlap vertically, the bounding box distance is taken.
- *Point distance*: the distance between the last point of the first component and the first point of the second component. This distance can be modified by using the mean of the last/first n points.

In addition to geometrical information, it can be helpful to use the time information of the gaps to define a gap metric. Two possibilities are investigated to include time information. First, only the time distance is used. Second, the time distance is scaled with a factor and added to the geometric distance. This factor is optimized on the validation set.

Three methods are investigated for calculating the initial threshold that is used to split a line of text into sequences of connected components. First a fixed value f is used as in most handwriting recognition systems. This is reasonable since width normalization takes place during preprocessing.

As an alternative, the thresholds proposed in [Marti and Bunke (2001a); Varga and Bunke (2005)] are taken for offline representation of the handwriting. Both thresholds are based on the white run-lengths between the upper and lower baseline of the handwriting. These lines separate the ascenders and the descenders from the middle part of the handwriting. The thresholds are based on the following statistics:

- *Median white run-length (MWR)*: the median of the set of white run-lengths between the two lines.
- *Average white run-length (AWR)*: the median of the number of white pixels in a row divided by the median number of black-white transitions in a row.

In the basic version of the segmentation method (see below) the text line is divided at all gaps that are larger than the threshold $\gamma \cdot f$, where $\gamma > 0$ is a parameter optimized on a separate validation set in the experiments and f is either equal to MWR or AWR.

4.4.3 Word Extraction Method

The word segmentation algorithm is based on the assumption that for all words w_i the gaps within w_i are smaller than the gaps between w_i and its left and right neighbor w_{i-1} and w_{i+1}. In the algorithm, first the text line is divided at all gaps that are larger than the initial threshold. Then all remaining sequences of consecutive connected components are taken into account. For each remaining sequence S the maximal gap *maxgap* inside the sequence and the gaps *leftgap* and *rightgap* to the left and right hand side of S are considered. If they fulfill the condition

$$\alpha * maxgap \geq \min\{leftgap, rightgap\}, \tag{4.7}$$

the sequence is further divided into two subsequences, where α is a predefined parameter. This is repeated recursively until no more sequences fulfill the condition in Eq. (4.7). Note that α is optimized on a separate validation set in the experiments.

Figure 4.12 illustrates how the algorithm works. First, all gaps larger than the initial threshold are considered as segmentation points. This results in the three sequences of connected components "the", "work should", and "have been". Then the largest gap of each sequence is tested if it fulfills

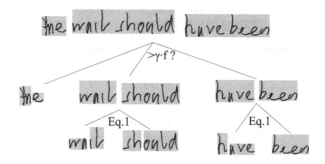

Fig. 4.12   Proposed segmentation method for an example text line

the condition of Eq. (4.7). As a result the sequences "work should" and "have been" are further divided. The algorithm stops at this point, because the remaining gaps are too small. Note that the blanks denote the gaps which are considered in the next step.

4.4.4   *Word Extraction Experiments*

All experiments were conducted on a subset of the the IAM-OnDB. The selected subset consists of 100 handwritten texts with about eight lines each. For optimizing the parameters γ and α of Sections 4.4.2 and 4.4.3, an additional validation set of 20 writers was used. Each text was produced by a different writer. Hence a total of 120 writers were involved.

Several methods for measuring the performance of a segmentation algorithm exist. In the experiments described in this section, three different performance measures were used:

- *Word extraction rate (WER)*: with this measure the segmentation task is considered as a word extraction task [Kim *et al.* (2002); Varga and Bunke (2005)]:

$$\text{WER} = \frac{\text{number of correctly extracted words}}{\text{number of all words}} \qquad (4.8)$$

- *Gap classification rate (GCR)*: the segmentation task is considered as a gap classification task which classifies the gaps as inter-word gaps or intra-word gaps [Mahadevan and Srihari (1996)]:

$$\text{GCR} = \frac{\text{number of correctly labeled gaps}}{\text{number of all gaps}} \qquad (4.9)$$

Table 4.7   Performance of the segmentation methods for the three measures of Eqs. (4.8)-(4.10) on the test set

Method measure	threshold	Basic	New	Error reduction
WER	FIX	85.36	**86.42**	7.24
	MWR	85.32	**86.08**	5.18
	AWR	85.95	**86.58**	4.48
GCR	FIX	95.64	95.69	1.15
	MWR	95.54	95.66	2.69
	AWR	95.69	95.75	1.39
GA	FIX	87.22	**87.50**	2.19
	MWR	86.95	**87.55**	4.60
	AWR	87.41	**87.73**	2.54

- *Gap accuracy (GA)*: the segmentation task is considered as an inter-word gap finding task:

$$GA = \frac{\text{correctly found gaps - gaps wrongly found}}{\text{all gaps}} \quad (4.10)$$

Depending on the underlying performance measure, the results vary. Usually, the best results are reported with the second measure, since it is rather simple to classify most short gaps as intra-word gaps. Note that for a two-stage handwriting recognition system the WER is the best measure, because it directly yields an upper bound on the word recognition rate.

First, the gap metrics presented in Section 4.4.2 were investigated. The results show that the bounding box distance was the best metric on the validation set. Integrating online information, i.e., temporal information, into the distance measure did not increase the performance. A possible reason for this observation is that, on the one hand, the writers sometimes make a break within a word for moving to the right in front of the whiteboard. On the other hand, sometimes they quickly write a couple of words without pausing. Thus the online information is not helpful for word extraction. In this respect the whiteboard handwriting data may be different from handwriting produced on an electronic tablet.

Table 4.7 shows the results of all segmentation methods using different thresholds and accuracy measures. The baseline method only uses the initial threshold for segmentation. The average white run-length turned out to be the best choice for the initial threshold computation (column 'Basic' in Table 4.7). However, using a fixed threshold also produced good results, because the text lines are width normalized before segmentation.

Table 4.8 Results of the offline word recognition
systems including a statistical language model

System	Recognition rate (%)
Baseline system	63.57
Two-stage approach	64.05

In Table 4.7 it can be observed that the system using the new method always outperformed the baseline system. Bold entries denote that the increase, when compared to the corresponding baseline system, is statistically significant on the 5 % level (using a standard Z-test). This confirms the hypothesis that applying a more refined method improves the word segmentation rate.

The differences of the three performance measures can be clearly seen in the results. The highest values were obtained by using the gap classification measure, while the word extraction measure and the gap accuracy were nearly on the same level. A possible reason for the high accuracy of the gap classification measure is the existence of many small intra-word gaps. For those gaps the classification is rather simple. However, the WER is a measure that directly gives an upper bound on the word recognition rate of a two-stage system, because a word is usually not recognized correctly if it is not segmented correctly.

4.4.5 *Word Recognition Experiments*

To measure the performance of the two-stage recognition system, experiments were performed on the dataset of the previous section. For this purpose the set was split into a training set of 64 texts, a validation set containing 96 texts, and a test set consisting of 32 texts. The other parameters of the experimental set up, e.g., vocabulary and letters, were the same as in the experiments of the IAM-OnDB-t1 benchmark.

The recognition system that was trained and tested on unsegmented data served as a reference system. Two different methods exist for the two-stage approach to train the recognizer of the second stage. First, the system may be trained on unsegmented data, and second, the system may be trained on segmented data. During the validation process it turned out that the latter method shows higher performance, and thus it was used in the experiments described this section.

Table 4.8 shows the performance of the two-stage approach compared to the baseline system. The recognition rate slightly improved by 0.48 %. However, this improvement is not statistically significant.

4.5   Conclusions

In this chapter a handwriting recognition system for whiteboard notes was presented. The proposed system is based on an offline handwriting recognition system, which has been developed in previous work. Some online preprocessing methods are added to recover from artifacts produced by the recording system. Next, the online data are transformed into gray-scale offline images. To achieve an improved recognition performance, state-of-the-art methods are applied, such as the optimization of the number of states and Gaussian mixture components, and the inclusion of a statistical language model.

To further improve the performance, the training data were enhanced in several ways. First, additional data from the IAM-DB were used. In the experiments the recognition rate was significantly increased by 4.2 % to 68.5 % by training on mixed training data. Second, a larger database of handwritten notes acquired on a whiteboard (IAM-OnDB) was used. With the second database, the recognition rate increased by 2.1 % to 66.4 %. This increase is also statistically significant. Additionally both databases were combined into one large training set. A recognition rate of 68.6 % was achieved, which is the best rate obtained in all experiments reported in this chapter.

At the end of this chapter a two-stage recognition system was investigated based on a word extraction system for online data. In the literature little attention has been paid to this specific task of online handwriting recognition. State-of-the-art methods are applied for initial threshold computation and for hierarchically segmenting a text line.

The word extraction results show that there is a significant potential for increasing the segmentation performance over simple heuristic methods. More precisely, the word extraction rate was increased from 85.36 % in the baseline method, where a fixed threshold is used, to 85.95 % by computing the initial threshold with the AWR method. By applying the new word segmentation algorithm the word extraction rate further increased to 86.58 %, which is statistically significant. It is shown that the definition of the measure has a great impact on the level of the reported results. While the word extraction rate was about 86 %, the gap classification rate was already over 95 %. This should be considered when results of different reports are compared with one another.

The two-stage system first applies the word extraction methods and then applies the same offline recognition system as in the other experiments. The recognition rate of this two-stage system was higher than the recognition rate of the baseline system. However, this improvement is not statistically significant.

To make the results of the single-stage offline recognition system comparable to the results obtained with other systems, the recognizer was evaluated on the IAM-OnDB-t1 benchmark. In the experiments the mixed system outperformed the other systems, i.e., mixing the original training set with the IAM-DB increased the recognition rate by 5.94 % to 67.85 %. This recognition rate serves as a baseline for the remaining chapters of this book.

Chapter 5

Online Approach

In this chapter an online handwriting recognition system for whiteboard notes is presented. This system uses state-of-the-art preprocessing and feature extraction methods. These methods are supplemented with special preprocessing procedures to handle particular problems arising from whiteboard data. Since all the preprocessing methods have been developed for text lines, the acquired whiteboard texts must be segmented into text lines first. For this purpose a novel approach based on dynamic programming is proposed in the beginning of this chapter.

Two classifiers are applied to recognize the data. The first classifier is based on HMMs and is similar to the recognition system described in the previous chapter. The second classifier is based on neural networks. It uses BLSTM combined with CTC (see Section 2.2). This type of recognition system has been applied to the recognition of handwritten data for the first time. To investigate the influence of the individual components of the novel approach, a detailed experimental analysis is performed and discussed in this book.

This chapter is organized as follows. First, a novel approach for line segmentation is proposed in Section 5.1. Parts of this section follow the description in [Liwicki *et al.* (2007b)]. Next, Section 5.2 presents the preprocessing and normalization steps. Subsequently, the set of extracted features is introduced in Section 5.3. Sections 5.2 and 5.3 follow the description given in [Liwicki and Bunke (2006)]. Then, Section 5.4 reports on experimental results with the HMM-based system. Following, an experimental study based on the neural network approach is described in Section 5.5. Finally, Section 5.6 concludes this chapter and discusses the two different recognition methods.

5.1   Line Segmentation

Line segmentation, also called text line detection, is an essential preprocessing step in nearly all recognition systems for handwritten text. In general online handwriting recognition systems, text line detection is usually
handled by simple heuristics, e.g., if the pen-movement to the left and to
the bottom exceeds a certain threshold it is assumed that a new text line
starts [Liwicki and Bunke (2006); Plamondon and Srihari (2000)]. However,
these simple methods fail if the user switches between different lines. This
typically happens when a missing letter or word is inserted later. For such
a scenario a more refined method must be applied.

For the offline case rather simple methods can be applied if the gap between consecutive neighboring text lines is large enough [Marti and Bunke
(2001a)]. Other approaches for offline text line detection are based on
connected components [Manmatha and Rothfeder (2005)] or on projection
histograms [Yu and Jain (1996)]. In [Kavallieratou *et al.* (2002)] an approach based on finding a segmentation path has been introduced, but this
method has many problems if the text lines are close to each other. Recently a new general algorithm for detecting text lines has been introduced
in [Li *et al.* (2006)].

As online data can be easily converted into offline format, any offline
method can be applied to online data. However, in order to segment online data, one can – and should – take additional benefit from the online
information. The approach proposed in this section is based on finding an
optimal path between two consecutive text lines. The optimal path between
two lines is found using dynamic programming. The input to the proposed
algorithm consists of online data, but additionally offline information is
taken into account. Most of the steps are performed on the offline version
of the data. This is motivated by the fact that the spatial information is
not dependent on the order of the strokes, and that humans also use the
offline information for this task.

The rest of the section is organized as follows. First, Section 5.1.1
gives an overview of the text line detection system. Next, the dynamic
programming procedure is introduced in Section 5.1.2 in greater detail and
the cost functions to find an optimal path are described in Section 5.1.3.
Following, Section 5.1.4 outlines some postprocessing steps, and finally,
experimental results are presented in Section 5.1.5.

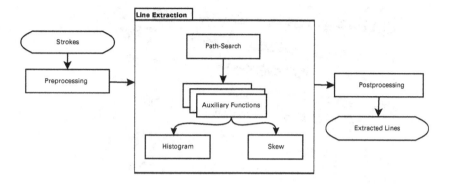

Fig. 5.1   Line segmentation system overview

5.1.1   *System Overview*

Figure 5.1 gives an overview of the text line detection system. The input is a handwritten text in online format. First some preprocessing steps are applied to filter out noise (see Section 4.1.1). Another preprocessing step is the initial estimation of the starting point of each text line. This estimation is needed because the dynamic programming paths will start between the starting points of each pair of consecutive lines. The starting points of the text lines are estimated by calculating the vertical histogram of the foreground pixels in the left part of the document. To prevent the skipping of lines, a new starting point is generated if the gap size between two consecutive starting points exceeds the median gap size. It is usually no problem if too many starting points have been found because this often results in empty spaces between two paths, which can be easily detected and deleted.

As the last preprocessing step, the skew of the document is estimated. Two methods for skew estimation have been investigated, i.e., linear regression and a new approach. In the new approach two histograms of the foreground pixels are calculated. One histogram is in the middle of the left-hand side of the text area, i.e., it covers the area from 12.5 % to 37.5 % of the text width; the other histogram is situated in the middle of the right-hand side, i.e., it covers the area from 62.5 % to 87.5 % of the text width. The maxima of these two histograms are then matched using a greedy search algorithm, which iteratively matches the maxima with the lowest y-difference and the largest number of strokes intersecting the connecting line. The approach is illustrated in Fig. 5.2, where the areas considered for

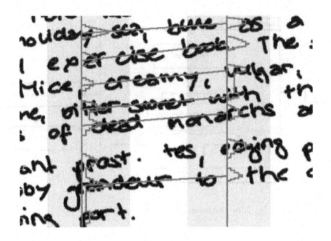

Fig. 5.2   Skew estimation using two histograms

the histograms are highlighted with a gray background. In the text line detection experiments the second approach based on histograms performed better than linear regression.

After preprocessing, a dynamic programming procedure is applied to detect the text lines. It searches an optimal path guided by a cost function that consists of a combination of several auxiliary functions. The dynamic programming procedure is outlined in Section 5.1.2, while the cost functions including the auxiliary functions are described in detail in Section 5.1.3. The dynamic programming procedure already outputs lines of good quality. At the end, however, some postprocessing steps are applied to further improve the results. These steps also take the online information into account.

5.1.2 *Dynamic Programming*

Dynamic programming is a well established technique for solving optimization problems [Bellman and Dreyfus (1962)]. It has been successfully applied in various subfields of image analysis, particularly in edge detection [Ballard and Brown (1982)]. Dynamic programming is applicable wherever the given optimization problem consists of similar sub-problems and the optimal solution can be determined using the optimal solutions of the sub-problems. In general the optimal solution for a given function $h(x_1, \ldots, x_N)$, i.e., the tuple $(\widehat{x}_1, \ldots, \widehat{x}_N)$ for which the function assumes

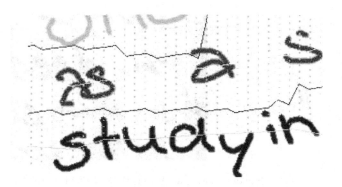

Fig. 5.3 Example grid for a path

its minimal or maximal value, can only be found using an exhaustive search through all parameters x_i, resulting in an exponential calculation time. If it is known that the problem can be divided into sub-problems $h_1, \ldots, h_{N-1}$ and the optimal values of $h_{n-1}(x_{n-1}, x_n)$ are greater then zero and independent of all other parameters, the problem can be solved in $O(N * k^2)$ time, where k is the number of discrete values each x_i can take on.

Dynamic programming works according to the following formula:

$$\min_{x_i, 1 \leq i \leq N} h(x_1, \ldots, x_N) = \min_{x_N} f_{N-1}(x_N) \tag{5.1}$$

where $f_0(x_1) = 0$ and

$$\min_{x_n} f_{n-1}(x_n) = \min_{x_{n-1}} (f_{n-2}(x_{n-1}) + h_{n-1}(x_{n-1}, x_n)) \tag{5.2}$$

In the problem considered in this section, the N parameters are the possible y-positions of the path in the y-vicinity of the path's start position. This is repeated at each horizontal position, resulting in a grid of $N * K$ possible positions for the best path, where K is a predifined parameter. Figure 5.3 illustrates a grid for an example text[1]. Note that the grid has been adjusted to the skew.

5.1.3 *Cost Function*

The function $h_{n-1}(x_{n-1}, x_n)$ for the sub-problems is calculated using three auxiliary functions. These functions are described in this section. Since the optimization problem is to find a path with minimal cost, each function can

---

[1]Note that in this and the following figures, different shades of gray have been used to represent the individual lines detected by the algorithm.

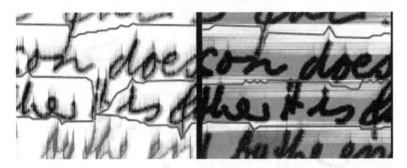

Fig. 5.4   Effects of the evade-function; note that there is the same text on the left and right - only the gray background that represents the penalty function differs

be seen as a penalty for any deviation from the optimal path. Eventually, the path with the smallest overall penalty, or cost, is the desired solution.

To avoid very high differences in y-direction between consecutive points on the path, the vertical distance between two adjacent positions is used for the calculation of the first auxiliary function. After subtracting the skew the penalty is calculated according to the following formula:

$$h_{y-difference}(x_{n-1}, x_n) = d(y_{n-1}, y_n)^3 \qquad (5.3)$$

In the letters of the Roman alphabet, delayed strokes, such as i-dots and quotation marks, usually belong to the text line below. Only punctuation marks, such as dots and commas, sometimes need to be assigned to the text above, but in most cases they are already at the correct y-position. One can benefit from this property if the optimal path of the dynamic programming procedure is closer to the text line above than to the text line below. This idea is captured in the *evade*-function, which adds more penalty if the path gets closer to strokes below. To avoid jumping to another line, another penalty is added to the grid points to the right and to the left. This penalty in horizontal direction decreases with distance. More formally, the penalty added to a given point x_n is defined as follows:

$$h_{evade}(x_{n-1}, x_n) = \max_{p \in P}((C - d(x_n, p_x)) + (C - 2 * d(y_n, p_y))) \qquad (5.4)$$

where P is the set of foreground pixels in the area below x_n where both summands are greater than or equal to 0, and C is a constant. Thus the penalty decreases if the distance becomes larger. Figure 5.4 illustrates the effect of adding this penalty. In the left-hand side of this figure only the distance in vertical direction is taken into account, while on the right-hand

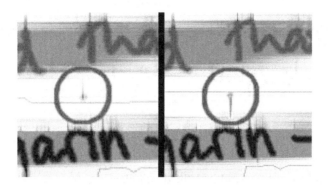

Fig. 5.5   The i-dot is correctly assigned with the special handling for small strokes

side both distances are considered. In this figure the penalty for all grid points is displayed in light gray. The darker a point, the higher is the corresponding penalty. A segmentation error in the left part of Fig. 5.4 can be observed, where the word "it" is assigned to the upper text line by mistake. However, thanks to the influence of the penalty in horizontal direction, this error is avoided in the right-hand side. In the area of small strokes this penalty is applied in the opposite direction, because most likely these strokes are points corresponding to the line below. Figure 5.5, on the left-hand side, illustrates what happens if this special handling for small strokes is not applied. Here an i-dot is assigned incorrectly to the upper text line. The correct segmentation obtained under the extended procedure is shown on the right-hand side.

The third auxiliary function is derived from the assumption that the words have roughly been written next to each other. To prevent the path from jumping into the text line above or below, a fixed penalty is added if the path crosses space of a supposed text line. It is assumed that large strokes that have their center of gravity in vertical direction near the maximum of the vertical histogram are all in the same text line. This initial guess is similar to connected component based approaches [Manmatha and Rothfeder (2005)]. Thus the third auxiliary function is defined as:

$$h_{cross}(x_{n-1}, x_n) = \begin{cases} 1 \text{ if there is a crossing} \\ 0 \text{ otherwise} \end{cases} \quad (5.5)$$

The effect of this auxiliary function is illustrated in Fig. 5.6.

Finally, the cost function $h_{n-1}(x_{n-1}, x_n)$ used in the dynamic programming procedure consists of a linear combination of the three auxiliary

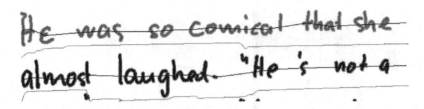

Fig. 5.6　Cost function for preventing the crossing of lines

functions introduced above and is defined as follows:

$$h_{n-1}(x_{n-1}, x_n) =$$

$$h_{y-difference}(x_{n-1}, x_n) + h_{evade}(x_{n-1}, x_n) + c * h_{cross}(x_{n-1}, x_n) \quad (5.6)$$

where c is a parameter that is optimized on an independent validation set.

5.1.4　*Postprocessing*

After the dynamic programming approach has detected the text lines as described above, some postprocessing operations are performed to eliminate a few common mistakes which may have occurred during preprocessing and the search for the optimal path. The first correction is the removal of empty text lines, which appear if too many starting points have been found.

Another effect of too many starting points is the existence of pseudo text lines which consist of quotation marks and i-dots only. These lines usually contain only a small number of strokes, and the strokes have a few points only. To recover from errors of this kind these lines are merged with the corresponding text lines below.

The last postprocessing step is the only one which directly uses online information. Since some i-dots and punctuation marks may have been assigned to a wrong text line, the strokes in the online vicinity of each stroke s_i are considered. If these strokes are also nearby in space, but in another estimated line, s_i is reassigned to the other text line. In the next section the effect of this online postprocessing step is demonstrated.

5.1.5　*Experiments and Results*

The text line extraction experiments were conducted on the IAM-OnDB (see Section 3.3). A set of 100 documents was used for testing. Each

Table 5.1 Results on 100 documents: stroke and document classification rate

System	Stroke	Document
Online reference	93.40 %	62 %
Proposed system	99.79 %	90 %
With online postpr.	99.94 %	98 %

document has about six to ten text lines with an average number of 25 strokes each. A different set was used for validating the parameters of the dynamic programming approach.

In order to compare the performance of the proposed system, an online reference system was implemented. This reference system is based on simple heuristics, i.e., if the pen-movement to the left is larger than N pixels and there is a pen-movement to the bottom it starts a new text line. This is a common procedure found in many online systems [Liwicki and Bunke (2006); Plamondon and Srihari (2000)]. The reference system usually fails if a punctuation mark has been written later than the words next to it, or if a letter or a word has been forgotten and inserted later.

The parameters of the proposed method and the reference system have been optimized manually on the validation set. The weights of the first two auxiliary functions of Section 5.1.3 have been set to 1, while the last one has been found to be optimal at 1,000. The proposed system was tested under two different settings. While in the first test dynamic programming and the offline postprocessing was applied, in the second test also the online post processing was executed.

Table 5.1 shows the classification rates of the proposed system and the reference system on the stroke level and on the document level. The stroke classification rate is the number of correctly assigned strokes divided by the total number of strokes. Similarly, the document classification rate is the number of correctly processed documents divided by the total number of documents. A very remarkable improvement from 93.40% (62 %) to 99.79 % (90 %) has been achieved with the proposed system without online postprocessing. Adding the online postprocessing step, the performance is further improved. Note that the improvement from 99.79 % to 99.94 % is statistically significant at a significance level of 5 %.

In the system with online postprocessing only two documents contained small mistakes. Figure 5.7 shows some examples of the errors. Even for a human it is not easy to assign the misclassified strokes to the correct text

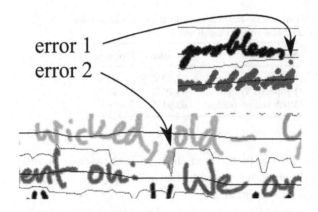

Fig. 5.7   Examples of misclassified strokes

line without reading the text. The first error is a period which has been treated as an i-dot and assigned to the text line below. The second error is a pair of misclassified quotation marks from the line below which have been treated as commas.

As a result of the proposed method, the text lines are extracted from the data originally recorded. Since the handwriting recognition system in this chapter works on complete text lines, this result can be used in the following processing steps.

5.2   Preprocessing

Having the extracted text lines at hand, the next step of the recognition system can be applied. It consists in text line normalization. This is a very important step in every handwriting recognition system because the style of the writers differs with respect to skew, slant, height, and width of the characters. Most preprocessing steps are similar to state-of-the-art online handwriting recognition systems reported before [Jäger *et al.* (2001); Plamondon and Srihari (2000); Schenkel *et al.* (1995)]. In the literature there is no standard way of preprocessing the data, but many systems use similar techniques. The basic preprocessing steps and the special procedures introduced for the handling of whiteboard data are explained in Section 5.2.1. Next, the normalization steps are described in Section 5.2.2.

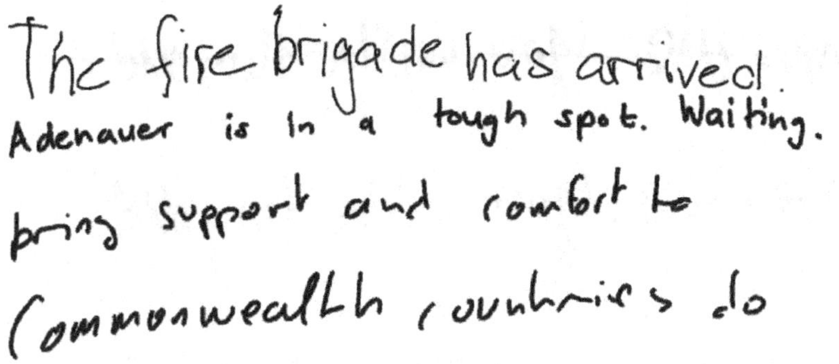

Fig. 5.8 Examples of handwritten texts acquired from a whiteboard

5.2.1 *Online Preprocessing*

The recognition of notes written on a whiteboard is a relatively new task. As people stand, rather than sit, during writing and the arm does not rest on a table, handwriting rendered on a whiteboard differs from handwriting produced with a pen on a writing tablet. It has been observed that the baseline usually cannot be interpolated with a simple quadratic polynomial. Furthermore, the size and width of the characters become smaller the more the writer moves to the right. Figure 5.8 shows some examples of handwritten text lines acquired from a whiteboard. There the baseline of the first line does not follow a simple curve and the letters on the left hand side are larger than those on the right hand side. These problems require methods specifically adapted to whiteboard data in addition to the usual preprocessing steps.

The text lines on a whiteboard usually have no uniform skew. Therefore they are split into smaller parts and the rest of the preprocessing is done for each part separately. To accomplish the splitting, all gaps within a line are determined. The text line is then split at a gap if the size of this gap is larger than the median gap size. Furthermore the size of both parts must be greater than a predefined threshold. An example of the splitting process is shown in Fig. 5.9 with the resulting parts indicated by lines below the first text line.

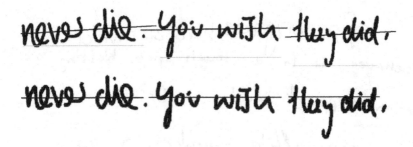

Fig. 5.9   Splitting a text line into components and skew correction

5.2.2 *Normalization*

As a first normalization step the parts are corrected with respect to their skew. A linear regression computed through all the points before the correction of the text line orientation according to the regression parameters. This process is illustrated in Fig. 5.9 with the resulting text line in the lower part. The black lines in the upper text line indicate the function of the linear regression computed for each part of the text line. (Note that the baseline and corpus line detection, which are performed at later stage, usually give a better estimation of the skew.)

For slant normalization, which is the next preprocessing step, a histogram is used. This approach computes the histogram over all angles enclosed by the lines connecting two successive points of the trajectory and the horizontal line [Jäger *et al.* (2001)]. An illustration of an example text line histogram is given in Fig. 5.10. The histogram ranges from $-90\,°$ to $90\,°$ with a step size of $2\,°$. In the online recognition system described in this chapter, each histogram entry is smoothed using its direct neighbors and a weighting window $(0.25, 0.5, 0.25)$. This is done because in some cases the correct slant is at the border of two angle intervals, and a single peak at another interval may be slightly higher. The single peak will become smaller after smoothing. The histogram values are additionally weighted with a Gaussian whose mean is at the vertical angle and whose variance is chosen empirically. This is beneficial since some words are not properly corrected if a single long straight line is drawn in the horizontal direction, which results in a large histogram value. The effects of the two histogram processing steps are shown in Fig. 5.10. The resulting histogram is smoothed and the maximum is near the vertical angle. Figure 5.11 shows a text line before and after slant correction. The gray lines indicate the estimated slant angle.

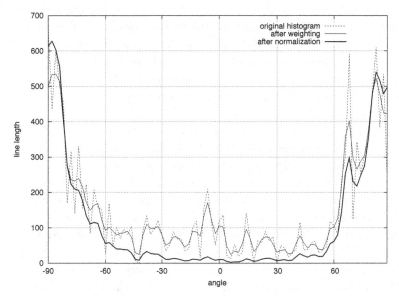

Fig. 5.10   Angle histogram for an example text line

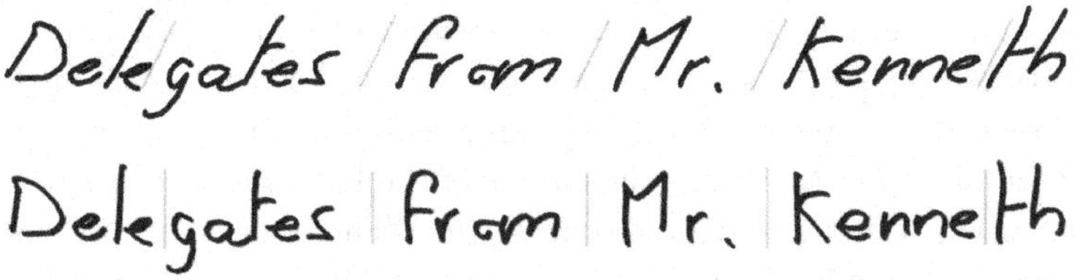

Fig. 5.11   Slant correction

Delayed strokes, e.g., the crossing of a "t" or the dot of an "i", are a well known problem in online handwriting recognition. These strokes cause an additional variation of the temporal information because the writing order of delayed strokes varies between different writers. Therefore delayed strokes are removed in most online handwriting recognition systems. In the recognition system described in this chapter the removal is done using simple heuristics. Strokes written above already existing parts, followed by a pen-movement to the right, are removed. To retain the information of delayed strokes for the recognizer, the *hat-feature* is used in the feature set (see Section 5.3).

Since online data are equidistant in time but not in space, the number of captured points varies depending on the writing speed. This variation should be removed in order to normalize the data. For the normalization of the number of points, the sequence of captured points is replaced by a new sequence where each two consecutive points on the trajectory have the same distance to each other. The optimal value for the distance has been empirically optimized.

The next important step is the computation of the baseline and the corpus line. The baseline corresponds to the original guiding line on which the text has been written. The corpus line goes through the top of the lower case letters, e.g., "a" or "c". These lines are utilized in order to normalize the size of the text. The minima and maxima of the y-coordinates of the strokes are calculated to obtain the baseline and the corpus line. Then two linear regressions through the minima and maxima are computed with the constraint that the two resulting lines have to have the same slope. After the regression lines have been determined, the least fitting points are removed and another linear regression is performed. This correction step is done twice, which then results in the estimated baseline (minima) and corpus line (maxima). Figure 5.12 illustrates the estimated baseline and the corpus line of part of the example shown in Fig. 5.9.

The baseline is subtracted from all y-coordinates to make it equal to the x-axis. Based on the baseline and the corpus line the text is divided into three areas: the upper area, which mainly contains the ascenders of the letters; the median area, where the corpus of the letters is present; and the lower area with the descenders of some letters. The upper area is then scaled to have the same height as the median area. The lower area is only scaled to the corpus height if it is larger than than the corpus height. This prevents the system from an unnecessary scaling of the lower area if there are no descenders.

The last preprocessing step consists of normalizing the width of the characters. This is done by scaling the text horizontally with a fraction of the number of strokes crossing the horizontal line between the baseline and the corpus line. This preprocessing step is needed because the x-coordinates of the points are taken as a feature.

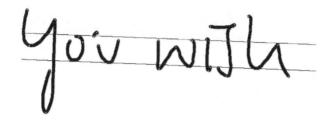

Fig. 5.12   Baseline and corpus line of an example part of a text line

5.3   Features

State-of-the-art feature extraction methods are applied to extract the features from the preprocessed data. The feature set input to the recognizer
consists of 25 features which utilize information from both the real online
data stored in XML format, and pseudo offline information automatically
generated from the online data. For each (x, y)-coordinate recorded by the
acquisition device a set of 25 features is extracted, resulting in a sequence
of 25-dimensional vectors for each given text line.

The set of extracted features can be divided into two classes. The
first class consists of features extracted for each point by considering the
neighbors with respect to time. It is presented in Section 5.3.1. The second
class takes the offline matrix representation into account, i.e., it is based
on spatial information. This class is described in Section 5.3.2.

5.3.1   *Online Features*

The features of the first class are the following (the numbers in parenthesis
will be used to refer to selected features later in this chapter):

- *pen-up/pen-down (1):* a binary feature indicating whether the pen-tip
  touches the board or not. Consecutive strokes are connected with
  straight lines for which this feature has the value *false*.
- *hat-feature (2):* this binary feature indicates whether a delayed stroke
  has been removed at the same horizontal position as the considered
  point.
- *speed (3):* the velocity is computed before resampling and then interpolated.
- *x-coordinate (4):* the *x*-position is taken after high-pass filtering, i.e.,

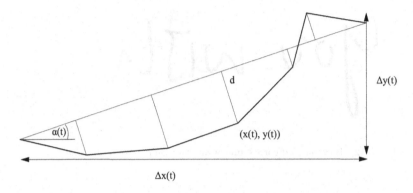

Fig. 5.13   Features of the vicinity

after subtracting a moving average from the real horizontal position.

- *y-coordinate (5):* this feature represents the vertical position of the point after normalization.
- *writing direction (6,7):* this pair of features is given by the cosine and sine of the angle between the line segment starting at the point and the *x*-axis.
- *curvature (8,9):* similarly to the writing direction, this is a pair of features given by the cosine and sine of the angle between the lines to the previous and the next point.
- *vicinity aspect (19):* this feature is equal to the aspect of the trajectory in the vicinity of a fixed size (see Fig. 5.13):

$$\frac{\Delta y(t) - \Delta x(t)}{\Delta y(t) + \Delta x(t)}$$

The vicinity aspect is large for strokes that are nearly straight in horizontal or vertical direction.

- *vicinity slope (20,21):* this pair of features is given by the cosine and sine of the angle α of the straight line from the first to the last vicinity point (see Fig. 5.13).
- *vicinity curliness (22):* this feature is defined as the length of the trajectory in the vicinity divided by $\max(\Delta x(t), \Delta y(t))$ (see Fig. 5.13).
- *vicinity linearity (23):* here the average squared distance d^2 of each point in the vicinity to the straight line from the first to the last vicinity point is used (see Fig. 5.13).

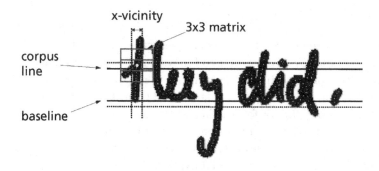

Fig. 5.14   Features of the offline matrix

5.3.2   *Pseudo Offline Features*

The features of the second class are all computed by using a two-dimensional matrix $B = b_{i,j}$ representing the offline version of the data. For each position $b_{i,j}$ the number of points on the trajectory of the strokes is stored. This can be seen as a low-resolution image of the handwritten data. The following features are used:

- *ascenders/descenders (24,25):* these two features count the number of points above the corpus line (ascenders) and below the baseline (descenders). Only points which have an x-coordinate in the vicinity of the current point are considered. Additionally the points must have a minimal distance to the lines to be considered as a part of ascenders or descenders. This can be seen as a tolerance area. The corresponding distances as well as the vicinity area are set to a predefined fraction of the corpus height.
- *context map (10-18):* the two-dimensional vicinity of the current point is transformed to a 3×3 map. The number of black points in each region is taken as a feature value. Altogether nine features of this type are obtained.

Figure 5.14 illustrates the extracted features. Note that the strokes are widened for ease of visualization.

5.4   HMM-Based Experiments

The writer-independent experiments were performed on the IAM-OnDB. This database and the benchmarks used for evaluating the performance are described in Section 3.3. Initial experiments were performed to measure the influence of the new preprocessing steps, and then the performance was measured on the benchmark tasks. Finally, feature selection was applied to the set of 25 features to find the best subset of features.

Before reporting the experimental results, Section 5.4.1 summarizes the recognition parameters. The initial experiments are presented in Section 5.4.2 and the results on the benchmarks are given in Section 5.4.3. The feature selection experiments are summarized in Section 5.4.4.

5.4.1   *Recognition Parameters*

For the experiments described in this section, an HMM-based recognition system was used. One HMM was built for each character in the character set. In all HMMs the linear topology was used. In the emitting states, the observation probability distributions were estimated by mixtures of Gaussian components. The character models were concatenated to represent words, and word models were concatenated to represent text lines. For training, the Baum–Welch algorithm was applied. In the recognition phase, the Viterbi algorithm was used to find the most probable word sequence. The output of the recognizer is a sequence of words. A statistical language model supports the Viterbi decoding step. The integration of this language model was optimized on a validation set as described in Section 2.4.3.

As stated above, the recognition system used HMMs with diagonal covariance Gaussian probability distributions. The number of states per HMM has been optimized globally on the validation set. The final value was eight states per HMM. Since the number of Gaussian mixtures and also the number of training iterations have an effect on the recognition results of an HMM recognizer, they were optimized in the experiments described in this section. The number of Gaussian components was incremented stepwise by one by splitting the Gaussian component with the highest weight at each step into two components. After each increase, four training iterations were performed. Here this step was repeated up to 36 Gaussian components.

Table 5.2 Recognition rate of different online recognition systems on the validation set

System	Recognition rate (%)
Preprocessing and features as in [Schenkel *et al.* (1995)]	50.0
All features of Section 5.3.1	50.5
All features	65.3
All features, new preprocessing	66.7

Table 5.3 Recognition rate on the test set (WPG = word pair grammar, LM = language model)

System	Using a WPG	Including LM
Conventional preprocessing	62.3	64.8
New preprocessing	63.6	66.4
Trained on large set	67.3	70.8

5.4.2 *Initial Experiments*

The test set in the first experiments consisted of 6,204 word instances in 1,258 lines produced by 20 different writers. The tests were conducted using a dictionary consisting of the 2,337 words that appear in the test set. The language model was generated from the LOB Corpus [Johansson (1986)]. This is the same setting as the one used for the initial experiments with the offline recognizer in Section 4.3.3. Hence the results can be compared to one another.

Several recognition systems were trained on a subset of the IAM-OnDB consisting of the 20 writers mentioned above. The different recognition systems result from different preprocessing steps and feature sets. Table 5.2 shows the results of the systems on the validation set. The inclusion of offline information (rows 3 and 4) led to a substantial improvement of the word recognition rate. "Conventional preprocessing" denotes the preprocessing steps of Section 5.2.2 which are known from literature, and "new preprocessing" includes the splitting of text lines into subparts and the improved slant correction.

In Table 5.3 the results on the test set are given. The last row shows the results of the same recognition system as the one used in the second row, but trained on a larger training set of about 50,000 words in about 7,800 text lines written by 132 writers. The improvement resulting from the larger training set is quite substantial. Yet the improvement of the new

Table 5.4   Word recognition accuracy on IAM-OnDB-t1

System	Recognition rate (%)	Accuracy (%)
Best offline	67.85 %	61.36 %
Online	73.13 %	63.14 %
Online with LM	76.42 %	72.98 %

Table 5.5   Word recognition accuracy on IAM-OnDB-t2

System	Recognition rate (%)	Accuracy (%)
Online	52.23 %	31.32 %
Online with LM	71.69 %	63.86 %

preprocessing methods (63.6 % vs. 62.3 % with a simple word pair grammar and 66.4 % vs. 64.8 % including the statistical language model) is already statistically significant at the 5 % level.

5.4.3   *Results on the Benchmarks of the IAM-OnDB*

In order to make the results of the offline recognition system comparable to the results obtained by other systems, the recognizer was evaluated on the IAM-OnDB-t1 benchmark and the IAM-OnDB-t2 benchmark.

For the experiments on the IAM-OnDB-t2 benchmark, the language model was trained and optimized on the second validation set. The training is based on three different corpora (LOB Corpus, Brown Corpus, Wellington Corpus). To guarantee that the test data are not used for training, the texts of the IAM-OnDB were removed from the LOB Corpus.

Table 5.4 shows the results of the online recognition system compared to the offline recognition system on the IAM-OnDB-t1 benchmark. The recognition rate is significantly higher, which can be explained by the additional information included in the online data. The results on the IAM-OnDB-t2 benchmark are shown in Table 5.5. The results on the second benchmark are significantly lower because of the larger vocabulary size. However, including a bigram language model led to a substantial improvement on a larger vocabulary.

5.4.4 *Feature Subset Selection Experiments*

The recognition system is based on 25 features extracted from the online and offline vicinity of each sampling point. It is an open question whether the extracted features are optimal or near-optimal. Actually, the features may be dependent on one another or may be redundant. Some of the features may even have an adverse effect on the recognition accuracy. In this section the set of features is analyzed and a sequential forward search is performed for feature subset selection [Kudo and Sklansky (2000)].

First, the correlation of the features is investigated. Figure 5.15 illustrates the correlation matrix of these 25 features. Note that the features are ordered according to their numbers (see above), beginning in the bottom-left corner. In this figure darker values indicate a stronger correlation between corresponding features. The matrix shows that most features are only weakly correlated.

Next, a sequential forward search (SFS) is applied on a validation set for selecting feature subsets. Given a set of features $S_1 = \{f_1, \ldots, f_n\}$ the algorithm proceeds as follows:

(1) Start with the feature f_s that individually performs best on the validation set and put it into the set of best features B_1; then set $S_2 = S_1 \backslash \{f_s\}$.
(2) For $k = 2, \ldots, n-1$ do:

   - For all $f_i \in S_k$ calculate the performance of $B_{k-1} \cup \{f_i\}$ on the validation set and rank the features according to their performance.
   - Add the best performing feature $f_{\hat{i}}$ to the set of best features $B_k = B_{k-1} \cup \{f_{\hat{i}}\}$ and set $S_{k+1} = S_k \backslash \{f_{\hat{i}}\}$.

The feature subset B_k finally selected is the one that performs best among all subsets considered by the algorithm. For a general description of feature selection algorithms see [Pudil *et al.* (1994)] and [Kudo and Sklansky (2000)].

As mentioned above, the number of Gaussian mixtures and training iterations have an effect on the recognition results of an HMM recognizer. Often the optimal value increases with the number of features and the amount of training data since more variations are encountered. The optimization of this value is very time consuming. Therefore it has been empirically set for each number of features equal to the optimal values of previous recognition experiments. However, after the optimal feature subset of a given size was

correlation matrix for all features

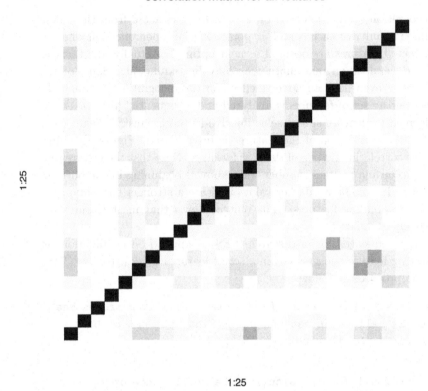

1:25

Fig. 5.15   Correlation matrix for all features; light colors imply low correlation

found by SFS, the number of Gaussian mixtures was optimized for this set.

Similarly to the previous section, the IAM-OnDB-t1 was used for the recognition experiments. The development of the recognition rate on the validation set during the sequential forward search is shown in Fig. 5.16. Using a subset of only five features, the recognition rate is already close to the recognition rate of the reference system. The highest performance was reached with 16 features. Table 5.6 shows the recognition rates of these three systems on the test set. The recognition rate of 73.88 % is statistically significantly higher than the recognition rate using all features (at a significance level of 5 %).

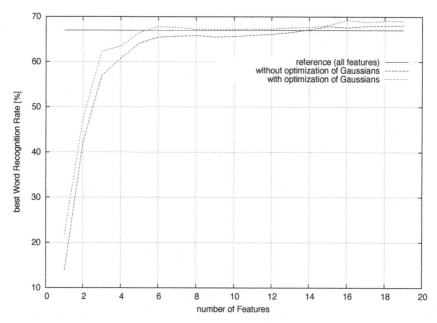

Fig. 5.16 Results of the best combination for each number of features on the validation set

A detailed analysis of the results shows that during the first iterations of the search algorithm the ranking of the first five features did not change (see Table 5.7). From this observation it can be concluded that each of the features is quite stable. Also these features give diverse information, which is more important for the recognition than the information provided by other features. The best five features are the cosine angle of the writing direction (6), the normalized y-position (5), the density in the center of the 3×3-matrix (14), the pen-up/down information (1), and the sine angle of the curvature (9).

Other features often did not increase the performance and even sometimes lead to lower recognition scores. These are the cosine angle of the curvature (8), the ascenders (24) and descenders (25), the linearity (23), the curliness (22), and the aspect (19) of the online vicinity. A possible explanation for the fact that the cosine angle of the curvature is not a good choice, while the sine angle of the curvature is one of the best features, is that the sine angle clearly distinguishes between a right turn and

Table 5.6   Performance of selected feature subsets on the test set

Subset	Recognition rate in %
Reference system	73.13
5 best features	71.83
Best subset (16)	73.88

Table 5.7   Ranking of features in step two for the first feature subsets during validation

Iteration k	Best subset B_k	Ranking of remaining features
1	$\{6\}$	$5, 14, 1, 9, 23, 3, \ldots$
2	$\{6, 5\}$	$14, 1, 9, 23, 3, \ldots$
3	$\{6, 5, 14\}$	$1, 9, 3, \ldots$
4	$\{6, 5, 14, 1\}$	$9, 18, 17, \ldots$

a left turn, while the cosine angle does not change significantly for small angles (which is the usual case in handwriting). Thus it does not provide additional information for the recognizer.

5.5   Experiments with Neural Networks

In the work described in this book, BLSTM combined with CTC was applied to word sequence recognition for the first time in the domain of handwriting recognition. Various experiments were conducted to analyze the influence of the different parameters on the recognition performance. The aim of the experiments is to evaluate the complete RNN handwriting recognition system, illustrated in Figure 5.17, on online handwriting.

This section is organized as follows. First, the parameters of the CTC approach are given in Section 5.5.1. Second, results using different recognition configurations are reported in Section 5.5.2. Next, Section 5.5.3 analyzes the effect of using LSTM units, and finally, Section 5.5.4 reports results using different vocabularies. Note that this section follows the report on the experiments in [Graves *et al.* (2008)].

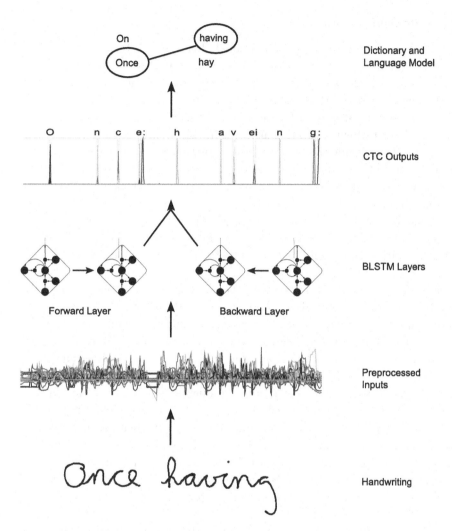

Fig. 5.17 The complete RNN handwriting recognition system. First the online hand-writing data are preprocessed with the techniques described above. The resulting sequence of feature vectors is scanned in opposite directions by the forward and backward BLSTM hidden layers. The BLSTM layers feed forward to the CTC output layer, which produces a probability distribution over character transcriptions. This distribution is passed to the dictionary and language model, using the token passing algorithm, to obtain the final word sequence.

5.5.1   *Recognition Parameters*

The neural network uses a bidirectional Long Short-Term Memory (BLSTM) architecture with a Connectionist Temporal Classification (CTC) output layer. The forward and backward hidden layers each contain 100 LSTM memory blocks. Each memory block consists of a memory cell, an input gate, an output gate, a forget gate and three peephole connections. The hyperbolic tangent function is used for the block input and output activation functions, while the gate activation function is the logistic sigmoid. The CTC output layer has 81 nodes (one for each character occurring in the training set, and one extra for 'blank'), while the size of the input layer is determined by the data.

For the online data there are 25 inputs. The input layer is fully connected to both hidden layers, and these are fully connected to themselves and to the output layer. This gives a total of 117,681 weights for the online data.

Note that, unlike an HMM system, the number of parameters was not directly determined by the data. The general tendency with RNNs is for performance to improve smoothly with the number of weights, up to a certain point when no further significant gains are recorded. The choice of hidden layer size, and hence number of weights, was therefore determined by a tradeoff between final performance and training time.

The network was trained using online gradient descent with a learning rate of e^{-4} and a momentum of 0.9. The error rate was recorded every five epochs on the validation set and training was stopped when performance has ceased to improve on the validation set for 50 epochs. The network weights have been initialized with a Gaussian distribution of mean 0 and standard deviation 0.1. Because of the random initialization, all RNN experiments were repeated four times, and the results were recorded as the mean $\pm$ the standard error.

The CTC network was trained to recognize individual characters. Once training was complete, the word recognition rate was recorded by finding the most probable sequences of dictionary words, given the character level transcription.

For the experiments with the language model, the word sequence probabilities were multiplied directly by the combined transition probabilities given by the bigram language model. This contrasts with the HMM system, where a language model weighting factor was found empirically.

Table 5.8 Word recognition accuracy on IAM-OnDB-t2

System	Accuracy
HMM	63.9 % –
CTC	79.7 % ± 0.3 %

Table 5.9 Character recognition accuracy on IAM-OnDB-t2 with different CTC architectures

Architecture	Character accuracy	Training iterations
Forward only	81.3 ± 0.3 %	182.5 ± 97.1
Reverse only	85.8 ± 0.3 %	228.8 ± 206.6
Bidirectional	88.5 ± 0.05 %	41.25 ± 9.6

5.5.2 *Results on the IAM-OnDB-t2 Benchmark*

Table 5.8 shows the results of the CTC approach compared to the HMM-based system. The word recognition accuracy of 79.7 % with the 20,000 word dictionary is a significant improvement (using a standard z-test with $\alpha < 0.001$). Note that CTC requires no task specific tuning to achieve this result. For the HMM, various meta parameters such as the language model weight, the number of Gaussian mixtures, the insertion penalty etc. must be specifically optimized for the data. For CTC, on the other hand, all training parameters are standard, and are imported unchanged from other domains, such as speech recognition [Graves *et al.* (2006)].

Table 5.9 shows the character recognition accuracy of the CTC network with unidirectional and bidirectional LSTM architectures without including a language model. The "Forward only" ("Reverse only") network was created by including only the forward (reverse) hidden layer in the BLSTM architecture. Unsurprisingly, the bidirectional network gave the best performance. However it is interesting that significantly better results were achieved with the "Reverse only" network than with the "Forward only" network. This suggests that the right-to-left dependencies are more important to the network than the left-to-right ones. While the number of parameters is larger if the bidirectional network is used, the training is also much faster for these networks. The number of training iterations needed is only about one fifth of the number required using unidirectional LSTM.

Figure 5.18 shows the decrease in training and validation error over time

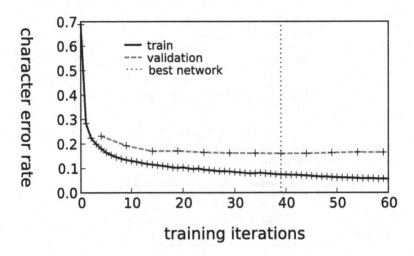

Fig. 5.18   CTC character error rate during training

for a typical CTC training run. The network was already near convergence after only 15 passes through the training data.

5.5.3   *Analysis*

It has been previously asserted that one of the key advantages of BLSTM RNNs is their ability to access long-range, bidirectional context. This can be substantiated by analyzing the derivatives of the network outputs y_k^t at a particular point t in the data sequence with respect to the inputs $x_k^{t'}$ at all points t' in the sequence. The matrix $J = \frac{\partial y_k^t}{\partial x_{k'}^{t'}}$ of these derivatives is referred to as the *sequential Jacobian*. Intuitively, the larger the values of the sequential Jacobian, the more the network output at time t depends on the input at time t'.

Figure 5.19 shows the value of the sequential Jacobian for a single output during the transcription of a line from the IAM-OnDB. In this figure the Jacobian is evaluated at time step $t = 86$ for the output corresponding to the label '1'. The curves for all cells k are overlaid in this figure, while each curve represents the value of J for $t' = 1, \ldots, T$. The network makes use of contextual information from about the first 120 time steps of the sequence, which corresponds roughly to the length of the first word. Moreover, the context extends in both directions from the chosen output.

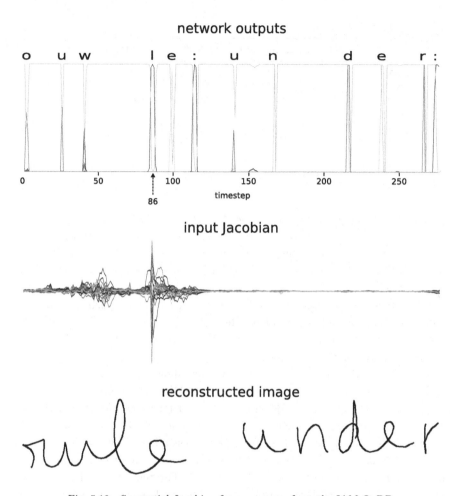

Fig. 5.19 Sequential Jacobian for a sequence from the IAM-OnDB

5.5.4 *Influence of the Vocabulary*

To gauge the effect of varying the dictionary size, two sets of experiments were carried out. In the first experiments open dictionaries were generated including between 5,000 and 30,000 words by taking the n most common words in the three corpora mentioned above (LOB Corpus, Brown Corpus, Wellington Corpus). In the other experiments, a closed dictionary was taken containing the 5,597 words in the IAM-OnDB-t2 test set, and the change in performance was measured when this is padded to 20,000 words,

Table 5.10   Online word accuracy with open dictionaries

Dictionary size	Coverage(%)	RNN(%)	HMM(%)
5,000	86.1	66.2 ± 0.4	47.7
10,000	90.7	70.3 ± 0.4	54.8
15,000	92.9	72.5 ± 0.3	60.6
20,000	94.4	74.0 ± 0.3	63.7
25,000	95.1	74.6 ± 0.3	65.0
30,000	95.7	75.0 ± 0.3	61.5

to measure the influence of the out of vocabulary word (OOVs). Note that the language model is not used for the RNN results in these experiments, which would be substantially higher otherwise (for example, the accuracy for the 20,000 word open lexicon is 79.7% with the language model and 74.0% without).

Table 5.10 shows the number of OOVs for each vocabulary size. It can be observed that the upper bound on the recognition accuracy is about 96 % for the largest vocabulary. Only for the closed vocabulary would a perfect recognition accuracy be possible.

The results for the first set of experiments are shown in Table 5.10 and plotted in Figures 5.20 and 5.21. In all cases the RNN system significantly outperforms the HMM system, despite the lack of language model. Both RNN and HMM performance increased with size (and test set coverage) up to 25,000 words. Note however that the RNN is less affected by the dictionary size, and that for the 30,000 word dictionary, performance continues to increase for the RNN but drops for the HMM. The tendency of HMMs to lose accuracy for very large handwriting lexicons has been previously observed [Zimmermann *et al.* (2003)].

The results of the second set of experiments are shown in Table 5.11. Unsurprisingly, the closed dictionary containing only the test set words gave the best results for both systems. The scores with the 20,000 word closed dictionary were somewhat lower in both cases, due to the increased perplexity, but still better than any recorded with open dictionaries.

In summary the RNN retained its advantage over the HMM regardless of the dictionary used. Moreover, the differences tended to be larger when the dictionary had higher perplexity. This may be due to the fact that the RNN is better at recognizing characters, and is therefore less dependent on a dictionary or language model to constrain its outputs.

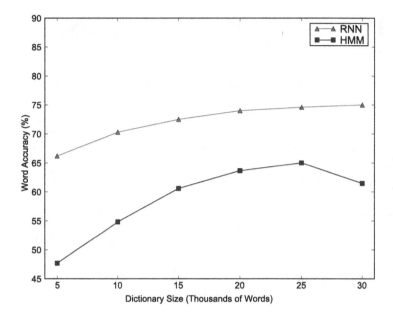

Fig. 5.20 HMM and RNN word accuracy plotted against dictionary size

Table 5.11 Online word accuracy with closed dictionaries

Dictionary size	RNN(%)	HMM(%)
5,597	85.3 ± 0.3	70.1
20,000	81.5 ± 0.4	68.8

5.6 Conclusions and Discussion

In this chapter, online recognition systems for handwritten texts acquired from a whiteboard have been presented. The recognition of notes written on a whiteboard is a relatively new task. Whiteboard data differ from usual pen-input data as people stand, rather than sit, during writing and the arm does not rest on a table. While the proposed system uses some

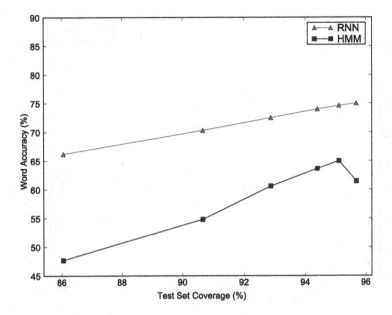

Fig. 5.21   HMM and RNN word accuracy plotted against dictionary test set coverage

state-of-the-art methods for preprocessing and feature extraction, some new preprocessing steps especially for whiteboard data have also been introduced. These preprocessing techniques can significantly increase the word recognition rate.

A new approach for detecting text lines in online handwritten documents has been proposed. This approach is based on dynamic programming and uses both the offline and online information of the strokes in a handwritten document. The system tries to find a path between two consecutive text lines based on a heuristic cost function that takes different criteria into account. In addition to two other criteria, which enforce the smoothness of the optimal path and prevent it from crossing a text line, the novel *evade*-function is proposed which adds more penalty if the path is closer to strokes belonging to the text line below. Using this function the path is forced to run closer to the text line above and many punctuation marks and i-dots are correctly assigned. In the experiments on 100 documents a commonly used online approach based on simple heuristics was outperformed. The correct assignment rate of strokes was 99.94 %. Only two documents contain small mistakes. While the proposed system already works very well, it is a hard problem to detect text lines perfectly. It can be argued that significant improvements in text line segmentation can be achieved only if text line detection and text recognition are integrated with each other. Such an integration is a challenging direction for future research.

Feature selection was applied in the experiments described in this chapter. During the sequential forward search a best performing subset of 16 features was found. This subset outperformed the reference system which uses all 25 features. Another interesting outcome for the handwriting research community was that a subset of five features already produced good results. These five features are not highly correlated and are the top choices during the first iterations of the forward search. Because of the small number of features the classifier becomes more efficient with respect to both computation time and memory requirements. In future the feature selection experiments could be extended using other strategies, such as Sequential Backward Search (SBS), Sequential Floating Forward Search (SFFS), and Sequential Floating Backward Search (SFBS) [Pudil *et al.* (1994)].

In this chapter a novel approach using a recurrent neural network (RNN) has also been described. The key innovation is a recently introduced RNN objective function known as Connectionist Temporal Classification (CTC). CTC uses the network to label the entire input sequence at once. This means the network can be trained with unsegmented input data, and the final label sequence can be read directly from the network output. In the experiments a performance significantly higher than the performance of the HMM-based system was achieved. The word recognition accuracy of the CTC approach was 79.7 % with the 20,000 word dictionary.

The results of the experiments show that the neural network approach achieved a performance significantly higher than the performance of the HMMs. Some of the key differences between the systems are discussed below to shed some light on this disparity. Note that this discussion follows the discussion given in [Graves *et al.* (2008)].

Firstly, standard HMMs are generative, while an RNN trained with CTC is discriminative. This means the HMM attempts to model the conditional probability of the input data given the internal state sequence, then uses this to find the most probable output label sequence. The RNN, on the other hand, directly models the probability of the labels given the observed data. Advantages of the generative approach include the possibility of adding extra models to an already trained system and being able to generate synthetic data. However, given that only the output distribution is required for sequence labeling tasks, determining the input distribution can be a huge modeling effort. Additionally, for tasks such as handwriting recognition where the prior data distribution is hard to determine, generative approaches can only provide unnormalized likelihoods for the label sequences. Discriminative approaches, on the other hand, yield normalized label probabilities, which can be used to assess prediction confidence, or to combine the outputs of several classifiers. In most cases, discriminative methods achieve better classification performance than generative methods.

A second difference is that RNNs provide more flexible models of the input features than the mixtures of diagonal Gaussian mixtures used in standard HMMs. In general, mixtures of Gaussian components can model complex, multi-modal distributions; however, when the Gaussian mixtures have diagonal covariance matrices (as is usually the case) they are limited to modeling distributions over independent variables. This assumes that the input features are decorrelated, but this can be difficult to ensure for real world tasks such as handwriting recognition. RNNs, on the other hand, do not assume that the features come from a particular distribution, or that they are independent, and can model non-linear relationships among features. Nonetheless, RNNs typically perform better using input features with simple properties and relationships.

A third difference is that the internal states of a standard HMM are discrete and single valued, while those of an RNN are defined by the vector of activations of the hidden units and are therefore continuous and multivariate. This means that for an HMM with n states, only $O(\log n)$ bits of information about the past observation sequence are carried by the internal state. For an RNN, on the other hand, the amount of internal information grows linearly with the number of hidden units.

Another difference is that with standard HMMs, the probability of remaining in a particular state decreases exponentially with time. Exponential decay is in general a poor model of state duration, and various measures have been suggested to alleviate this [Johnson (2005)]. For an RNN trained with CTC, the required output consists only of the sequence of labels, so the duration is never explicitly modeled and the problem does not arise.

A final, and perhaps most crucial, difference is that unlike RNNs, HMMs assume that the probability of each observation depends only on the current state. Consequently, data consisting of continuous trajectories (such as the sequence of pen coordinates for online handwriting) are difficult to model with standard HMMs, since each observation is heavily dependent on those around it. Similarly, data with long-range contextual dependencies are troublesome, because the observations relating to individual sequence elements (e.g., letters or phonemes) are influenced by the elements surrounding them. The second problem can be solved by adding extra models to account for each sequence element in all different contexts (e.g.,using triphones instead of phonemes for speech recognition). However, increasing the number of models exponentially increases the number of parameters that must be inferred which, in turn, increases the amount of data required to reliably train the system. For RNNs, on the contrary, modeling continuous trajectories is natural, since their own hidden state is itself a continuous trajectory. Furthermore, the ability of RNNs to incorporate contextual information is limited only by the choice of architecture. Since LSTM is capable of bridging time lags in excess of a thousand time steps [Hochreiter and Schmidhuber (1997)], and BRNNs allow for equal time-lags in both directions, a BLSTM RNN is in principle able to access context from the entire input sequence.

In summary, the observed difference in performance between RNNs and HMMs in unconstrained handwriting recognition can be explained by the fact that, as researchers approach handwriting recognition tasks of increasing complexity, the assumptions HMMs are based on lose validity. For example, unconstrained handwriting or spontaneous speech are more dynamic and show more marked context effects than hand-printed scripts or read speech.

Chapter 6

Multiple Classifier Combination

Having the offline recognition system of Chapter 4 and the online recognition system of Chapter 5 available, it may be beneficial to combine both systems. From such a combination, an improved recognition performance can be expected [Velek *et al.* (2003); Vinciarelli and Perrone (2003)]. In this chapter the combination of different systems derived from the recognizers introduced in the previous two chapters is described.

Several combination methods for character, numeral and word recognition have been proposed in the literature [Günter and Bunke (2004b); Huang and Suen (1995); Marti and Bunke (2001b); Vinciarelli and Perrone (2003); Ye *et al.* (2002)]. A general overview and an introduction to the field of multiple classifier systems (MCS) is given in [Kuncheva (2004)]. However, little work has been reported on the combination of classifiers for general handwritten text line and sentence recognition. The combination of the outputs of multiple handwritten text line and sentence recognizers differs from standard multiple classifier combination, because the output of a text line recognizer is a sequence of word classes rather than just one single word class, and the number of words may differ among several recognizers. Therefore, an additional alignment procedure is needed. In the work presented in this book, the recognizer output voting error reduction (ROVER) [Fiscus (1997)] framework is applied. To combine the output of the recognizers, the word sequences are incrementally aligned using a standard string matching algorithm. The word occurring most often at a certain position is used as the final result. In addition to using the frequency of occurrence, other voting strategies are investigated in this chapter.

In the initial experiments three HMM-based recognition systems are combined. To the best of the authors' knowledge these are the first experiments in the field of online sentence recognition combining systems based on offline and online features. In the second set of initial experiments, neural networks are used. In a broader experimental study, more recognition systems are combined. Beside the HMM-based recognizers, the new approach based on neural networks is used. Furthermore, external recognition systems from Microsoft© and Vision Objects© are included in the combination experiments. Since these recognizers are based on different features and classification methods, it can be expected that the performance increases, even if the individual recognition rates are significantly lower than those of the neural network based approach. This difference is caused by the diversity of the recognizers.

This chapter is organized as follows. First, the methodology for combining the different recognition systems is introduced in Section 6.1. Second, a description of all recognition systems for the combination experiments is given in Section 6.2. Note that parts of Section 6.2 closely follow [Liwicki *et al.* (2008a)]. Next, Section 6.3 describes initial experiments combining three different HMM-based systems, and three different neural network based recognizers, respectively. Following, Section 6.4 presents the results of the large-scaled experiments, and Section 6.5 proposes more elaborated voting strategies. These two sections follow the experimental description given in [Liwicki *et al.* (2008a)]. Finally, Section 6.6 draws some conclusions and gives an outlook to future work.

6.1 Methodology

Multiple classifier systems have been successfully used to improve the recognition performance in difficult tasks [Kuncheva (2004)]. There are two issues in multiple classifier systems research. First, individual classifiers that exhibit a high degree of diversity need to be constructed. The classifiers used in this work are described in the next section. As these classifiers are based on different features and classification paradigms, and have largely been developed independently of each other, it can be expected that their diversity is quite high. The second issue to be addressed in a multiple classifier system is classifier combination. A large number of combination schemes have been proposed [Kuncheva (2004)]. However, these schemes are restricted in the sense that they only address the classification of single objects. By contrast, in the application considered in this book, sequences of objects, i.e., whole text lines, need to be classified. This means that the task of the recognizer is not only word recognition, but also the

$$\mathcal{I}n \quad mid\text{-}april \quad Anglesey$$

W_1:   In mid-april Angle say
W_2:   It mid-april Anglesey
W_3:   I a mid-April Anglesey

WTN$_1$ = W$_1$ + W$_2$:

| In | mid-april | Angle | say |
| It | mid-april | Anglesey | ϵ |

WTN$_2$ = WTN$_1$ + W$_3$:

In	ϵ	mid-april	Angle	say
It	ϵ	mid-april	Anglesey	ϵ
I	a	mid-April	Anglesey	ϵ

Fig. 6.1   Example of iteratively aligning multiple recognition results

segmentation of a line of handwritten text into individual words. Because of segmentation errors, the word sequences output by the individual recognizers may consist of a different number of words. Therefore, an alignment procedure is needed as the first step in classifier combination. For aligning the outputs of the individual classifiers, the ROVER combination strategy is chosen. This strategy consists of two stages. Because the recognizers output word sequences for whole text lines and because there may be a different number of words in each sequence, the output sequences are aligned into a *word transition network* (WTN) in the first stage. A voting strategy is then applied in the second stage to select the best scoring word for the final transcription. The alignment process is described in Section 6.1.1, and several voting strategies are proposed in Section 6.1.2.

6.1.1   *Alignment*

Finding the optimal alignment for n sequences is NP-complete [Wang and Jiang (1994)]. Thus an approximate solution for the alignment is chosen. This solution aligns the multiple sequences incrementally by building WTNs. At the beginning, the first and the second word sequence are aligned in a single WTN, using the standard string matching algorithm described in [Wagner and Fischer (1974)]. The resulting WTN is aligned with the next word sequence giving a new WTN, which is then aligned with the next recognition result, and so on. This method does not guarantee an optimal solution, but in practice the suboptimal solution often provides a good alignment accuracy. An example alignment of the output of three recognizers (denoted by W_1, W_2, and W_3) is shown in Fig. 6.1. The columns in the WTNs denote *correspondence sets* (sets of corresponding words) that are identified by the alignment process. Note that the ϵ marks *null*-transitions, i.e., transitions where an empty string is chosen as alternative.

Figure 6.1 contains examples for all possible correspondence set categories that occur during string alignment. The four categories are:

(1) Correct: the word transcriptions are the same ("mid-april" in **WTN₁**)
(2) Insertion: an additional word occurs in the new word sequence, resulting in an additional column with *null*-transitions ("a" in **WTN₂**)
(3) Deletion: fewer words occur in the new word sequence, an consequently a *null*-transition is inserted ("say" in **WTN₁**)
(4) Substitution: the word transcriptions at the same position differ ("Angle"/"Anglesey" and "In"/"It" in **WTN₁**)

6.1.2 *Voting Strategies*

After alignment a voting module extracts the best scoring word sequence from the WTN. In the first experiments described in Section 6.4, only the number of occurrences of a word w was taken into account for making a decision. Under this strategy, in the case of ties, the output of the best performing system on the validation set is taken. In the example of Fig. 6.1 it would be the "In" from W_1 which yields the final output "In mid-april Anglesey". Note that this is the correct transcription, which is not present in the recognition results of any single recognizer.

In addition to the frequency of occurrence, the confidence of the recognizers can be used as a voting strategy. The trade off between the frequency of occurrence and the confidence score is weighted with one parameter $\alpha \in [0, 1]$. Let c be a correspondence set of the WTN containing n word classes $w_1, \ldots, w_n$. The number of occurrences of each word class w_i is denoted by N_i. Then the score $S(w_i)$ of a word w_i is:

$$S(w_i) = \alpha * \frac{N_i}{\sum_{j=1}^{n} N_j} + (1 - \alpha) * C(w_i), \qquad (6.1)$$

where $C(w_i)$ is the combined confidence score of word class w_i. There exist several methods to calculate $C(w_i)$. First, the average of all confidence scores of the occurrences of word class w_i can be used. Second, the maximum of these confidence scores may be chosen. Setting $\alpha = 1$ results in a voting procedure that takes only the number of occurrences into account, while $\alpha = 0$ corresponds to the case where only the confidence counts.

Another parameter is the confidence score of the *null*-transition $C(\epsilon)$. It determines how often the *null*-transition is taken instead of another word class. If no *null*-transition is taken, i.e., $C(\epsilon)$ is very low, the output transcription tends to be longer and more insertion errors occur. On the contrary, if $C(\epsilon)$ is too large, more deletions occur. The two parameters α and $C(\epsilon)$ are optimized on a validation set in this chapter.

6.2 Recognition Systems

Several recognizers are used for a more detailed investigation of the combination. Beside the recognizers of the previous chapters based on HMMs and neural networks, the Microsoft© handwriting recognition engine and the Vision Objects© recognizer are used.

This section gives a more detailed overview of the recognition systems. First, Section 6.2.1 summarizes the recognition systems developed in this book. Next, Section 6.2.2 introduces the Microsoft© handwriting recognition engine. Finally, the Vision Objects© recognizer is presented in Section 6.2.3.

6.2.1 *Hidden Markov Models and Neural Networks*

The recognizers presented in this book are based on three different feature sets. First, the offline recognizer of Chapter 4 uses nine features extracted from automatically generated offline images. For feature extraction a sliding window is used. The other two feature sets, which are based on online information, have been presented in Chapter 5. They differ from each other in the way of preprocessing. While the former is the system without the newly introduced preprocessing steps, the latter system includes novel preprocessing. Both feature sets consist of 25 individual features. The feature vectors are already in writing order, since they are extracted in the same order as the points are acquired. Note that the offline features extracted from the sliding window are not exactly in writing order, since the left-movements of some characters, e.g., "a" and "e", are not imitated by the left-to-right moving window. The length of the sequences of the offline recognizer differs from the length of the sequences in the online case. Thus the time information cannot be used for the alignment of the output sequences. Furthermore, for the offline recognizer the training set is mixed with the IAM-DB as described in Section 4.2.1.

In the initial experiments only the HMM-based systems were applied, while two recognition systems were applied in the broader experimental study: the HMM-based recognizer and a recognizer based on neural networks. The former uses a linear topology for the character HMMs, and the continuous observation functions are modeled with diagonal Gaussian mixtures. The number of Gaussian mixtures and the parameters (GSF, WIP) for including a language model are optimized on a validation set. The latter recognizer uses BLSTM combined with CTC to recognize the label sequence. The number of hidden cells is fixed to 100. The only parameter that is optimized on the validation set is the number of training iterations.

Using three feature sets combined with two classifiers results in a total of six classification systems. However, since the neural networks turned out to be the best individual classifiers, several networks were used for each feature set. These networks were generated by using different random initializations.

6.2.2 *Microsoft© Handwriting Recognition Engine*

The Microsoft© Tablet PC Software Development Kit (SDK) provides an interface for ink-enabled applications for the tablet PC[1]. It includes an application programming interface (API) to the Microsoft© handwriting recognition engine (HWR), which exists on any computer running Microsoft Windows XP Tablet Edition©[Pittman (2007)].

To support a wide range of writing styles, a large neural network has been trained on a very large data set. The training set contains ink samples from thousands of people with a diverse range of writing styles. An illustration of how the recognizer works is given in Fig. 6.2 [Pittman (2007)]. First, a stroke is cut into separate segments whenever it moves downward in y dimension and then reverses its direction back upward. Then a set of features is extracted for each individual segment. Generally the

---

[1] The Microsoft Windows XP© Tablet PC Edition SDK is available for download at http://www.microsoft.com/windowsxp/tabletpc/default.mspx

Input

Ink Segments

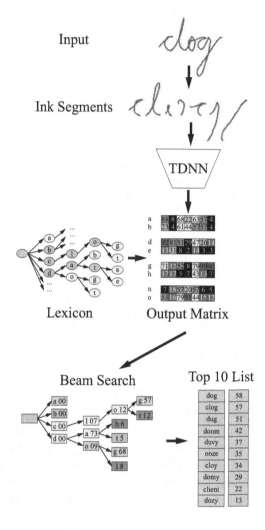

Fig. 6.2 Illustration of the Microsoft© HWR recognition architecture

measurements for the features are based on the direction and curvature of the ink trace, along with various measurements of size. Finally, to accomplish the recognition of connected letters in cursive script, a neural network based recognizer is used. The top part of Fig. 6.2 shows how the electronic ink is processed and fed through the neural network.

In the Microsoft© HWR, a *time delay neural network* (TDNN) with a

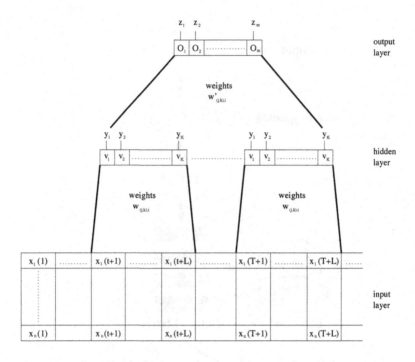

Fig. 6.3   Architecture of a time delay neural network

window size of five is used. A TDNN is a multi-layer feed-forward network with local connections in time and shared weights (see Fig. 6.3). Its layers perform successively higher-level feature extraction and produce scores for each class at the output. The TDNN outputs consist of a matrix, where each column represents one ink segment and each row represents one digit or character. The outputs are estimates of probability for each possible digit or character.

The TDNN is further supported by integrating a language model in form of a lexicon, organized in the form of a trie (see left part of Fig. 6.2). The nodes of the trie contain a Boolean flag indicating whether or not the corresponding letter is the end of a word. Optionally, some of these end-of-word nodes also contain a word unigram probability or other information. The lexicon is combined with the output of the TDNN by means of a beam search, an approach that most commercial speech-recognition systems use [Haeb-Umbach and Ney (1994)]. The bottom part of Fig. 6.2 illustrates how the beam search moves through the TDNN output matrix, column by

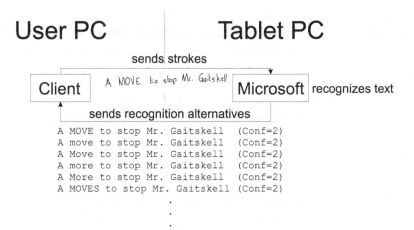

Fig. 6.4 Communication with the Microsoft© HWR

column, from left to right. At each column, it consults the lexicon on the left to find out what letters might be next and looks up the probability estimates for these letters in the matrix. It builds a copy of the lexicon trie (shown on the right-hand side in Fig. 6.2), with the scores stored in the nodes of this copy trie. At any one time, the scores in that trie are the cumulative scores of each character of the current column, and all characters up to that character, for each possible word in the lexicon. When a parent node produces a child node, the score in the child node is computed taking the current score in the parent node into account. After the child node has been generated, parent and child operate independently. They may even compete, because it is possible that the column (segment) still represents part of the parent letter, or is now part of the child letter. Early on, the scores higher up in the trie will be stronger, representing shorter words. Progressing from left to right in the output matrix, the scores further down in the trie will become stronger, and the scores of previously strong letters will weaken, as too many segments for such short words have been seen. Once the last column in the matrix is completed, the trie contains the final hypotheses about what the word might be. At this point, it is simply a matter of traversing the trie to find the n best-scoring words.

A simplified illustration of the communication process with the Microsoft© HWR is given in Fig. 6.4. The client application on the user PC sends online stroke information to the recognition engine on the tablet PC where the recognition is performed. The recognition engine answers with several recognition alternatives and their confidences. However, there are only three confidence values available (the number in parenthesis denotes the actual confidence value of the recognizer):

- *strong*(0): only about 25 % of the text lines in the test set of IAM-OnDB-t2 benchmark task are recognized with a strong confidence
- *intermediate* (1): this confidence is given for less then 3 % of these text lines only
- *poor* (2): in most cases a poor confidence is assigned

For handwritten text lines the alternatives represent different transcriptions of a given input. The confidence value assigned to a transcription represents the lowest confidence level of a recognized segment found in the input. Thus a strong confidence is rarely given, since it is not likely for a recognizer to be confident for a whole text line.

The Microsoft© HWR allows a user to define a vocabulary and a character set. In this book the same vocabulary is used as provided for the other recognizers. However, the Microsoft© HWR is not confined to recognizing only words from the given vocabulary. Therefore, often out of vocabulary words (OOVs) occur in the recognition alternatives.

6.2.3   *Vision Objects© Recognizer*

The MyScript recognizer from Vision Objects© is an online recognizer that processes digital ink and supports a large spectrum of languages and functionalities for applications that vary from forms processing and note taking to mobile data capture. Application programming interfaces exist for all major operating systems on the market, both for PC/Server architectures (Linux, Windows, Mac OS) and mobile platforms (Embedded Linux, Symbian, Windows CE/Mobile, and many others)[2].

The overall recognition system is built on the principles presented in [Knerr *et al.* (1997)]. Some of the more important concepts are:

- use of a modular and hierarchical recognition system,
- use of soft decisions (often probabilistic) and deferred decisions by means of considering concurrent hypotheses in the decision paths,

---

[2]The MyScript Builder SDK© is available for purchase at
http://www.visionobjects.com/

- use of complementary information at all stages of the recognition process, and
- use of global optimization criteria, making sure that the recognizer is trained in order to perform optimally on all levels.

The recognizer was trained on many millions of writing samples that were collected from native writers in the target countries. The processing chain of the Vision Objects recognizer starts out with some of the usual preprocessing operations, such as text line extraction and slant correction. Then the online handwriting is pre-segmented into strokes and sub-strokes. Here the general idea is to over-segment the signal and let the recognizer decide later on where the boundaries between characters and words are. This is followed by feature extraction stages, where different sets of features are computed. These feature sets use a combination of online and offline information. The feature sets are processed by a set of character classifiers, which use Neural Networks and other pattern recognition paradigms. All the information accumulated in the various processing steps is then processed by dynamic programming on the word and sentence level in order to generate character, word, and sentence level candidates with corresponding confidence scores. A global discriminant training scheme on the word level with automatic learning of all classifier parameters and meta parameters of the recognizer, in the general spirit of what has been described in [S.Knerr and E.Augustin (1998)], is employed for the overall training of the recognizer.

The Vision Objects recognizer uses a state-of-the-art statistical language model that incorporates lexical, grammatical and semantic information. This model is partially described in [Perraud *et al.* (2006)]. By means of the language model, the recognizer uses context information on all recognition levels, from the character to the word, and to the sentence level. The employed language model also supports the recognition of terms that are not explicitly covered by the lexicons (in this book a lexicon for British English), albeit the recognizer has a tendency to convert handwriting into text that is covered by the lexicons.

The communication with the client is similar to the communication of the Microsoft© recognizer (see Fig. 6.5). The client sends the stroke information to the recognition engine and gets a recognition result as an answer. This answer is divided into several segments. Each segment contains alternatives for the word at this position. The candidates come together with a normalized recognition score. This allows the Vision Objects© recognizer

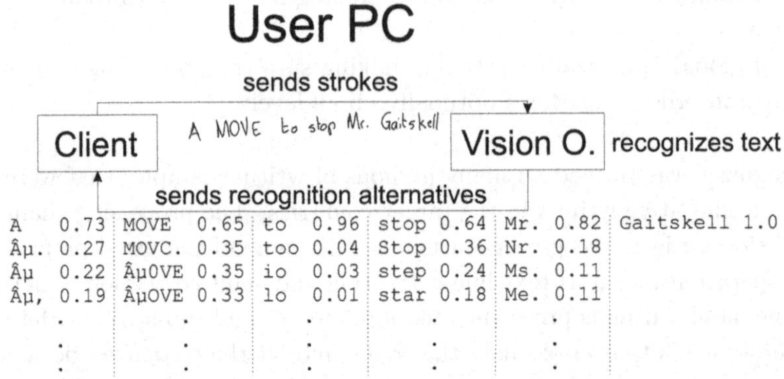

User PC

sends strokes

| Client | A MOVE to stop Mr. Gaitskell | Vision O. | recognizes text |

sends recognition alternatives

```
A     0.73  MOVE   0.65  to   0.96  stop 0.64  Mr.  0.82  Gaitskell 1.0
Âμ.   0.27  MOVC.  0.35  too  0.04  Stop 0.36  Nr.  0.18
Âμ    0.22  ÂμOVE  0.35  io   0.03  step 0.24  Ms.  0.11
Âμ,   0.19  ÂμOVE  0.33  lo   0.01  star 0.18  Me.  0.11
  .          .          .          .          .
  .          .          .          .          .
  .          .          .          .          .
```

Fig. 6.5   Communication with the Vision Objects© recognizer

to be used for advanced combination strategies where the confidence plays an important role.

6.3   Initial Experiments

The initial set of experiments was performed to validate the assumption that combining online and offline features leads to improved recognition results. First, a combination of three different systems derived from the HMM-based recognizers of the previous chapters was used (see Section 6.3.1). While the three recognition systems use the same HMM-based classifier, they differ in the way of preprocessing and feature extraction. These differences are described in Section 6.2.1. Second, the same three feature sets were used for experiments with neural networks (see Section 6.3.2).

6.3.1   *Combination of HMM-Based Recognizers*

These experiments were performed on the IAM-OnDB. This database and the benchmarks used for evaluating the performance are described in Section 3.3. For the initial experiments the sets of the benchmark task IAM-OnDB-t1 with the closed vocabulary were used. There the data are divided into four independent sets: one set for training, two sets for validation, and a test set. Since no writer appears in more than one set, a writer-independent

Table 6.1 Accuracy of combination of HMMs

System	Accuracy
Offline	61.4 %
1st online	65.1 %
2nd online	65.2 %
Combination	66.8 %

recognition task is considered. The size of the vocabulary is 11,059 words. In the initial experiments a simple word pair grammar was used. For the alignment and construction of the WTN, the rover tool from the National Institute of Standards and Technology (NIST) implementing the ROVER framework [Fiscus (1997)] was used[3].

Table 6.1 shows the results of the three individual recognition systems and their combination. For measuring the performance of the combined system, the accuracy is used since it also takes inserted words into account. (If just the recognition rate was used, one could easily increase the performance by never including any *null*-transitions in the WTN, because this only affects the number of insertions.) By combining the recognizers, the accuracy increased by 1.6 % to 66.8 %, which is statistically significant using the standard *z-test* with a significance level of 5 %.

6.3.2 *Combination of Neural Networks*

The IAM-OnDB-t2 benchmark task (see Section 3.3) was used for the second set of experiments. The parameters for the recognition and the combination were optimized on the first validation set. A bigram language model was included in the experiments. This language model was optimized on the second validation set.

Altogether 30 neural network classifiers were involved in the experiments, i.e., ten randomly initialized classifiers for each feature set. The best neural network classifier had an accuracy of 81.26 %. Note that a detailed overview of the individual recognition results is given in the next section.

Several parameters of the MCS must be optimized during validation. First, there are the parameters for voting described in Section 6.1. Then, the order of the classifiers for the alignment needs to be chosen. Finally,

---

[3]The rover tool is part of the NIST Scoring Toolkit available for download at ftp://jaguar.ncsl.nist.gov/current_docs/sctk/doc/sctk.htm

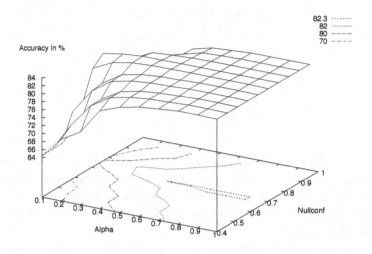

Fig. 6.6   Optimization of the parameters α and $C(\epsilon)$ (Nullconf)

the number of classifiers to be included in the ensemble must be decided. In the following these issues will be described in greater detail.

The parameters for the voting, α and $C(\epsilon)$, are optimized on the validation set for each ensemble of classifiers. Before voting can be applied, the outputs of the recognizers need to represent a confidence measure. Since not all of the individual recognizers provide useful confidence scores, the performance on the validation set was used as a confidence score for each of the classifiers. The final voting strategy includes taking the maximum rather than the average of the individual confidence scores in Eq. (6.1), because it returned better recognition results in all experiments on the validation set. Figure 6.6 illustrates the accuracy on the validation set of different parameter combinations for an example classifier ensemble. It is observed that the values do not change significantly for $\alpha > 0.8$. The highest accuracy in this example is already reached at $(\alpha = 0.5, C(\epsilon) = 0.7)$.

The order of the classifiers has an influence on the alignment, for only a suboptimal alignment strategy is chosen. A commonly used strategy begins with the best classifier on the validation set and sequentially adds the next best classifier. This strategy has been adopted in this section.

Table 6.2 Accuracy of combination of neural networks

System	Validation set accuracy	Test set accuracy
Best individual classifier	74.63 %	81.26 %
Three classifiers	77.03 %	81.27 %
Optimized weighting	77.20 %	81.18 %
Optimized mix	80.40 %	83.64 %

To get the number of individual classifiers to be included in the ensemble, several strategies were investigated. First, only the best classifier for each feature set was selected, resulting in an ensemble of three classifiers (second row in Table 6.2). Note that this is the same strategy as used in the HMM-based experiments of the previous section. This ensemble has a higher recognition accuracy on the test set than the best single classifier (first row in Table 6.2). Second, the weighing of these classifiers was optimized using weights from 0 to 1 with a step size of 0.1. The best weights were found to be 0.6 for "offline", 0.5 for "1st online", and 0.5 for "2nd online". However, there was only a small performance increase on the validation set and a small decrease on the test set (third row in Table 6.2), compared to the first strategy. Finally, the number $n_c (c = 1, 2, 3)$ of individual classifiers from each feature set was varied from one to ten, e.g., if $n_1 = 3$, the three best "offline" systems are used. This results in 10^3 combinations that were tested on the validation set. The results on the validation set show a promising increase of the recognition accuracy (last row in Table 6.2).

The optimized combination performed statistically significantly better than the best individual classifier at a significance level of 1 %. The recognition accuracy was 83.64 %, corresponding to error reduction of more than 12 %.

6.4   Experiments with All Recognition Systems

The second series of experiments was performed using the IAM-OnDB-t2 benchmark task with the open vocabulary. This vocabulary contains the 20,000 most frequent words out of three corpora (LOB Corpus, Brown Corpus, Wellington Corpus). All systems described in Section 6.2 were used for these experiments. The parameters for the recognition and the combination were optimized on the first validation set. For the recognizers

Table 6.3   Recognizers used for the combination experiments

System		Number of recognizers
CTC	offline	10
	1st online	10
	2nd online	10
HMM	offline	1
	1st online	1
	2nd online	1
Microsoft©		1
Vision Objects©		1

of this section a language model is included. This language model was optimized on the second validation set. The language model training is based on three different corpora (LOB Corpus, Brown Corpus, Wellington Corpus). To guarantee that the test data are not used for training, the texts of the IAM-OnDB were removed from the LOB Corpus.

This section is organized as follows. First, Section 6.4.1 reports on the recognition results of the individual recognizers. Next, the optimization on the validation set is presented in Section 6.4.2. Finally, the results on the test set are given in Section 6.4.3.

6.4.1   *Individual Recognition Results*

A total of six classification systems from this book are used for the combination, three HMM-based systems and three systems based on neural networks. Since the neural networks have been found to be the best individual classifiers and because of the outcomes of the experiments in Section 6.3.2, it is advisable to use more than one neural network for each feature set. Thus ten neural networks were trained with each of the three feature sets.

A summary of the individual recognition systems is given in Table 6.3. Altogether 35 classifiers were involved in the experiments: 30 randomly initialized CTC networks, three HMM-based classifiers, the Vision Objects© recognizer, and the Microsoft© recognizer. The different feature sets are denoted by "offline" for offline features, "1st online" for conventional online features and preprocessing, and "2nd online" for online features extracted after applying additional preprocessing steps (see Section 6.2.1).

Table 6.4 shows the recognition accuracy of the individual recognition systems on the validation set and on the test set. For ease of visualization the best performing neural network classifiers are marked with bold numbers. Surprisingly, the best neural network classifier was trained with conventional preprocessing (marked with 3 in Table 6.4). It performed at 81.26 %, which is 0.19 % higher than the best CTC with novel preprocessing. This performance is perhaps an outlier, since the average accuracy of the "new online" CTC was 80.05 %, compared to 79.84 % of the "old online" CTC. However, this difference is not statistically significant. The offline CTC systems performed with an average accuracy of 73.64 %.

The HMM-based recognizer had the lowest accuracy, as observed in the previous chapters. The recognition rates of the "offline" and "old online" system are significantly lower than the "new online" system. During the experiments only the "new online" HMM-based recognizer increased the performance in the combination.

The Vision Objects© recognizer was the best external recognizer on the IAM-OnDB-t2 benchmark task. The accuracy of 79.18 % on the test set is significantly higher than the Microsoft© recognizer with 71.32 %.

6.4.2 *Optimization on the Validation Set*

As stated above, several parameters need to be optimized during validation, namely the parameters for voting of Section 6.1, the order of the classifiers for the alignment, and the choice of classifiers to be used for the ensemble. This section describes the choices made during the development of the MCS.

In the experiments reported in this section, the frequency of occurrence was used for voting. Other voting strategies are investigated in the next section.

Because the order of the classifiers has an influence on the alignment, the strategy of Section 6.3.2 was used leading to the following sequence of recognition systems:

(1) the online CTC systems
(2) the Vision Objects© recognizer
(3) the offline CTC systems
(4) the Microsoft© recognizer
(5) the HMM-based recognizers

Table 6.4   Accuracies of the individual recognizers

System		Validation set	Test set
CTC offline	1	66.99 %	74.73 %
	2	69.77 %	73.88 %
	3	72.81 %	76.43 %
	4	67.96 %	72.84 %
	5	70.72 %	75.05 %
	6	67.13 %	71.26 %
	7	67.34 %	71.95 %
	8	69.06 %	72.72 %
	9	72.33 %	76.17 %
	10	70.90 %	74.97 %
CTC 1st online	1	74.04 %	79.11 %
	2	75.26 %	80.90 %
	3	76.60 %	81.26 %
	4	74.40 %	79.87 %
	5	72.67 %	78.47 %
	6	75.11 %	80.50 %
	7	75.34 %	80.53 %
	8	73.57 %	79.80 %
	9	73.93 %	79.42 %
	10	72.99 %	79.10 %
CTC 2nd online	**1**	76.09 %	80.99 %
	2	74.97 %	81.07 %
	3	74.50 %	79.84 %
	4	74.46 %	80.77 %
	5	74.83 %	80.44 %
	6	73.56 %	79.91 %
	7	73.36 %	79.90 %
	8	73.79 %	79.27 %
	9	74.92 %	80.58 %
	10	72.00 %	77.82 %
HMM offline		51.47 %	57.34,%
HMM 1st online		57.20 %	63.20 %
HMM 2nd online		58.84 %	63.86 %
Microsoft©		68.51 %	71.32 %
Vision Objects©		73.05 %	79.18 %

As explained previously (see also Table 6.3), there are 35 individual classifiers available for potential inclusion in the ensemble. However, it is well known that ensemble performance is not necessarily monotonically increasing with ensemble size. Therefore, the question arises which of the individual classifiers to actually include in the ensemble. It can be expected that taking just the best recognition systems does not necessarily yield the optimal performance, because the CTC systems would be too dominant. On the other hand, validating all possible combinations is computationally very expensive. Therefore, the decision of which classifiers to include in the ensemble leads to the following two questions:

- Which of the systems from Table 6.3 are to be taken for the classifier ensemble? (Each row of Table 6.3 corresponds to one recognition system, resulting in ten candidates.)
- How many instances of the CTC system are used for a particular ensemble?

The influence of the HMM-based systems was investigated to gradually solve the first problem stated above. Adding the 2nd online HMM-based system to the ensemble of Section 6.3.2 led to a performance increase on the validation set. On the other hand, if the other two HMM-based systems were added to the ensemble, the performance on the validation set dropped dramatically. Consequently, only the HMM-based system with the novel preprocessing was used for other experiments.

The following automatic strategy was chosen to solve the second problem. All possible combinations of up to six instances of each system were validated automatically. Note that this is an implicit weighting for each of the non-CTC classifiers, because the same classifier can be included several times. The upper bound of six is motivated by the experiments of Section 6.3.2 where there was no performance increase when more than six classifiers were used. The best combination on the validation set was: five "2nd online" CTC systems, one "1st online" CTC system, five Vision Objects© recognition systems, four offline CTC systems, three Microsoft© recognition systems, and two "2nd online" HMM-based system. The accuracy of this ensemble on the validation set was 83.34 %, which is remarkably higher than the accuracy of the best individual classifier on the validation set, i.e., a CTC with only 76.60 %.

Table 6.5   Results of the best combination on the test set

System	Accuracy
Best individual classifier	81.26 %
Optimal combination	85.88 %
Oracle	92.03 %

Table 6.6   Test set performance using only CTC compared to using only the other recognizers

System	Accuracy
Best individual classifier	81.26 %
Vision Objects© Recognizer	79.18 %
Combining CTC only	83.64 %
Combining all other systems	79.51 %
Combining all systems	85.88 %

6.4.3   *Test Set Results*

After finding the optimal combination of recognizers on the validation set, the corresponding MCS was tested on the independent test set. The results on the test set appear in Table 6.5. The optimized combination performed statistically significantly better than the best individual classifier at a significance level of 0.1 %. The recognition accuracy was 85.88 %, resulting in a remarkable relative error reduction of 24.65 %.

Note that in the last row in Table 6.5 the result of an oracle voting is presented. The oracle is assumed to know the transcription and always takes the correct word if at least one individual classifier recognized it. Hence the oracle performance is an upper bound on the combination of the classifiers given the alignment. The results show that there is a possible further improvement of about 7 %.

One interesting aspect investigated in this chapter is the influence of the CTC systems compared to the other systems. Therefore, the number of instances of the CTC system was optimized on the validation set as described above. Table 6.6 shows the performance of this optimized CTC combination in the third row. The performance of 83.64 % is already significantly higher than the performance of the best individual network at a significance level of 1 %. The improvement of the combination of the other (non-CTC) recognizers only led to an increase that is significant on the 5 % level, compared to the best individual classifier of this ensemble. Note that the improvement of the overall combination (+4.62 %) was larger than the addition of the improvement of these two combinations (2.38 %+0.33 %). The individual strengths of the systems involved in the two combinations showed to bring more advantage in the overall combination.

6.5   Advanced Confidence Measures

In the previous section, only the frequency of occurrence was used to decide which word in a correspondence set is chosen as the final output. However, it is advisable to also take the confidences of the individual classifiers into account. In the following, Section 6.5.1 first summarizes the voting strategies, and then Section 6.5.2 reports the experimental results.

6.5.1   *Voting Strategies*

Three strategies for making a decision which word to choose have been investigated in the work described in this section. First, only the frequency of occurrence has been used. In the second and third strategy, confidence scores have been used. Under these strategies the outputs of the recognizers need to be augmented with a confidence measure.

The second strategy uses the performance of each individual classifier on the validation set as a confidence measure. This means that for all words in the output sequence of a classifier the same confidence score is taken.

The third strategy uses more elaborated confidence values, i.e., it takes the confidence values output by the recognizers into account. This is not an easy task, because the confidences of the individual recognition systems are not directly comparable. While the CTC and Vision Objects© systems output a normalized recognition score, the HMM-based system gives a likelihood, which is barely useful for combination. However, the most difficult problem is the Microsoft© recognizer, which only gives three discrete values on the text line level. We have solved the problem as follows. The range of confidence scores of each classifier is divided into several intervals. For each interval, the accuracy on the validation set is calculated. This accuracy is then taken as the final confidence score during testing.

An example of a curve obtained with the third strategy is shown in Fig. 6.7. In this example the interval $[-0.2, 0]$ of the log confidences of a

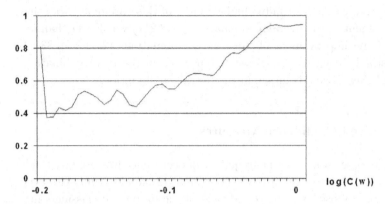

Fig. 6.7   Accuracy on the validation set for several confidence intervals

Table 6.7   Test set performance of the advanced voting strategies

System	Accuracy
Voting 1	85.88 %
Voting 2	85.86 %
Voting 3	**86.16 %**

CTC system is divided into 40 sub-intervals. As can be seen the accuracy increases if the confidence increases. Surprisingly, for the lowest confidence interval there is a higher accuracy on the validation set. This is caused by words with a low frequency. Often such words are correct, but they have only small language model probabilities. Note that the curve is smoothed to avoid discontinuities at the borders of each interval.

6.5.2   *Experiments*

Again the IAM-OnDB-t2 benchmark task with the open vocabulary was used to evaluate the performance of the system. The experimental setup, the validation of parameters, and the individual classifiers were the same as in Section 6.4.

The results on the test set appear in Table 6.7. The three different voting strategies described in Section 6.5.1 are denoted by "voting 1" for voting based on the number of occurrences, "voting 2" for voting using the accuracy on the validation set as a confidence measure, and "voting 3" for advanced voting taking also the confidence of the classifiers into account.

The second voting strategy, which uses the accuracy on the validation set as a confidence score, performed with 85.86 %, which is almost as good as "voting 1". However, while there was a performance increase on the validation set, there was a small decrease on the test set. This motivates to take more elaborated voting strategies.

The third strategy led to a relative error reduction of more than 26.14 %, compared to the best individual classifier, which is significant at the 0.1 % level. Note that the additional effort made by the more elaborated combination method also brought a significant performance increase, compared to "voting 1". The final recognition accuracy of 86.16 % was the highest performance achieved on the test set.

6.6 Conclusions

In this chapter a multiple classifier system (MCS) for the recognition of handwritten notes written on a whiteboard has been presented. The ROVER framework has been used to combine the output sequences of the recognizers. This framework first aligns the word sequences incrementally in a word transition network and then, at each output position, applies a voting strategy to select the final result.

One offline and two online HMM-based recognition systems are combined in the initial experiments on the IAM-OnDB-t1 benchmark task. The number of occurrences of each word was chosen for voting. The recognition accuracy of the combined system was significantly higher than the accuracy of the best single system. It increased significantly from 65.2 % to 66.8 % by using only a word pair grammar. This motivates involving more systems of different nature in order to further improve the MCS.

In the second set of initial experiments, several neural network recognizers (CTC combined with BLSTM) were combined on the IAM-OnDB-t2 benchmark. For these experiments a language model was included. The experimental results on the test set show a highly significant improvement of the recognition performance. The final recognition accuracy was 83.64 %, corresponding to an error reduction of more than 12 % compared to the best individual classifier. An interesting outcome of these experiments is that applying an MCS using only three classifiers did not increase the performance significantly, even if the weighting is optimized. It can be concluded that simply applying an MCS is not helpful in all cases. However, using different recognizers by changing the initialization of the network led to better recognition rates.

The second series of experiments was performed on the IAM-OnDB-t2 benchmark. Beside the HMM-based recognizers and the CTC system, external recognition systems from Microsoft© and Vision Objects© were included for the combination using the original and some modified transcriptions for both systems. Since the CTC system performed best on the validation set, ten instances were generated with each of the three feature sets. This results in eight different recognition systems with altogether 35 instances. For this set of experiments a language model was included which was trained on the second validation set. The first validation set was used to optimize the individual systems and the combination parameters.

The results of the individual recognizers show that the CTC systems based on online features had the best accuracy, followed by the Vision Objects© recognizer. A possible explanation for this ranking is that CTC systems take advantage of already being optimized on whiteboard data. The HMM-based systems had the lowest accuracy. During validation it turned out that one online HMM-based system is sufficient for the combinations.

The experimental results on the test set show a highly significant improvement of the recognition performance. The optimized combination performed with 85.88 %, representing a relative error reduction of 24.65 %. Combining just the online and offline CTC systems already led to a significant performance increase. The improvement of the combination of all other recognizers also led to a significant increase. Noteworthy the improvement of the overall combination was larger than the addition of the improvement of these first two combinations. The individual strengths of the systems involved in the two combinations show to bring more advantage in the overall combination.

Experiments with advanced voting strategies have shown another significant performance increase on the test set. While using the recognition accuracy on the validation as a confidence score did not lead to an improved performance of the combination, a significantly higher performance was achieved with an advanced approach. This approach takes also the confidence scores of the individual recognizers into account. The optimized combination performed with 86.16 %, representing a relative error reduction of 26.15 % over the best individual classifier.

While the main goal of this research is to achieve higher recognition performance, an interesting aspect of the recognition system is the computation time needed for obtaining the recognition result. The individual recognizers differ in computation time, i.e., the commercial systems need about 500 ms, the neural networks need about two seconds and the HMMs need more than a minute for the recognition of one text line. Combining the systems leads to a longer computation time, for all individual times are accumulated. However, if a parallel computing architecture is available, the recognizers can be run in parallel. This results in no significant overhead as only a negligible time is needed for combination.

In addition to the MCS recognition accuracy, the performance of an oracle system was investigated. It performed with 92.02 %, i.e., 6 % higher than the performance of the best combination. This shows that there is still a high potential in the combination, which is a promising research topic for future work. For example, other confidence measures proposed in the literature [Bertolami *et al.* (2006); Gorski (1997); Pitrelli and Perrone (2003)] could be considered for advanced combination strategies.

Chapter 7

Writer-Dependent Recognition

In the recognition tasks of the previous chapters, the handwriting of an unknown person is considered. However, in the domain of smart meeting rooms, where only a few persons have access to the whiteboard, it would be reasonable to identify the writer first and then apply a recognition system optimized for this writer. It is thus interesting to investigate the performance of a writer-dependent system.

A writer-dependent recognition system is presented in this chapter. The system operates in two stages. First, a writer identification system that has been developed in collaborative work [Liwicki *et al.* (2006b); Schlapbach *et al.* (2008)] identifies the person writing on the whiteboard. Then a recognition system adapted to the individual writer is applied. It is expected that this recognition system has a better performance compared to a writer-independent recognition system, because writer-dependent recognizers have a better knowledge of the writer's individual writing style and show a better performance than general recognizers.

Furthermore, in this chapter the topic of automatically identifying subcategories of the set of writers is addressed. This research topic has been investigated for many decades and it is interesting how an automated system succeeds in this task. The result of such a classification can also be used to improve a handwriting recognition system. The variability within a certain category is smaller than within a complete population, which allows the training of specialized recognizers. Having the writer identification system available, it can be easily applied to the handwriting classification task.

This chapter is organized as follows. First, Section 7.1 is devoted to the writer identification system. Next, experiments and results of several recognition approaches are stated in Section 7.2. Note that the first two sections follow the presentation given in [Liwicki *et al.* (2008c)]. Following, automatic methods for classifying the handwriting are proposed in Section 7.3. Note that this section follows [Liwicki *et al.* (2008b)]. Finally, conclusions are given in Section 7.4.

7.1   Writer Identification

The topic of writer identification for given online whiteboard data has not been addressed in the literature to the best of the authors' knowledge. However, much research has been performed in related fields, such as identification and verification of signatures and general handwriting [Gupta and McCabe (1997); Leclerc and Plamondon (1994); Plamondon and Lorette (1989); Plamondon and Srihari (2000)]. Some of the ideas used in this section, such as the selection of features, are inspired by work in online handwriting recognition [Jain *et al.* (2002); Richiardi *et al.* (2005)] and signature verification [Jäger *et al.* (2001); Schenkel *et al.* (1995)]. The features have been chosen because they have shown to adequately capture the form of a person's handwriting. To model the distribution of the features extracted from the text lines, powerful but simple Gaussian mixture models (GMMs) are used which had a good performance in signature verification [Richiardi *et al.* (2005)] and offline writer identification [Schlapbach and Bunke (2006)].

This section is outlined as follows. Section 7.1.1 gives an overview of the writer identification system. First, the feature sets are described in Section 7.1.2. Next, a short summary of writer identification experiments is presented in Section 7.1.3. For a more intensive experimental study, including different feature sets, see [Schlapbach *et al.* (2008)].

7.1.1   *System Overview*

The distribution of the features extracted from the handwriting of a person is modeled by one GMM for each writer. The models are obtained by the following two-step training procedure (a detailed description of the training procedure has been presented in Section 2.3). In the first step, all training data from all writers are used to train a single, writer-independent universal background model (UBM). In the second step, a writer-specific model is obtained for each writer by adaptation using the UBM and training data from that writer. The result of the training procedure is a model for each

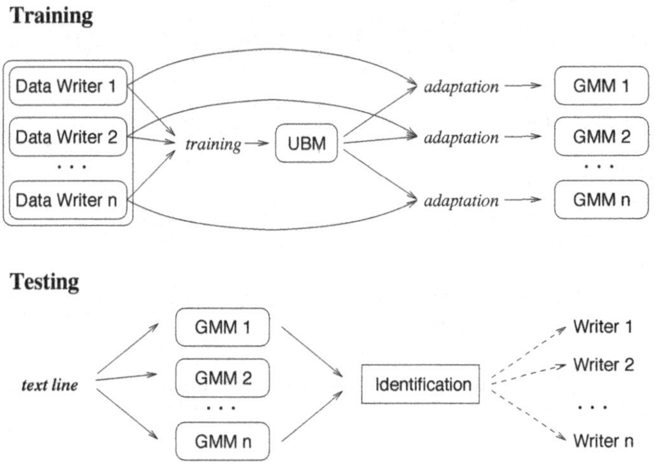

Training

Testing

Fig. 7.1 Schematic overview of the training and the testing phase

writer. In the testing phase, a text of unknown identity is presented to each model. Each model returns a log-likelihood score, and these scores are sorted in descending order. Based on the resulting ranking, the text is assigned to the person whose model produces the highest log-likelihood score. A schematic overview of the training and the testing phase is shown in Fig. 7.1.

To train the models, different feature sets are extracted from the text which are described below. Before feature extraction, a series of normalization operations are applied. The operations are designed to improve the quality of the extracted features without removing writer-specific information. For this reason, no resampling of the data points is performed. The following preprocessing steps are performed (for a description see Section 5.2):

- removal of noisy points and gaps within strokes
- division of the text line into parts
- skew correction
- baseline and corpus line detection
- width and height normalization

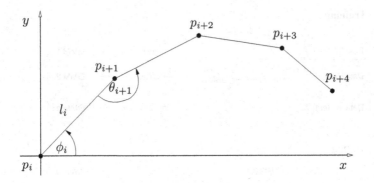

Fig. 7.2   Illustration of point-based features

7.1.2   *Feature Sets for Whiteboard Writer Identification*

Two different feature sets are presented in this subsection, the *point-based feature set* and the *point-based feature set*. In the remainder of this section, the number in parenthesis behind the name of a feature indicates the number of individual feature values.

The features of the *point-based feature set* are similar to the ones used in online handwriting recognition systems and signature verification systems. For a given stroke s consisting of points p_1 to p_n, a set of features is computed for each consecutive pair of points (p_i, p_{i+1}). The angle ϕ_i denotes the angle between the horizontal line and the line (p_i, p_{i+1}), and the angle θ_i denotes the angle between the lines (p_{i-1}, p_i) and (p_i, p_{i+1}) (see Fig. 7.2 for an illustration).

The following features are calculated:

- *speed (1):* the speed v_i of the segment

$$v_i = \frac{\Delta(p_i, p_{i+1})}{t}$$

  where t equals the sampling rate of the acquisition device.
- *writing direction (2):* the writing direction at p_i, i.e., the cosine and sine of θ_i:

$$\cos(\theta_i) = \frac{\Delta x(p_i, p_{i+1})}{l_i}$$

$$\sin(\theta_i) = \frac{\Delta y(p_i, p_{i+1})}{l_i}$$

- *curvature (2):* the curvature, i.e., the cosine and the sine of the angle ϕ_i. These angles are derived by the following trigonometric formulas:

$$\cos(\phi_i) = \cos(\theta_i) \cdot \cos(\theta_{i+1}) + \sin(\theta_i) \cdot \sin(\theta_{i+1})$$

$$\sin(\phi_i) = \cos(\theta_i) \cdot \sin(\theta_{i+1}) - \sin(\theta_i) \cdot \cos(\theta_{i+1})$$

- *x/y-coordinate (2):* the relative x/y-position of the point p_i. The relative x-coordinate is calculated by subtracting the x-coordinate of a point from a moving average coordinate.
- *speed (1):* the speed v_i of the segment
- *speed in x/y-direction (2):* the speed v_{i_x}/v_{i_y} in x/y-direction
- *acceleration (1):* the overall acceleration a_i
- *acceleration in x/y-direction (2):* the acceleration a_{i_x}/a_{i_y} in x/y-direction
- *log curvature radius (1):* is the log of the radius r_i of the circle which best approximates the curvature at the point p_i. The curvature $c_i = 1/r_i$ is derived from the local velocities and the local accelerations as follows:

$$c_i = \frac{(v_{i_x} \cdot a_{i_y} - a_{i_x} \cdot v_{i_y})}{\sqrt{(v_{i_x}^2 + v_{i_y}^2)}^3}$$

- *writing direction (2):* the cosine and the sine of the angle between the line segment of the starting point and the x-axis
- *curvature (2):* the cosine and the sine of the angle between the lines to the previous and to the next point
- *vicinity features (5):* the aspect, the curliness, the linearity, and the slope (2) as described in Section 5.3.1.
- *offline features (11):* the ascenders/descenders and the context map (9) as described in Section 5.3.1.

In total the *point-based feature set* consists of 29 feature values.

In the *stroke-based feature set* the individual features are based on strokes. For each stroke $s = p_1, \ldots, p_n$ the following features are calculated (for an illustration see Fig. 7.3):

- *accumulated length (1):* the accumulated length l_{acc} of all lines l_i:

$$l_{acc} = \sum_{i=1}^{n-1} l_i$$

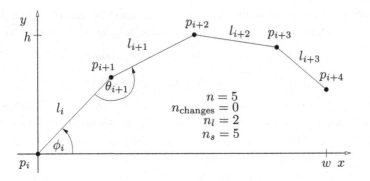

Fig. 7.3   Illustration of stroke-based features

- *accumulated angle (1):* the accumulated angle θ_{acc} of the absolute values of the angles of the writing directions of all lines:

$$\theta_{acc} = \sum_{i=1}^{n-1} |\theta_i|$$

- *width and height (2):* the width $w = x_{\max} - x_{\min}$ and the height $h = y_{\max} - y_{\min}$ of the stroke
- *duration (1):* the duration t of the stroke
- *time to previous stroke (1):* the time difference Δt_{prev} to the previous stroke
- *time to next stroke (1):* the time difference Δt_{next} to the next stroke
- *number of points (1):* the total number of points n
- *number of curvature changes (1):* the number of changes n_{changes} in the curvature
- *number of up strokes (1):* the number of angles n_l of the writing direction larger than zero
- *number of down strokes (1):* the number of angles n_s of the writing direction smaller than zero

The *stroke-based feature set* thus contains 11 feature values.

7.1.3   *Experiments*

In the experiments, data from 200 different writers of the IAM-OnDB was used. The task is to identify which person out of these 200 individuals has written a given text. It can be argued that even in large organizations there are rarely more than 200 potential participants to a meeting held in a smart meeting room.

For each writer, there are eight paragraphs of text, i.e., in total 1,600 paragraphs of text consisting of 11,170 text lines. A text line contains 627 points and 24 strokes on average.

The division into training data, validation data, and test data is based on paragraphs of text. Four paragraphs of text were used for training, two paragraphs were used to validate the meta parameters of the GMMs and the remaining two paragraphs formed the independent test set. Training, validation and test set were iteratively rotated.

All training data from all writers were used to train the UBM. The model of each writer was then obtained by adapting the UBM with writer-specific training data. Two meta parameters were systematically varied. First, the number of Gaussian mixture components was increased from 50 to 300 by steps of 50. Second, the variance flooring factor was increased from 0.001 to 0.031 in steps of 0.002. As there was a high amount of training data available, full adaptation was performed, i.e., the MAP factor was set to 0.0. The other meta parameters were set to standard values [Collobert *et al.* (2002)].The optimal number of Gaussian mixture components and the optimal variance flooring factor were determined by averaging the writer identification rates achieved on the four validation sets. The final writer identification rate is the average of the writer identification rates on the four test sets.

In order to measure the performance of the identification system if fewer data is available during recognition, each paragraph was split into its individual text lines for the experiments on the text line level. The training set, the validation set, and the test set thus consisted no longer of full paragraphs, but of the individual text lines. While the amount of data available for training is identical to the first experimental setup, the models were optimized and tested on the text line level. The rest of the experimental setup is identical to the first experimental setup.

Three aspects of the identification system are investigated in this section. First, the choice of the feature set is evaluated in Section 7.1.3.1. Next, the training method is investigated in Section 7.1.3.2, and finally, the performance of the system based on different training set sizes is analyzed in Section 7.1.3.3.

Table 7.1   Writer identification rates for different feature sets on the paragraph level

Feature set	Validation set	Test set
stroke-based feature set (11)	92.31 % (100, 0.015)	92.56 %
point-based feature set (29)	98.31 % (300, 0.007)	98.56 %

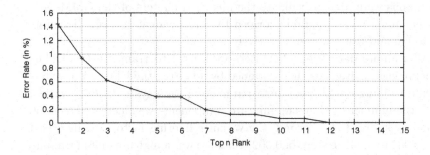

Fig. 7.4   *n*-best list for the *point-based feature set* on the paragraph level.

7.1.3.1   *Evaluation of Feature Set*

In Table 7.1 the writer identification rates of the two feature sets are given on the paragraph level, and in Table 7.2 the results on the text line level are shown. The number in parenthesis in the feature set column denotes the number of features in a feature vector. The number in parenthesis in the validation set column denotes the number of Gaussian mixture components and the variance flooring factor that achieved the highest writer identification rate on the validation set. The last column describes the results achieved on the test set.

Table 7.1 gives the results of the experiments on the paragraph level. The highest writer identification rate of 98.56 % was obtained using the *point-based feature set*. In this case, only a few text paragraphs were classified incorrectly.

An *n*-best list measures the identification rate not only based on the first rank, but based on the first *n* ranks. As can been seen in Fig. 7.4, for the *point-based feature set* the error rate dropped below 0.2% if the first seven ranks were considered and all paragraphs were identified correctly if the first twelve out of a total of 200 ranks were considered.

The writer identification rates shown in Table 7.2 were calculated on the text line level. The *stroke-based feature set* produced rather low writer

Table 7.2 Writer identification rates for different feature sets on the text line level

Feature set	Validation set	Test set
stroke-based feature set (11)	61.80 % (100, 0.001)	62.55 %
point-based feature set (29)	86.45 % (300, 0.027)	88.96 %

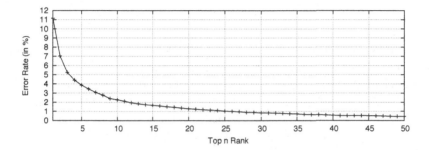

Fig. 7.5   *n*-best list for the *point-based feature set* on the text line level

identification rates. The highest writer identification rate of 88.96 % was again obtained by the *point-based feature set*.

In Fig. 7.5, the *n*-best list for the *point-based feature set* on the text line level is shown. The error rate dropped below 4% if the first five ranks were considered, and below 1% if the first 27 ranks were taken into account.

7.1.3.2 *Evaluation of Training Methods*

In the approach used in this book, the client models were obtained from the UBM by adapting the mean values of the diagonal covariance matrix. The variance, as well as the weight values, were not adapted. In order to evaluate the training method, two alternative approaches to obtain the client models have been investigated in the work described in the following.

In the first alternative approach, the client models were obtained from the UBM by adapting the weights of the diagonal covariance matrix. The mean and the variance values of the covariance matrix were not adapted. The number of Gaussian mixture components was varied from 50 to 300 in steps of 50 and the variance flooring factor from 0.001 to 0.031 in steps of 0.002 which is identical to the first series of experiments.

The second alternative approach does not use any UBM at all. Instead, for every writer, the client models are trained from scratch using the EM

Table 7.3   Evaluation of three different trainings methods to obtain the client models

Training method	Parameters	Average	Std. dev.
UBM, learn means	300G, 0.027VF	86.96 %	2.64 %
UBM, learn weights	300G, 0.031VF	74.43 %	3.06 %
No UBM	300G, 0.001VF	66.32 %	2.41 %

algorithm (see Section 2.3). Again the number of Gaussian mixture components is increased from 50 to 300 in steps of 50 and the variance flooring factor is varied from 0.001 to 0.031 in steps of 0.002.

In Table 7.3 the identification rates achieved using three different training methods are shown on the validation sets and the test sets, respectively. The first row in Table 7.3 shows the results that are achieved if the client models are obtained by only updating the weights in the adaptation process (denoted by *UBM, learn means*). The second row presents the results that are achieved if the client models are obtained by adapting the weights (denoted by *UBM, learn weights*), and in the third row, the identification rate for the case where each client model is trained without the use of a UBM is given (denoted by *No UBM*). The best performance of 88.96 % was achieved if the client models were obtained by adaptation from a UBM compared to an approach where every client model was trained from scratch. Furthermore, the experimental results show that significantly higher writer identification rates were achieved if the mean values instead of the weights were updated in the UBM adaptation process.

7.1.3.3   *Evaluation of Reducing Training Data*

The third set of experiments measures the influence of using less data to train the GMMs. In the previous two sets of experiments, text from four paragraphs were used for training. In this experimental setup, the amount of data available for training was reduced from four paragraphs to one paragraph in steps of one.

In this series of experiments, no cross validation was performed to reduce the computational complexity. The initial training set consists of four paragraphs, and the validation and the test set each consist of two paragraphs. The *point-based feature set* was used in this set of experiments. The experiments were performed on the text line level. Only the mean values were updated during adaptation. The rest of the setup is identical to the previous two sets of experiments.

Table 7.4   Influence of the amount of data available for training on the writer identification rate

Number of paragraphs	Parameters	Validation set	Test set
One paragraph	150G, 0.2MAP	70.50 %	69.23 %
Two paragraphs	300G, 0.2MAP	81.57 %	80.75 %
Three paragraphs	300G, 0.1MAP	87.62 %	86.18 %
Four paragraphs	250G, 0.0MAP	90.36 %	87.68 %

In Table 7.4 the results of reducing the number of training data from four paragraphs to one paragraph is shown using the *point-based feature set*. The parameters in the second column indicate the number of Gaussian mixture components and the MAP adaptation factor which produced the highest writer identification rates on the validation set. The third column presents the results on the validation and the fourth row the results on the test set. The results show that reducing the number of paragraphs for training from four to three paragraphs did not significantly reduce the writer identification rate.

A deeper analysis of the influence of the UBM on the system's performance was performed on the validation set (see Fig. 7.6). For each validation experiment, the writer identification rate as a function of the number of Gaussian mixture components and the MAP adaptation factor is plotted with one to four paragraphs of training data. If only one or two paragraphs of text were used for training then the highest writer identification rates were achieved with a MAP adaptation factor of 0.2. If three paragraphs of text were available for training the best result was achieved with a MAP adaptation factor of 0.1. For four paragraphs, full adaptation to the writer specific data, i.e., a MAP adaptation factor of 0.0, produced the best writer identification rate.

7.2   Writer-Dependent Experiments

Having a good writer identification system available, a writer-dependent recognition system for smart meeting room environments can be developed. In smart meeting rooms it is known beforehand who may attend the meeting. We assume that the recognition system has a small amount of training data from each writer available. These data need to be acquired only once. Thereupon, the identification system can use these data for

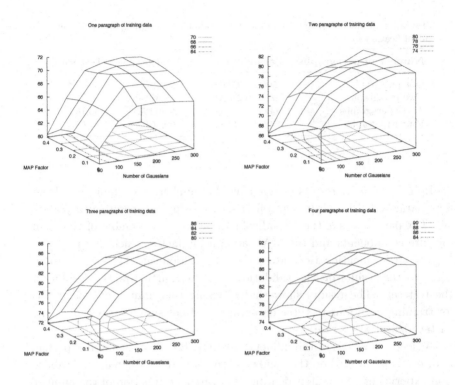

Fig. 7.6   Writer identification rate on the validation set as a function of the number of Gaussian mixtures and the MAP adaptation factor

training the identification system, and the handwriting recognition system can be created on these data.

Two different methods exist for generating a writer-dependent recognition system. The first is to use the available data to train a new recognition system from scratch. Following this method an individual handwriting recognition system has been generated for each writer in the considered population, using the approach described in Chapter 5.

The second method takes a writer-independent recognizer and adapts it with the data from the considered writer. HMM adaptation is a method to adjust the model parameters θ of a given background model (here the HMMs of the writer-independent recognizer) to the parameters θ_{ad} of the adaptation set of observations O (the data of the individual writer). More information about adaptation can be found in Section 2.1.4. The adaptation parameter τ weights the influence of the background model on the adaptation data. Whereas τ has been set empirically in previous work [Vinciarelli and Bengio (2002)], it is optimized on a validation set in in the work described in this section.

Both methods, training from scratch and adaption, have their advantages and drawbacks. While the first method succeeds if enough training data are available, the second method is better if only a small amount of writer-specific training data is present.

This section describes the writer-dependent experiments that were performed on the test set of the whiteboard data. First, Section 7.2.1 gives an overview of the experimental setup. Finally, the results are presented and discussed in Section 7.2.2.

7.2.1 *Experimental Setup*

The experiments were performed on both benchmark tasks of the IAM-OnDB (see Section 3.3). The division into a training, a validation, and a test set is the same in both benchmarks, IAM-OnDB-t1 and IAM-OnDB-t2. Since the benchmark tasks have been designed for writer-independent recognition systems, some modifications on the tests set are needed to perform writer-dependent experiments. All the other parameters of the benchmark task, e.g., the vocabulary, the letters, and the training and validation sets, were left untouched.

The test set was changed as follows. Each writer contributed eight texts, so the data can be separated on the paragraph level. The data ware divided into four sets for each writer, containing two paragraphs each. A cross validation similar to the experiments in Section 4.3.3 was performed on the four sets (s_0, ..., s_3). It was performed in the following way (combinations c_0, ..., c_3). For $i = 0$, ..., 4, sets $s_{i \oplus 2}$, and $s_{i \oplus 3}$ were taken for training the system, set $s_{i \oplus 1}$ was used as a validation set, i.e., for optimizing the training or adaptation parameters, and set s_i was used as a test set for measuring the system performance. This cross validation procedure guarantees that each paragraph of the test set is used once for recognition. Therefore the results may be compared to the results of the writer-independent recognition system tested only once on the whole test set.

The background model for the writer identification step, as well as the recognition system for the adaptation experiments, were trained on the training set of the benchmarks. Optimization of these models was also performed on the validation sets of the benchmarks.

For both benchmarks, first a word pair grammar was used and later a bigram language model was included. For the IAM-OnDB-t1 task the

Table 7.5   Word recognition accuracy on IAM-OnDB-t1

System	Recognition rate (%)	Accuracy (%)
Reference	73.1	63.1
Trained from scratch	37.8	0.2
Adapted from reference	75.0	66.7
Including a language model	77.0	73.2

Table 7.6   Word recognition accuracy on IAM-OnDB-t2

System	Recognition rate (%)	Accuracy (%)
Reference	56.2	31.3
Trained from scratch	26.1	−36.8
Adapted from reference	59.7	37.7
Including a language model	72.6	64.8

bigram language model was trained on the LOB Corpus, while it was trained on three corpora for the IAM-OnDB-t2 task. Note that these are the same conditions as in Section 5.4.3, where the results of the HMM-based recognition system are reported.

7.2.2   *Results*

The results of this section are reported as word recognition rates and word level accuracies, as in the previous chapters. The writer-independent recognition system evaluated in Section 5.4.3 serves as a reference system.

Tables 7.5 and 7.6 show the results of the writer-dependent recognition systems on the two benchmark tasks IAM-OnDB-t1 and IAM-OnDB-t2. The first stage always gave a perfect identification rate on the test set of 68 writers. Hence, the correct specialized recognition system was always applied. As it can be seen in the tables, training the writer-dependent recognizers from scratch resulted in lower recognition rates in all cases. This is mainly due to the low amount of training data. However, adapting the reference system on the writer-specific training data led to a significant improvement of the accuracy and the recognition rate in all cases (using a standard *z-test* at a significance level of 5 %). By integrating a bigram language model, the recognition rate was further improved.

7.3 Automatic Handwriting Classification

A population of individuals can often be partitioned into sub-categories based on various criteria. Such a division is interesting for numerous reasons, for example, if a researcher is only interested in one specific sub-category, or if specifically processing each sub-category leads to improved results. For example, in the field of face recognition, much research has been conducted on classifying a face image according to gender [Wiskott *et al.* (1995); Wu *et al.* (2003)]. Classification results up to 94% have been reported for this two-class problem.

For handwriting there exist several criteria for sub-categories. Whereas in KANSEI the sub-categories are feelings for character patterns [Hattori *et al.* (2004)], handwriting can also be divided into writer-specific sub-categories including gender, handedness, age and ethnicity [Scheidat *et al.* (2006)]. Correlations between these sub-categories and handwriting features have been presented in [Huber (1999)]. Special interest has been focused on determining the gender of the writer. In [Hamid and Loewenthal (1996)] human persons were asked to classify the writer's gender from a given handwriting example. A classification rate of about 68 % was reported. Further studies in [Beech and Mackintosh (2005)], which inlcude a detailed analysis of the raters' background, reported results in the same range.

Beside being an interesting research topic of its own, automatically identifying sub-categories can be used to improve a handwriting recognition system. The variability within a certain category is smaller than within a complete population, which allows the training of specialized recognizers. Another application is demographic studies. A concrete example would be to study the handwriting available on the world wide web and to find out how many people from each category contributed to the data.

Especially the classification of gender from handwriting has been a research topic for many decades [Broom *et al.* (1929); Newhall (1926); Tenwolde (1934)]. However, there exist conflicting results ranging from slightly more than 50 % to more than 90 %. An overview of several manual approaches to detect gender from handwriting can be found in [Hecker (1996)]. The approach proposed in [Hecker (1996)] tries to semi-automatically classify the handwriting, while it is done automatically in this section.

Little work exists on automatically identifying sub-categories, such as gender or handedness, from handwriting. In [Cha and Srihari (2001)] a system for classifying the handwriting based on images of individual letters is presented. Results of 70.2 % for gender classification and 59.5 % for handedness have been achieved. If longer texts are available and multiple classifier approaches are applied even better results are reported [Bandi and Srihari (2005)]. However, these systems are restricted to the offline case and either the transcription of the text must be known or even identical texts must be provided by all writers.

In this section, a system that classifies the gender of online, Roman handwriting is presented. This problem is a two class problem, i.e., *male/female*. The handwriting is unconstrained, thus any text can be used for classification. Two sets of features are investigated in this Section. While the first feature set is based on online data, the second set of features is extracted from offline images generated from the online data. Gaussian Mixture Models (GMMs) are used to model the classes. Furthermore, both feature sets are combined and several combination strategies are investigated. For the purpose of comparison, an experiment with human persons classifying the same data set is also performed.

The rest of the section is organized as follows. First, Section 7.3.1 shortly summarizes the features used and the GMM classifier. Second, the combination strategy is described in Section 7.3.2. Finally, experiments and results are presented and discussed in Section 7.3.3.

7.3.1   *Classification Systems*

The normalization and feature extraction procedure is motivated by previous work in writer identification. Both, the online and offline feature sets used in this sections have shown excellent performance on the writer identification and verification task [Schlapbach *et al.* (2008); Schlapbach and Bunke (2006)]. The gender identification task is related to the task of writer identification and can be posed as a two-class problem ("female" writer vs. "male" writer). Therefore it is reasonable to apply these normalization and feature extraction methods to the gender identification task.

A series of normalization operations are applied before feature extraction. The operations intend to improve the quality of the features without removing writer specific, i.e., class specific information. In this section the same methods as in Section 7.1 are used. The individual text lines are then processed differently for both feature sets.

For the online features, the same normalization and feature extraction methods as described in Section 7.1 are performed. The online feature set contains online features as well as pseudo offline features extracted from an offline representation of the online data. Overall the feature set consists of 29 features.

For the offline features, the preprocessed data needs to be transformed into an offline image, so that it can be used as input for the offline recognizer. Unlike the online data, the normalization operations for the offline data are applied to entire text lines at once. Only the following steps of the normalization processes described in Section 4.1 are performed:

- skew correction
- baseline and corpus line detection
- width and height normalization

A sliding window is used to extract the feature vectors from a normalized image. The width of the window is one pixel, and nine geometrical features are computed at each window position. Each text line image is therefore converted to a sequence of 9-dimensional vectors. (The features are introduced in Section 4.1.3.)

A *generative* approach based on GMMs is used to model the handwriting of each sub-category of the underlying population. The distribution of the feature vectors extracted from a sub-category's handwriting is modeled by a Gaussian mixture density. (The GMM based method is described in Section 7.1.)

7.3.2 *Combination*

After decoding, each classifier returns a log-likelihood score, i.e., the online classifier returns ll_{online} and the offline classifier returns ll_{offline}. Having online and offline classification systems available, it may be beneficial to combine both systems. From such a combination, an improved performance can be expected. For a general overview and an introduction to the field of multiple classifier systems (MCS) see [Kuncheva (2004)].

To combine the results of the online and the offline classifier, the following standard rules for the classifier combination on the score level are applied [Czyz *et al.* (2004)]:

- *Average Rule*
  The log-likelihood scores of both the online and the offline classifiers are averaged: $ll_{\text{sum}} = \frac{1}{2} * (ll_{\text{online}} + ll_{\text{offline}})$.

- *Maximum Rule*
  The largest log-likelihood score is chosen:
  $ll_\mathrm{max} = \max(ll_\mathrm{online}, ll_\mathrm{offline})$.

- *Minimum Rule*
  The smallest log-likelihood score is chosen:
  $ll_\mathrm{min} = \min(ll_\mathrm{online}, ll_\mathrm{offline})$.

The range of log-likelihood scores of both classifiers varies greatly. Therefore, before combination, the results of both classifiers are normalized in respect to mean and standard deviation. Due to the fact that only two classifiers are used, other combination rules such as the median rule or voting are not applicable in this case.

7.3.3   *Experiments and Results*

The experiments were conducted on the IAM-OnDB. Each text consists of seven text lines on average. The classification task is to identify the correct gender for a given text line.

For the task of gender classification 40 male and 40 female writers were randomly selected for training the classifiers. Furthermore, 10 male and 10 female writers were randomly selected for the validation of meta parameters, and 25 male and 25 female writers were randomly selected for testing the final system. This ensures that both classes (male/female) are equally distributed in all sets, i.e., the training, the validation, and the test set.

For the GMM the number of Gaussian mixture components G were optimized between 1 and 250. Next, the variance flooring factor φ was varied between 0.001 and 0.011 in steps of 0.002. Furthermore, the MAP adaptation factor α was varied from full adaptation ($\alpha = 0$) to no adaptation ($\alpha = 1$) in steps of 0.2. All these optimization operations were carried out on the validation set.

The optimization of the MAP adaptation factor and the number of Gaussian mixtures is illustrated in Fig. 7.7. This figure shows that, first, a higher number of Gaussian mixture components led to higher classification results. Second, a small MAP adaptation factor improved the performance as long as it was larger than zero which would imply that no adaptation to the client specific samples was made. This result shows that adaptation

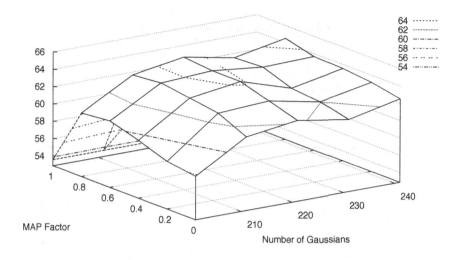

Fig. 7.7 Optimizing the number of Gaussian mixtures and the MAP adaptation factor

Table 7.7   Gender classification rates

Classifier	Classification rate
Online	64.25 %
Offline	55.39 %
Combination	67.57 %

to the UBM is important as only few training data are available to train client models from scratch.

Table 7.7 shows the classification results for the gender classification task on the test set. The best combination achieved a performance of 67.57 %. This result is significantly higher than the classification of the best individual classifier (using a *z-test* with $\alpha = 0.05$).

A deeper analysis of the different combination strategies is given in Table 7.8. As can be seen, the combination based on the *Average Rule* achieved the best performance. Using the *Minimum Rule* only led to a small increase of the performance and the *Maximum Rule* surprisingly led to a performance decrease, compared to the online recognizer. This may be due to the fact that the likelihoods were normalized before combination.

Table 7.8   Gender classification rates of
several combination approaches

Classifier	Classification rate
Average rule	67.57 %
Maximum rule	61.93 %
Minimum rule	65.58 %

Fig. 7.8   Illustration of the offline classification interface for human participants

To compare the performance of the classifiers to that of human persons, two manual classification tasks were performed. The first task was based on offline information and the second task was based on online information in form of a short movie.

In the first task, 30 persons were asked to classify 20 images from different writers each. For these images ten writers were chosen from each group, i.e., female and male. A screen shot of the interface is provided in Fig 7.8. For "training" purposes, these human participants also had classified images from other writers available (see Fig. 7.9 for an example) The classification rate of the human participants was about 57 %. These classification rates were similar to the offline classification rates of the automatic system. Note that the human participants did not perform the experiments on the same data set. Therefore the results are not directly comparable.

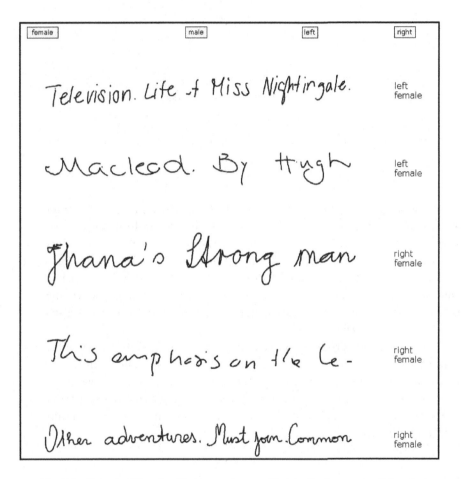

Fig. 7.9 Subset of the classified examples provided to the human participants

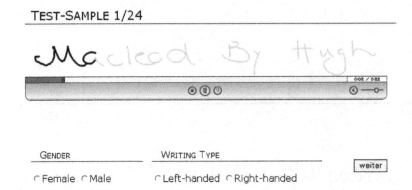

Fig. 7.10   Screen shot of the web interface for human classification based on online data

In the second task, 20 persons were asked to classify 24 movies of hand-writing from different writers. For these movies writers from the test set were chosen. Similarly to the offline task, the test subjects had classified images from other writers available. A screen shot of the web interface is given in Fig. 7.10. The movie could be viewed with standard Flash or Quicktime plugins. Navigation was possible to each position of the writing. Below the movie, the human participant could indicate his or her decision and submit the answers.[1]

The average classification rate of the human participants on the online data was about 63.88 % for the gender recognition task. This performance was lower than the performance of the automatic system. However, no direct comparison can be made because the test set for the human partici-pants contains 24 lines, while the test set for the automatic system contains data from 50 writers.

7.4   Conclusions

In this chapter a writer-dependent recognition system has been described. It benefits from the fact that usually the persons writing on the white-board are known to the smart meeting room system. The proposed sys-tem consists of two stages. In the first stage, the identity of the writer is

---

[1]The test is available under http://www.iam.unibe.ch/~smueller/

determined, and in the second stage, a writer-specific recognition system is applied to recognize the handwritten input.

For the first stage, a language and text-independent system to identify the writer of online handwriting has been presented. A set of features is extracted from the acquired data and used to train Gaussian mixture models (GMMs). GMMs provide a powerful but simple means of representing the distribution of the features extracted from handwritten text lines. All data are used to train a Universal Background Model (UBM), and a specific client model is adapted for each writer. During the identification, a text line of unknown origin is presented to each of the models. Each model returns a log-likelihood score for the given input, and the text line is assigned to the model which produces the highest score.

Two different feature sets have been investigated in this chapter. These feature sets are calculated from either the single points or the strokes of the writing. The highest writer identification rate was achieved with a point-based feature set consisting of 29 feature values, of which 11 features are were extracted from an offline representation of the online data. A writer identification rate of 98.56 % on the paragraph and of 88.96 % on the text line level was achieved.

While the identification system was developed for handwriting data acquired by the eBeam© whiteboard system, the approach can easily be applied to other online handwritten data, e.g., data acquired by a digitizing tablet or a Tablet PC [Schomaker (1998)]. The system can be expected to also show good performance on online signature data, as the features are partially inspired by work on signature verification.

The performance of the identification system can potentially be improved by using feature selection or extraction methods such as SBFS or FDA [Schlapbach *et al.* (2005)]. Another interesting topic is to fuse the different feature sets extracted from the online whiteboard data. The point-based and the stroke-based feature set contain an unequal number of vectors extracted from the same text. This means that the vectors of the different sets can not be fused by simply concatenating them to form one vector. Development of suitable feature fusion methods and comparison of their performance with fusion on other levels, such as score or decision level fusion, is left to future work.

For the second stage, a previously described HMM-based system has been used to train the writer-dependent recognizers. Two different methods for deriving the writer-dependent recognizers exist. The first method uses the available data to train a new recognition system from scratch. The second recognition system takes a writer-independent recognizer and adapts it with the data from the considered writer. Both methods were investigated in the experiments.

For the recognition experiments, the two benchmark tasks of the IAM-OnDB were used. On the test set of both tasks, the writer identification system produced a perfect identification rate. Thus, the correct writer-specific recognition system was always applied for the recognition.

The experiments show that training a writer-specific recognizer from scratch did not lead to a good performance. However, adapting the system from a good writer-independent recognition system led to significantly better results. The final word recognition rate on the IAM-OnDB-t1 was already close to 80 %, which means that only about one out of five words was not recognized correctly. It can be concluded that applying writer identification is a useful step if it is possible in the specific domain.

At the end of this chapter a system for the gender classification of handwriting has been presented. The data are given in online format and the same features are extracted as in the writer identification system. Two feature sets were extracted from the normalized data, offline and online features. In the experiments, classification results higher than those achieved by humans were obtained. The GMM results for gender classification were similar to results reported on another data set in [Cha and Srihari (2001)]. Furthermore, the offline and online systems were combined using several voting strategies for combining the likelihood scores. Applying the *average rule* led to significant improvement of the classification rate, compared to the best individual classifier. It is interesting to note that the other combination rules did not significantly increase the performance. A possible reason for this observation is the normalization of the likelihoods before the combination, which is necessary because the individual outputs are in different ranges. A potential solution is to use a weighted voting strategy or to include more individual classifiers, which is an interesting topic for future work.

The combination of classifiers' results on the score level has shown to increase the classification rates significantly. There exist other approaches to combine the classifier's results, such as combination on the feature or on the decision level. Comparison of the results presented in this paper with these approaches is left to future work. Another interesting topic for further research is the integration of other classifiers [Cha and Srihari (2001)] or the use of more features [Schlapbach *et al.* (2008)]. The number of classifiers could also be enlarged by the use of ensemble methods, such as bagging, boosting, or random feature subset selection. Related to this issue is the investigation of feature subset selection methods on its own. It could be possible that a smaller set of features leads to higher performance, as some features may have an adverse effect on the classification performance.

The promising classification rates achieved in this chapter motivates the use of specialized handwriting recognition systems. As the variability of handwriting within a certain category is smaller than within a complete population, a higher recognition performance can be expected from using a two-stage approach that first classifies the handwriting according to male/female, and subsequently applies a recognizer trained on handwriting from one sub-category.

Possible future work is to extend the experiments to other datasets. In the eBeam system there is no information about the pressure of the pen available. From this specific information one could expect higher classification results, especially for the gender detection task [Broom *et al.* (1929); Hecker (1996); Newhall (1926); Tenwolde (1934)].

Chapter 8

Conclusions

This book addresses the problem of processing online handwritten notes acquired from an electronic whiteboard. Notes written on a whiteboard is a new modality in handwriting recognition research which has received relatively little attention in the past. Obviously, handwriting on a whiteboard differs from handwriting on usual pen-input devices, because people stand during writing and the arm does not rest on a table. It has been observed that the baseline usually cannot be interpolated with a simple quadratic function. Furthermore, the size and width of the characters become smaller as the writer moves to the right.

The main motivation for this book is smart meeting room applications, where not only speech and video data of a meeting are recorded, but also notes written on a whiteboard are captured. The aim of a smart meeting room is to automate standard tasks usually performed by humans in a meeting. In a smart meeting room, one can typically find multiple acquisition devices used to record a meeting. In order to allow for retrieval of the meeting data by a browser, semantic information needs to be extracted from the raw sensory data, such as the transcription of speech or the identity of persons in video images. Whiteboards are commonly used in meeting rooms, so capture and automatic transcription of handwritten notes on a whiteboard are essential tasks in smart meeting room applications.

To solve the problem of recognizing handwritten notes, various approaches based on offline and online recognition are addressed in this book. In online recognition systems, a time ordered sequence of coordinates, representing the pen movement, is available. This may have been produced by any electronic sensing device, such as a mouse, or an electronic pen on a tablet. In offline recognition systems only the image of the text is present. Usually it is scanned or photographed from paper. Both problems have already been considered for many decades. While in the beginning the research was focused on isolated character or word recognition, more recently the problems of complete text line or sentence recognition have been considered. The latter task is the most complex one, and usually is not solvable without integrated recognition and segmentation. Sayre's paradox, saying that character segmentation cannot be completely separated from word recognition, can be applied to word segmentation in text line recognition as well.

In offline handwriting recognition a large variety of problems have been considered in research, and commercial systems have been developed. For example, there exist systems for postal address reading as well as for bank check and forms processing. Many systems have been developed in the last decades. Nonetheless, there is an increasing interest in the research community, and many open issues are unsolved in this field. Recent studies propose multiple classifier systems (MCS) or hybrid methods to get a better recognition performance. Other work concentrates on specific topics such as automated word spotting or mapping a given transcription to handwritten text.

In online handwriting recognition a significant growth of activities during the last two decades can be observed. For the task of isolated character and digit recognition, high recognition performances have been reported. In this field also highly accurate commercial systems have become available, such as recognizers running on PDAs. However, in the case of general word or sentence recognition, where no constraints are given and the lexicon is large, recognition rates are still rather low. In this domain also hybrid approaches, MCS, and additionally, novel preprocessing and feature extraction methods have been proposed in recent studies.

Throughout this book several contributions to the field of handwriting recognition are presented. To be more specific, in the context of the research described in this book, a novel online handwritten database has been compiled, and four individual handwriting recognition systems have been developed. This chapter gives a small summary of the book and provides an outlook for future work. First, an overview of the recognizers presented in this book is provided in Section 8.1. Second, the experimental findings are summarized in Section 8.2. Next, Section 8.3 concludes the overall content of this book. Finally, an outlook for future work is given in Section 8.4.

8.1 Overview of Recognition Systems

In this book four individual handwriting recognition systems have been proposed. The four systems consist of an offline and an online recognition system, a system combining offline and online data, and a writer-dependent recognition system. A short summary of these systems is provided in this section.

The first recognizer presented in this book is an offline recognizer for handwritten data. The motivation for using offline recognition is twofold. Firstly, online data can easily be converted into the offline format, and secondly, there was a state-of-the-art offline recognizer available, developed in the context of previous work. The offline recognizer consists of six main modules: online preprocessing, where noise in the raw data is reduced; transformation, where the online data are transformed into offline format; offline preprocessing, where various normalization steps take place; feature extraction, where the normalized image is transformed into a sequence of feature vectors; recognition, where an HMM-based classifier generates an n-best list of word sequences; and post-processing, where a statistical language model is applied to improve the results generated by the HMM. Based on this offline recognition system an extensive study was performed. Beside optimizing standard recognition parameters, several approaches to enhance the training data were investigated. First, the training data were enhanced with data from a large existing database of offline handwritten sentences (IAM-DB) by either adaptation or training on a mixed training set. Second, additional data from the large online database (IAM-OnDB) were used. Furthermore, both databases were combined into one large training set. Another study was performed on a two-stage recognition approach which first extracts the words and then recognizes the isolated words.

During the work described in this book an online recognition system for handwritten whiteboard notes has been developed. Therefore, as a first preprocessing method a novel approach for line segmentation has been proposed. This approach is based on dynamic programming. In line segmentation experiments, this approach performed better than using simple heuristics. The online handwriting recognition system uses state-of-the-art preprocessing and feature extraction methods, supplemented with special preprocessing procedures to handle the difficulties of whiteboard data. These methods comprise splitting of the text lines into several parts and improved slant correction. For each point sampled from the whiteboard, a set of 25 features is extracted which includes information about the online and offline vicinity of each point. This set of features was investigated in feature subset selection experiments. For the task of handwriting recognition, two systems were applied. The first one, similar to the offline recognition system, is based on HMMs. The second one is based on neural networks and is applied to the recognition of handwritten data for the first time. It uses BLSTM combined with CTC to recognize the label sequence. Because of its novelty the CTC approach was extensively experimentally investigated and a discussion about possible reasons for the higher performance was included in this book.

A multiple classifier system for the recognition of handwritten notes written on a whiteboard has also been proposed in this book. A number of individual classifiers are used in the combination. First, there are the HMM-based recognizers and the neural network-based recognizers proposed in this book. These recognizers are trained on different feature sets, i.e., offline features and online features. Furthermore, external recognizers from Microsoft© and Vision Objects© are used together with the other recognizers developed by the authors of this book. To combine the output sequences of the recognizers, the ROVER framework has been chosen. In this framework, first, the word sequences are incrementally aligned using a standard string matching algorithm. Then a voting strategy is applied at each output position to select the final result. Several voting strategies have been compared in this book. The first strategy takes the number of occurrences of each word into account. In the second and third strategies the confidence scores of the individual recognizers are used as well. While the second strategy employs the performance of each individual classifier on the validation set as a confidence measure, the third strategy takes the confidence values output by the recognizers into account. To normalize the recognition scores, the range of the scores of each classifier is divided into intervals and the accuracy on the validation set is taken for each interval.

Finally, a writer-dependent recognition system has been proposed in this book. The system operates in two stages. First, a writer identification system identifies the person writing on the whiteboard. Second, a recognition system adapted to the individual writer is applied. A GMM-based approach is used in the identification stage. In this approach the distribution of the features extracted from the handwriting of each writer is modeled with a GMM. Therefore a universal background model is trained on data from all writers and adapted to each writer's data. In the recognition stage the HMM-based online recognizer is applied.

Table 8.1   Accuracies of the recognizers presented in this book

System	IAM-OnDB-t1	IAM-OnDB-t2
offline features		
HMM	61.4,%	57.3,%
CTC	—	76.4 %
HMM two-stage approach	60.9,%	—
1st set of online features		
HMM	65.1,%	63.2 %
CTC	—	81.3 %
2nd set of online features		
HMM	65.2,%	63.9 %
CTC	—	81.1 %
HMM writer-dependent	73.2,%	64.8 %
HMM SFS	65.4,%	64.8 %
CTC SFS	—	81.7 %
CTC SBS	—	81.6 %
external recognizers		
Microsoft[©]		71.3 %
Vision Objects[©]		79.2 %
combination		
HMM only	66.8 %	—
CTC only	—	83.6 %
All (voting 1)	—	85.9 %
All (voting 2)	—	85.9 %
All (voting 3)	—	86.2 %
Oracle	—	92.0 %

8.2   Overview of Experimental Results

In order to provide a good experimental environment, a large handwriting data base, the IAM-OnDB, was acquired at the beginning of the work described in this book. The IAM-OnDB is the first large collection of handwritten whiteboard data publicly available to the research community. To allow a direct comparison of the experimental results obtained by different researchers, two benchmark tasks have been specified for the database. While the various sets for training, validating, and testing are identical in both benchmarks, the vocabulary and the encoding of the letters differ. For example, the first benchmark task (IAM-OnDB-t1) is defined on a closed vocabulary, while the second one (IAM-OnDB-t2) provides a vocabulary of the 20,000 most frequent words from three linguistic corpora.

Table 8.1 gives an overview of the most important recognition results reported in this book. The results are given for both benchmark tasks, if available. All classifiers summarized in this chapter include a statistical language model which was trained on the LOB Corpus for IAM-OnDB-t1 and on three corpora (LOB Corpus, Brown Corpus, Wellington Corpus) for IAM-OnDB-t2. Note that the two external recognizers were trained on restricted data sets and use different language models which are not publicly available.

The results in Table 8.1 are arranged in five groups. These are

(1) "offline features" for recognizers using the features described in Chapter 4
(2) "1st set of online features" for recognizers using the conventional preprocessing and features described in Chapter 5
(3) "2nd set of online features" for recognizers using the newly introduced preprocessing procedure and the features described in Chapter 5
(4) "external recognizers" for commercial recognizers that have not been developed by the authors
(5) "combination" for the multiple classifier systems described in Chapter 6

Beside the HMM and CTC performance of the best classifiers, additional results of further experiments are reported in Table 8.1. These include:

- "two-stage approach" for the two-stage approach described in Section 4.4
- "writer-dependent" for the writer-dependent experiments described in Section 7.2

- "SFS" and "SBS" for the feature subset selection experiments (sequential forward search and sequential backward search) described in Section 5.4.4; note that additional results of the CTC approach were computed
- "voting x" for the three voting strategies described in Chapter 6

As can be seen in Table 8.1, the CTC-based recognizer always outperformed the corresponding HMM-based system. The performance of the CTC was about 18 % higher than that of the HMM. Furthermore the general observation that online systems work better than offline systems has been confirmed, i.e., the best online recognizer performed with 81.3 % which is almost 5 % higher than the performance of the best offline recognizer.

The word segmentation followed by isolated word recognition did not lead to a significant increase of the performance. On the IAM-OnDB-t1 even a lower recognition accuracy was observed (60.9 % compared to 61.4 %). However, the other two-stage approach, namely the writer-dependent recognition, led to a performance increase of about 8 % on the IAM-OnDB-t1.

In the feature subset selection experiments the best recognizer always outperformed the reference system on the test set. The highest recognition accuracy was achieved by a sequential forward search with the CTC system. This recognizer performed with 81.7 %.

The Vision Objects© recognizer was the best external recognizer on the IAM-OnDB-t2 benchmark task. The accuracy of 79.18 % on the test set is significantly higher than the Microsoft© recognizer with 71.32 %. Both recognizers had an inferior performance to the online CTC-based recognizers proposed in this book. However, these results are not directly comparable because the CTC-based system was trained on whiteboard data while the external recognizers have been trained on other data.

During the combination experiments a significant performance increase was achieved in all cases. Combining all recognizers with a voting based on the number of occurrences led to a performance of 85.88 %. Experiments with advanced voting strategies have shown another significant performance increase on the test set. The optimized combination performed with 86.16 %, representing a relative error reduction of 26.15 % over the best individual classifier. However, the performance of an oracle system (92.02 %) is 6 % higher than the performance of the best combination. This shows the excellent potential of the combination, which is even not yet fully exploited.

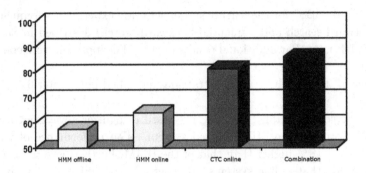

Fig. 8.1   Performance of selected recognizers on the IAM-OnDB-t2 benchmark task

8.3   Concluding Remarks

The main contributions of this book are a novel handwriting database and several recognition systems for handwritten whiteboard notes. Additional experiments have been performed in the area of text line detection and word detection, writer identification, and handwriting classification.

During different stages of the work described in this book the recognition accuracy has been increased enormously (see Fig. 8.1). On the IAM-OnDB-t2 benchmark task, the offline HMM-based system had a performance below 60 %. Using online information this was increased by more than 5 %. The largest performance increase was achieved by applying the novel neural network-based recognizer. It performed with more than 81 % accuracy. Finally, by combining these systems and commercial recognizers, another increase of about 5 % was achieved. The large performance increase mainly results from the following improvements:

- using larger training sets
- using online information
- applying a novel classifier
- combining the results of individual classifiers

Some improvements of the recognition performance were higher than others. Especially the novel neural network architecture led to a remarkable increase. A discussion of the main reasons has been provided in Section 5.6. The classifier combination experiments also show a highly significant improvement of the recognition performance. This suggests that the individual strengths of the systems involved in the combination bring a high advantage in the overall combination, i.e., the large difference is caused by the diversity of the recognizers, which are experts on different subsets of the data.

8.4 Outlook

While this book proposes different novel approaches to the recognition of whiteboard notes, there are many open issues left to future work. Especially in the area of smart meeting room research, systems which first separate the handwriting from drawings and other strokes need to be applied [Rossignol *et al.* (2004); Shilman *et al.* (2003)]. To further enhance the practical usefulness of the system in a smart meeting room scenario, the recognition of mathematical formulas [Tapia and Rojas (2003)] and tables [Zanibbi *et al.* (2004)] need to be considered.

A more detailed study on the online features for the recognition is a promising topic for future research. An interesting outcome of this book for the handwriting research community is that a subset of five features already produces good results. These five features are not highly correlated and were the top choices during the first iterations of the forward search. Perhaps better features can be found to further improve the recognition results. In the future the feature selection experiments could be extended by using other strategies, such as Sequential Backward Search (SBS), Sequential Floating Forward Search (SFFS), Sequential Floating Backward Search (SFBS), or even genetic algorithms. Another possibility is to apply feature extraction methods like principal component analysis (PCA) or multiple discriminant analysis (MDA). It is also advisable to apply the classifier based on neural networks in conjunction with better sets of features.

Concerning multiple classifier systems, there are also research topics for future work. During the combination it turned out that taking just the accuracy on the validation set as a confidence score does not lead to a significant increase, compared to a simple voting based on the number of occurrences of each word. However, it is difficult to get better confidence scores, because the outputs of the recognizers are not easily comparable and are given at different levels (text line, word). Thus finding better confidence scores is a challenging, but promising research topic. Another possibility to improve the recognition performance is to use even more systems for the combination. These may include other external recognizers as well as classifiers described in this book which have not yet been used. The systems derived from the feature selection experiments could be a useful starting point. Furthermore, several vocabulary sizes for the recognition can be used, as they turned out to influence the recognition accuracy of the classifier based on neural networks. Finally, it bears good prospects to include a language model during combination. The ROVER framework applies a voting strategy that disregards the neighboring words. Yet, a language model integrated in the voting procedure would use the information provided by the surrounding words.

The writer-dependent experiments have shown a significant increase of the recognition performance. The final recognition accuracy with the HMM-based systems is still below 70 %, while the CTC systems perfom with an accuracy around 80 %. A higher recognition performance can be expected if the CTC systems are also adapted to the specific writers. Developing adaptation strategies for BLSTM combined with CTC is therefore a challenging research topic for future work. Another possibility is to use writer-specific recognizers for the combination, which should result in a significantly better performance.

Bibliography

Alvarado, C. and Davis, R. (2006). Resolving ambiguities to create a natural computer-based sketching environment, in *Proc. Int. Conf. on Computer Graphics and Interactive Techniques*, pp. 24–30.

Aston, G. and Burnard, L. (1998). *The BNC Handbook: Exploring the British National Corpus with SARA* (Edinburgh Textbooks in Emperical Linguistics).

Bahlmann, C. and Burkhardt, H. (2004). The writer independent online handwriting recognition system *frog on hand* and cluster generative statistical dynamic time warping, *IEEE Trans. Pattern Analysis and Machine Intelligence* **26**, 3, pp. 299–310.

Bahlmann, C., Haasdonk, B. and Burkhardt, H. (2002). Online handwriting recognition with support vector machines – a kernel approach, in *Proc. 8th Int. Workshop on Frontiers in Handwriting Recognition*, pp. 49–54.

Baird, H. and Govindaraju, V. (eds.) (2004). *1st Int. Workshop on Document Image Analysis for Libraries*.

Bakis, R. (1976). Continuous speech recognition via centisecond acoustic states, *The Journal of the Acoustical Society of America* **59**, p. 97.

Baldi, P., Brunak, S., Frasconi, P., Pollastri, G. and Soda, G. (2001). Bidirectional dynamics for protein secondary structure prediction, *Lecture Notes in Computer Science* **1828**, pp. 80–104.

Baldi, P., Brunak, S., Frasconi, P., Soda, G. and Pollastri, G. (1999). Exploiting the past and the future in protein secondary structure prediction, *Bioinformatics* **15**, pp. 937–946.

Ball, G. R., Srihari, S. N. and Srinivasan, H. (2006). Segmentation-based and segmentation-free methods for spotting handwritten Arabic words, in *Proc. 10th Int. Workshop on Frontiers in Handwriting Recognition*, pp. 53–58.

Ballard, D. H. and Brown, C. M. (1982). *Computer Vision* (Prentice-Hall, Inc.).

Bandi, K. and Srihari, S. N. (2005). Writer demographic classification using bagging and boosting, in *Proc. 12th Conf. of the Int. Graphonomics Society*, pp. 133–137.

Bauer, L. (1993). *Manual of Information to Accompany the Wellington Corpus* of Written New Zealand English (Department of Linguistics, Victoria University, Wellington, New Zealand).

Beech, J. R. and Mackintosh, I. C. (2005). Do differences in sex hormones affect handwriting style? Evidence from digit ratio and sex role identity as determinants of the sex of handwriting, *Personality and Individual Differences* **39**, 2, pp. 459–468.

Bellman, R. and Dreyfus, S. (1962). Applied dynamic programming, *Princeton University Press* .

Bengio, Y. (1999). Markovian models for sequential data, *Neural Computing Surveys* **2**, pp. 129–162.

Bengio, Y., Simard, P. and Frasconi, P. (1994). Learning long-term dependencies with gradient descent is difficult, *IEEE Trans. Neural Networks* **5**, 2, pp. 157–166.

Bercu, S. and Lorette, G. (1993). On-line handwritten word recognition: an approach based on hidden Markov models, in *Proc. 3rd Int. Workshop on Frontiers in Handwriting Recognition*, pp. 385–390.

Bertolami, R. and Bunke, H. (2005). Multiple handwritten text recognition systems derived from specific integration of a language model, in *Proc. 8th Int. Conf. on Document Analysis and Recognition*, pp. 521–524.

Bertolami, R., Zimmermann, M. and Bunke, H. (2006). Rejection strategies for offline handwritten text line recognition, *Pattern Recognition Letters* **27**, 16, pp. 2005–2012.

Bourbakis, N. G. (1995). Handwriting recognition using a reduced character method and neural nets, in *Proc. SPIE Nonlinear Image Processing VI*, Vol. 2424, pp. 592–601.

Bourlard, H. A. and Morgan, N. (1994). *Connectionist Speech Recognition: a Hybrid Approach* (Kluwer Academic Publishers).

Brakensiek, A., Kosmala, A., Willett, D., Wang, W. and Rigoll, G. (1999). Performance evaluation of a new hybrid modeling technique for handwriting recognition using identical on-line and off-line data. in *Proc. 5th Int. Conf. on Document Analysis and Recognition, Bangalore, India*, pp. 446–449.

Brakensiek, A. and Rigoll, G. (2004). Handwritten address recognition using hidden Markov models, in A. Dengel et al. (ed.), *Reading and Learning, LNCS*, Vol. 2956 (Springer), pp. 103–122.

Bridle, J. S. (1990). Probabilistic interpretation of feedforward classification network outputs, with relationships to statistical pattern recognition, in F. F. Soulie and J. Herault (eds.), *Neurocomputing: Algorithms, Architectures and Applications* (Springer-Verlag), pp. 227–236.

Brill, E. (1992). A simple rule-based part of speech tagger, in *Proc. 3rd Conf. on Applied Natural Language Processing*, pp. 152–155.

Broom, M., Thompson, B. and et al. (1929). Sex differences in handwriting, *Journal of Applied Psychology* **13**, pp. 159–166.

Brown, P. F., deSouza, P. V., Mercer, R. L., Pietra, V. J. D. and Lai, J. C. (1992). Class-based n-gram models of natural language, *Computational Linguistics* **18**, 4, pp. 467–479.

Bunke, H. (2003). Recognition of cursive Roman handwriting – past present and future, in *Proc. 7th Int. Conf. on Document Analysis and Recognition*, Vol. 1, pp. 448–459.

Bunke, H., Roth, M. and Schukat-Talamazzini, E. G. (1995). Off-line cursive handwriting recognition using hidden Markov models, *Pattern Recognition* **28**, 9, pp. 1399–1413.

Caillault, E., Viard-Gaudin, C. and Ahmad, A. R. (2005a). MS-TDNN with global discriminant trainings, in *Proc. 8th Int. Conf. on Document Analysis and Recognition*, pp. 856–861.

Caillault, E., Viard-Gaudin, C. and Lallican, P. M. (2005b). Training of hybrid ANN/HMM systems for on-line handwritten word recognition, in *Proc. 12th Conf. of the Int. Graphonomics Society*, Vol. 1, pp. 212–216.

Cha, S.-H. and Srihari, S. N. (2001). Apriori algorithm for sub-category classification analysis of handwriting, in *Proc. 6th Int. Conf. on Document Analysis and Recognition*, pp. 1022–1025.

Chen, S. F. and Goodman, J. (1996). An empirical study of smoothing techniques for language modeling, in *Proc. 34th Annual Meeting of the Association for Computational Linguistics*, pp. 310–318.

Chevalier, S., Preteux, F., Geoffrois, E. and Lemaitre, M. (2005). A generic 2D approach of handwriting recognition, in *Proc. 8th Int. Conf. on Document Analysis and Recognition*, pp. 489–493.

Choisy, C. and Belaïd, A. (2000). Analytic word recognition without segmentation based on Markov random fields, in *Proc. 7th Int. Workshop on Frontiers in Handwriting Recognition*, pp. 487–492.

Collobert, R., Bengio, S. and Mariéthoz, J. (2002). Torch: a modular machine learning software library, IDIAP-RR 46, IDIAP.

Cramer, D. and Howitt, D. (2004). *The Sage Dictionary of Statistics: A Practical Resource for Students in the Social Sciences* (Sage Publications).

Czyz, J., Bengio, S., Marcel, C. and Vandendorpe, L. (2003). Scalability analysis of audio-visual person identity verification, in *Proc. 4th Int. Conf. on Audio-and Video-based Biometric Person Authentication*, pp. 752–760.

Czyz, J., Kittler, J. and Vandendorpe, L. (2004). Multiple classifier combination for face-based identity verification, *Pattern Recognition* **37**, 7, pp. 1459–1469.

Dempster, A. P., Laird, N. M. and Rubin, D. B. (1977). Maximum likelihood from incomplete data via the EM algorithm, *Journal of Royal Statistical Society B* **39**, 1, pp. 1–38.

Duda, R. O., Hart, P. E. and Stork, D. G. (2001). *Pattern Classification* (Wiley-Interscience Publication).

Esponda Argüero, M. (2004). *A New Algorithmic Framework for the Classroom and for the Internet*, Ph.D. thesis, Freie Universität Berlin, Institut für Informatik.

Fasel, B. and Luettin, J. (2003). Automatic facial expression analysis: a survey, *Pattern Recognition* **36**, 1, pp. 259–275.

Feng, H. and Wah, C. C. (2003). Online signature verification using a new extreme points warping technique, *Pattern Recognition Letters* **24**, pp. 2943–2951.

Fernández, S., Graves, A. and Schmidhuber, J. (2007). Sequence labelling in structured domains with hierarchical recurrent neural networks, in *Proc. 20th Int. Joint Conf. on Artificial Intelligence*, pp. 774–779.

Feynman, R. P., Leigthon, R. B. and Sands, M. (1977). *The Feynman Lectures on Physics 2 Volume II - Mainly Electromagnetism and Matter* (Massachusetts, Addison-Wesley Publishing Company).

Fink, G. A., Wienecke, M. and Sagerer, G. (2001). Video-based on-line handwriting recognition, in *Proc. 6th Int. Conf. on Document Analysis and Recognition*, pp. 226–230.

Fiscus, J. (1997). A post-processing system to yield reduced word error rates: recognizer output voting error reduction ROVER, in *IEEE Workshop on Automatic Speech Recognition and Understanding*, pp. 347–352.

Forney, G. D. (1973). The Viterbi algorithm, in *Proc. IEEE*, Vol. 61, pp. 268–278.

Francis, W. N. and Kucera, H. (1979). *Manual of Information to Accompany A Standard Corpus of Present-Day Edited American English, for use with Digital Computers* (Department of Linguistics, Brown University, Providence, USA).

Friedland, G., Knipping, L., Schulte, J. and Tapia, E. (2004). E-Chalk: a lecture recording system using the chalkboard metaphor, *Int. Journal of Interactive Technology and Smart Education (ITSE)* **1**, pp. 9–20.

Fukada, T., Schuster, M. and Sagisaka, Y. (1999). Phoneme boundary estimation using bidirectional recurrent neural networks and its applications, *Systems and Computers in Japan* **30**, 4, pp. 20–30.

Gauvain, J. and Lee, C. (1994). Maximum a-posteriori estimation for multivariate Gaussian mixture observation of Markov chains, *IEEE Trans. Specch & Audio Processing* **2**, pp. 291–298.

Gauvain, J.-L. and Lee, C.-H. (1992). MAP estimation of continuous density HMM: Theory and applications, in *Proc. of DARPA Speech and Natural Language Workshop*, pp. 272–277.

Gers, F., Schraudolph, N. and Schmidhuber, J. (2002). Learning precise timing with LSTM recurrent networks, *Journal of Machine Learning Research* **3**, pp. 115–143.

Gopisetty, S., Lorie, R., Mao, J., Mohiuddin, M., Sorin, A. and Yair, E. (1996). Automated forms-processing software and services, *IBM Journal of Research and Development* **40**, 2, pp. 211–230.

Gorski, N. (1997). Optimizing error-reject trade off in recognition systems, in *Proc. 4th Int. Conf. on Document Analysis and Recognition*, Vol. 2, pp. 1092–1096.

Graves, A., Fernández, S., Gomez, F. and Schmidhuber, J. (2006). Connectionist temporal classification: labelling unsegmented sequence data with recurrent neural networks, in *Proc. Int. Conf. on Machine Learning*, pp. 369–376.

Graves, A., Fernández, S. and Schmidhuber, J. (2005). Bidirectional LSTM networks for improved phoneme classification and recognition, in *Proc. Int. Conf. on Artificial Neural Networks* (Warsaw, Poland), pp. 799–804.

Graves, A., Liwicki, M., Fernández, S., Bertolami, R., Bunke, H. and Schmidhuber, J. (2008). Bidirectional long short-term memory networks for on-line handwriting recognition, *IEEE Trans. Pattern Analysis and Machine Intelligence* Accepted for publication.

Graves, A. and Schmidhuber, J. (2005). Framewise phoneme classification with bidirectional LSTM and other neural network architectures, *Neural Networks* **18**, 5–6, pp. 602–610.

Grudin, M. A. (2000). On internal representations in face recognition systems, *Pattern Recognition* **33**, 7, pp. 1161–1177.

Günter, S. and Bunke, H. (2004a). HMM-based handwritten word recognition: on the optimization of the number of states, training iterations and Gaussian components, *Pattern Recognition* **37**, pp. 2069–2079.

Günter, S. and Bunke, H. (2004b). Multiple classifier systems in off-line handwritten word recognition on the influence of training set and vocabulary size, *Int. Journal of Pattern Recognition and Artificial Intelligence* **18**, pp. 1303–1320.

Gupta, J. and McCabe, A. (1997). A review of dynamic handwritten signature verification, Tech. rep., Departement of Computer Science, James Cook University, Australia.

Guyon, I., Schomaker, L., Plamondon, R., Liberman, M. and Janet, S. (1994). Unipen project of on-line data exchange and recognizer benchmarks, in *Proc. 12th Int. Conf. on Pattern Recognition*, pp. 29–33.

Haeb-Umbach, R. and Ney, H. (1994). Improvements in beam search for 10000-word continuous-speechrecognition, *Trans. Speech and Audio Processing* **2**, pp. 353–356.

Hamid, S. and Loewenthal, K. M. (1996). Inferring gender from handwriting in Urdu and English, *The Journal of social psychology* **136**, 6, pp. 778–782.

Hammond, T. and Davis, R. (2002). Tahuti: a geometrical sketch recognition system for UML class diagrams, in *Papers from AAAI Spring Symposium on Sketch Understanding*, pp. 59–66.

Hattori, T., Izumi, T., Kitajima, H. and Yamasaki, T. (2004). Kansei information extraction from character patterns using a modified fourier transform, in *Proc. Sino-Japan Symposium on KANSEI & Artificial Life*, pp. 36–39.

Haykin, S. (1994). *Neural Networks: a Comprehensive Foundation* (Prentice Hall PTR).

Hecker, M. R. (1996). *Die Untersuchung der Geschlechtsspezifitt der Handschrift mittels Rechnergesttzter Merkmalsextraktionsverfahren*, Ph.D. thesis, Humboldt-University, Berlin.

Hochreiter, S., Bengio, Y., Frasconi, P. and Schmidhuber, J. (2001). Gradient flow in recurrent nets: the difficulty of learning long-term dependencies, in S. C. Kremer and J. F. Kolen (eds.), *A Field Guide to Dynamical Recurrent Neural Networks* (IEEE Press), pp. 237–243.

Hochreiter, S. and Schmidhuber, J. (1997). Long short-term memory, *Neural Computing* **9**, 8, pp. 1735–1780.

Hong, J. I. and Landay, J. A. (2000). SATIN: a toolkit for informal ink-based applications, in *Proc. 13th Annual ACM Symposium on User Interface Software and Technology*, pp. 63–72.

Hu, J., Lim, S. G. and Brown, M. K. (2000). Writer independent on-line handwriting recognition using an HMM approach, *Pattern Recognition* **33**, 1, pp. 133–147.

Hu, J. Y., Brown, M. K. and Turin, W. (1996). HMM based online handwriting recognition, *IEEE Trans. Pattern Analysis and Machine Intelligence* **18**, 10, pp. 1039–1045.

Huang, C. and Srihari, S. N. (2006). Mapping transkripts to handwritten text, in *Proc. 10th Int. Workshop on Frontiers in Handwriting Recognition*, pp. 15–20.

Huang, Y. S. and Suen, C. Y. (1995). A method of combining multiple experts for the recognition of unconstrained handwritten numerals, *IEEE Trans. Pattern Analysis and Machine Intelligence* **17**, 1, pp. 90–94.

Huber, R. A. (1999). *Handwriting Identification: Facts and Fundamentals* (CRC Press).

Hull, J. J. (1994). A database for handwritten text recognition research, *IEEE Trans. Pattern Analysis and Machine Intelligence* **16**, 5, pp. 550–554.

Ide, N. and Veronis, J. (1995). *Text Encoding Initiative: Background and Contexts* (Kluwer Academic Publishers Norwell).

Impedovo, S., Wang, P. and Bunke, H. (1997). *Automatic Bankcheck Processing* (World Scientific).

Jäger, S., Manke, S., Reichert, J. and Waibel, A. (2001). Online handwriting recognition: the NPen++ recognizer, *Int. Journal on Document Analysis and Recognition* **3**, 3, pp. 169–180.

Jain, A. K., Griess, F. D. and Connell, S. D. (2002). On-line signature verification, *Pattern Recognition* **35**, pp. 2663–2972.

Jain, A. K., Namboodiri, A. M. and Subrahmonia, J. (2001). Structure in on-line documents, in *Proc. 6th Int. Conf. on Document Analysis and Recognition*, pp. 844–848.

Jelinek, F. (1998). *Statistical Methods for Speech Recognition* (The MIT Press), ISBN 0262100665.

Johansson, S. (1986). *The tagged LOB Corpus: User's Manual* (Norwegian Computing Centre for the Humanities, Norway).

Johnson, M. T. (2005). Capacity and complexity of HMM duration modeling techniques, *IEEE Signal Processing Letters* **12**, 5, pp. 407–410.

K. Sirlantzis, M. C. F. and Hoque, M. S. (2001). Genetic algorithms for multi-classifier system configuration: a case study in character recognition, in *Proc. 2nd Workshop on Multiple Classifier Systems*, pp. 99–108.

Kavallieratou, E., Fakotakis, N. and Kokkinakis, G. (2002). An unconstrained handwriting recognition system, *Int. Journal on Document Analysis and Recognition* **4**, 4, pp. 226–242.

Kennard, D. J. and Barrett, W. A. (2006). Separating lines of text in free-form handwritten historical documents, in *Proc. 1st Int. Workshop on Document Image Analysis for Libraries*, pp. 12–23.

Kim, S.-H., Jeong, C. B., Kwag, H. K. and Suen, C. Y. (2002). Word segmentation of printed text lines based on gap clustering and special symbol detection, in *Proc. 16th Int. Conf. on Pattern Recognition*, Vol. 2, pp. 320–323.

Knerr, S., Anisimov, V., Baret, O., Gorsky, N., Price, D. and Simon, J. (1997).

The A2iA INTERCHEQUE system: Courtesy amount and legal amount recognition for french checks, *Int. Journal of Pattern Recognition and Artificial Intelligence* **11**, 4, pp. 505–548.

Knipping, L. (2005). *An Electronic Chalkboard for Classroom and Distance Teaching*, Ph.D. thesis, Freie Universität Berlin, Institut für Informatik.

Kornfield, E. M., Manmatha, R. and Allan, J. (2004). Text alignment with handwritten documents, in *Proc. 1st Int. Workshop on Document Image Analysis for Libraries*, pp. 195–205.

Krupina, O. (2005). *NeuroSim: Neural Simulation System with a Client-Server Architecture*, Ph.D. thesis, Freie Universität Berlin, Institut für Informatik.

Kudo, M. and Sklansky, J. (2000). Comparison of algorithms that select features for pattern classifiers, *Pattern Recognition* **33**, 1, pp. 25–41.

Kuncheva, L. I. (2004). *Combining Pattern Classifiers: Methods and Algorithms* (John Wiley & Sons Inc).

Lamere, P., Kwok, P., Walker, W., Gouvea, E., Singh, R., Raj, B. and Wolf, P. (2003). Design of the CMU Sphinx-4 decoder, in *Proc. 8th European Conf. on Speech Communication and Technology*, pp. 1181–1184.

Lavrenko, V., Rath, T. M. and Manmatha, R. (2004). Holistic word recognition for handwritten historical documents, in *Proc. 1st Int. Workshop on Document Image Analysis for Libraries*, pp. 278–287.

Leclerc, F. and Plamondon, R. (1994). Automatic signature verification: the state of the art 1989–1993, in R. Plamondon (ed.), *Progress in Automatic Signature Verification* (World Scientific Publ. Co.), pp. 13–19.

Lee, S.-W. (1996). Off-line recognition of totally unconstrained handwritten numerals using multilayer cluster neural network, *IEEE Trans. Pattern Analysis and Machine Intelligence* **18**, 6, pp. 648–652.

Leggeter, C. J. and Woodland, P. C. (1995). Maximum likelihood linear regression for speaker adaptation of continuous density hidden Markov models, *Computer Speech and Language* **9**, pp. 171–185.

Li, Y., Zheng, Y., Doermann, D. and Jğer, S. (2006). A new algorithm for detecting text line in handwritten documents, in *Proc. 10th Int. Workshop on Frontiers in Handwriting Recognition*, pp. 35–40.

Lin, J., Newman, M. W., Hong, J. I. and Landay, J. A. (2000). DENIM: finding a tighter fit between tools and practice for web site design, in *Proc. Conf. on Human Factors in Computing Systems*, pp. 510–517.

Liu, C.-L. and Nakagawa, M. (2001). Evaluation of prototype learning algorithms for nearest-neighbor classifier in application to handwritten character recognition, *Pattern Recognition* **34**, 3, pp. 601–615.

Liwicki, M. and Bunke, H. (2005a). Handwriting recognition of whiteboard notes, in *Proc. 12th Conf. of the Int. Graphonomics Society*, pp. 118–122.

Liwicki, M. and Bunke, H. (2005b). IAM-OnDB – an on-line English sentence database acquired from handwritten text on a whiteboard, in *Proc. 8th Int. Conf. on Document Analysis and Recognition*, Vol. 2, pp. 956–961.

Liwicki, M. and Bunke, H. (2006). HMM-based on-line recognition of handwritten whiteboard notes, in *Proc. 10th Int. Workshop on Frontiers in Handwriting Recognition*, pp. 595–599.

Liwicki, M. and Bunke, H. (2007a). Combining on-line and off-line systems for handwriting recognition, in *Proc. 9th Int. Conf. on Document Analysis and Recognition*, Vol. 1, pp. 372–376.

Liwicki, M. and Bunke, H. (2007b). Feature selection for on-line handwriting recognition of whiteboard notes, in *Proc. 13th Conf. of the Int. Graphonomics Society*, pp. 101–105.

Liwicki, M. and Bunke, H. (2007c). Handwriting recognition of whiteboard notes – studying the influence of training set size and type, *Int. Journal of Pattern Recognition and Artificial Intelligence* **21**, 1, pp. 83–98.

Liwicki, M. and Bunke, H. (2008). Writer-dependent handwriting recognition of whiteboard notes, Submitted.

Liwicki, M., Bunke, H., Pittman, J. A. and Knerr, S. (2008a). Combining diverse systems for handwritten text line recognition, Submitted.

Liwicki, M., Graves, A., Bunke, H. and Schmidhuber, J. (2007a). A novel approach to on-line handwriting recognition based on bidirectional long short-term memory networks, in *Proc. 9th Int. Conf. on Document Analysis and Recognition*, Vol. 1, pp. 367–371.

Liwicki, M., Indermühle, E. and Bunke, H. (2007b). On-line handwritten text line detection using dynamic programming, in *Proc. 9th Int. Conf. on Document Analysis and Recognition*, Vol. 1, pp. 447–451.

Liwicki, M. and Knipping, L. (2005). Recognizing and simulating sketched logic circuits, in *Proc. 9th Int. Conf. on Knowledge-Based Intelligent Information & Engineering Systems*, *LNCS*, Vol. 3683 (Springer), pp. 588–594.

Liwicki, M., Scherz, M. and Bunke, H. (2006a). Word extraction from on-line handwritten text lines, in *Proc. 18th Int. Conf. on Pattern Recognition*, Vol. 2, pp. 929–933.

Liwicki, M., Schlapbach, A. and Bunke, H. (2008b). Automatic gender detection using on-line and off-line information, Submitted.

Liwicki, M., Schlapbach, A. and Bunke, H. (2008c). Writer-dependent recognition of handwritten whiteboard notes in smart meeting room environments, Submitted.

Liwicki, M., Schlapbach, A., Bunke, H., Bengio, S., Mariéthoz, J. and Richiardi, J. (2006b). Writer identification for smart meeting room systems, in *Proc. 7th IAPR Workshop on Document Analysis Systems*, *LNCS*, Vol. 3872 (Springer), pp. 186–195.

Liwicki, M., Schlapbach, A., Loretan, P. and Bunke, H. (2007c). Automatic detection of gender and handedness from on-line handwriting, in *Proc. 13th Conf. of the Int. Graphonomics Society*, pp. 179–183.

Mahadevan, U. and Srihari, S. N. (1996). Hypothesis generation for word separation in handwritten lines, in *Proc. 5th Int. Workshop on Frontiers in Handwriting Recognition*, pp. 453–456.

Manmatha, R. and Rothfeder, J. L. (2005). A scale space approach for automatically segmenting words from historical handwritten documents, *IEEE Trans. Pattern Analysis and Machine Intelligence* **27**, pp. 1212–1225.

Mariéthoz, J. and Bengio, S. (2002). A comparative study of adaptation methods for speaker verification, in *Int. Conf. on Spoken Language Processing* (Denver, CO, USA), pp. 581–584.

Marti, U.-V. (2000). *Off-line Recognition of Handwritten Texts*, Ph.D. thesis, IAM, University of Bern.

Marti, U.-V. and Bunke, H. (2001a). Text line segmentation and word recognition in a system for general writer independent handwriting recognition, in *Proc. 6th Int. Conf. on Document Analysis and Recognition*, pp. 159–163.

Marti, U.-V. and Bunke, H. (2001b). Use of positional information in sequence alignment for multiple classifier combination, in J. Kittler and F. Roli (eds.), *2nd Int. Workshop on Multiple Classifier Systems*, LNCS 2096 (Springer), pp. 388–398.

Marti, U.-V. and Bunke, H. (2001c). Using a statistical language model to improve the performance of an HMM-based cursive handwriting recognition system, *Int. Journal of Pattern Recognition and Artificial Intelligence* **15**, pp. 65–90.

Marti, U.-V. and Bunke, H. (2002). The IAM-database: an English sentence database for offline handwriting recognition, *Int. Journal on Document Analysis and Recognition* **5**, pp. 39–46.

Marukatat, S., Artières, T., Dorizzi, B. and Gallinari, P. (2001). Sentence recognition through hybrid neuro-Markovian modelling, in *Proc. 6th Int. Conf. on Document Analysis and Recognition*, pp. 731–735.

McCowan, L., Gatica-Perez, D., Bengio, S., Lathoud, G., Barnard, M. and Zhang, D. (2005). Automatic analysis of multimodal group actions in meetings, *IEEE Trans. Pattern Analysis and Machine Intelligence* **27**, 3, pp. 305–317.

Melin, H., Koolwaaij, J., Lindberg, J. and Bimbot, F. (1998). A comparative evaluation of variance flooring techniques in HMM-based speaker verification, in *Proc. 5th Int. Conf. on Spoken Language Processing*, pp. 2379–2382.

Moore, D. (2002). The IDIAP smart meeting room, Tech. rep., IDIAP-Com.

Morgan, N., Baron, D., Edwards, J., Ellis, D., Gelbart, D., Janin, A., Pfau, T., Shriberg, E. and Stolcke, A. (2001). The meeting project at ICSI, in *Human Language Technologies Conf.*, pp. 246–252.

Munich, M. E. and Perona, P. (1996). Visual input for pen-based computers, in *Proc. 3rd Int. Conf. on Pattern Recognition*, pp. 33–37.

Murase, H. and Wakahara, T. (1986). Online hand-sketched figure recognition, *Pattern Recognition* **19**, 2, pp. 147–160.

Newhall, S. (1926). Sex differences in handwriting, *Journal of Applied Psychology* **10**, pp. 151–161.

Oh, I.-S. and Suen, C. Y. (2002). A class-modular feedforward neural network for handwriting recognition, *Pattern Recognition* **35**, 1, pp. 229–244.

Oudot, L., Prevost, L. and Milgram, M. (2004). An activation-verification model for on-line texts recognition, in *Proc. 9th Int. Workshop on Frontiers in Handwriting Recognition*, pp. 485–490.

Perraud, F., Viard-Gaudin, C. and Morin, E. (2006). Language independent statistical models for on-line handwriting recognition, in *Int. Workshop on Frontiers in Handwriting Recognition*, pp. 435–440.

Pitrelli, J. and Perrone, M. P. (2003). Confidence-scoring post-processing for off-line handwritten-character recognition verification, in *Proc. 7th Int. Conf. on Document Analysis and Recognition*, Vol. 1, pp. 278–282.

Pittman, J. A. (2007). Handwriting recognition: Tablet pc text input, *Computer* **40**, 9, pp. 49–54.

Plamondon, R. and Lorette, G. (1989). Automatic signature verification and writer identification – the state of the art, in *Pattern Recognition*, Vol. 22, pp. 107–131.

Plamondon, R. and Srihari, S. N. (2000). On-line and off-line handwriting recognition: a comprehensive survey, *IEEE Trans. Pattern Analysis and Machine Intelligence* **22**, 1, pp. 63–84.

Pudil, P., Novovičová, J. and Kittler, J. (1994). Floating search methods in feature selection, *Pattern Recognition Letters* **15**, 11, pp. 1119–1125.

Rabiner, L. R. (1989). A tutorial on hidden Markov models and selected applications in speech recognition, *Proc. IEEE* **77**, 2, pp. 257–286.

Rath, T. M. and Manmatha, R. (2003). Features for word spotting in historical manuscripts, in *Proc. 7th Int. Conf. on Document Analysis and Recognition*, pp. 218–222.

Reiter, S. and Rigoll, G. (2004). Segmentation and classification of meeting events using multiple classifier fusion and dynamic programming, in *Proc. 17th Int. Conf. on Pattern Recognition*, pp. 434–437.

Reppen, R. and Ide, N. (2004). The American national corpus: overall goals and the first release, *Journal of English Linguistics* **32**, pp. 105–113.

Reynolds, D. A. (1995). Speaker identification and verification using Gaussian mixture speaker models, *Speech Communication* **17**, pp. 91–108.

Reynolds, D. A., Quatieri, T. F. and Dunn, R. B. (2000). Speaker verification using adapted Gaussian mixture models, *Digital Signal Processing* **10**, pp. 19–41.

Richiardi, J. and Drygajlo, A. (2003). Gaussian mixture models for on-line signature verification, in *Proc. 2003 ACM SIGMM Workshop on Biometrics Methods and Applications*, pp. 115–122.

Richiardi, J., Ketabdar, H. and Drygajlo, A. (2005). Local and global feature selection for on-line signature verification, in *Proc. 8th Int. Conf. on Document Analysis and Recognition*, pp. 625–629.

Rigoll, G., Kosmala, A. and Willett, D. (1998). A new hybrid approach to large vocabulary cursive handwriting recognition, in *Proc. 14th Int. Conf. on Pattern Recognition*, pp. 1512–1514.

Robinson, A. J. (1994). An application of recurrent nets to phone probability estimation, *IEEE Trans. Neural Networks* **5**, 2, pp. 298–305.

Rojas, R. (1996). *Neural Networks – A Systematic Introduction* (Springer-Verlag).

Rojas, R., Knipping, L., Raffel, W. and Friedland, G. (2001). Elektronische Kreide: eine Java-Multimedia-Tafel für den Präsenz- und Fernunterricht, *Informatik: Forschung und Entwicklung* **16**, pp. 159–168.

Rosenfeld, R. (2000). Two decades of statistical language modeling: Where do we go from here? in *Proc. IEEE*, Vol. 88, pp. 1270–1278.

Rossignol, S., Willems, D., Neumann, A. and Vuurpijl, L. (2004). Mode detection and incremental recognition, in *Proc. 9th Int. Workshop on Frontiers in Handwriting Recognition*, pp. 597–602.

Sanderson, C. and Paliwal, K. K. (2003). Fast features for face authentication under illumination direction changes, *Pattern Recognition Letters* **24**, 14, pp. 2409–2419.

Sayre, K. M. (1973). Machine recognition of handwritten words: a project report, *Pattern Recognition* **5**, 3, pp. 213–228.

Scheidat, T., Wolf, F. and Vielhauer, C. (2006). Analyzing handwriting biometrics in metadata context, in *Proc. 8th SPIE conf. at the Security, Steganography, and Watermarking of Multimedia Contents*, Vol. 6072, pp. 182–193.

Schenk, J. and Rigoll, G. (2006). Novel hybrid NN/HMM modelling techniques for on-line handwriting recognition, in *Proc. 10th Int. Workshop on Frontiers in Handwriting Recognition*, pp. 619–623.

Schenkel, M., Guyon, I. and Henderson, D. (1995). On-line cursive script recognition using time delay neural networks and hidden Markov models, *Machine Vision and Applications* **8**, pp. 215–223.

Schlapbach, A. and Bunke, H. (2006). Off-line writer identification using Gaussian mixture models, in *Proc. 18th Int. Conf. on Pattern Recognition*, Vol. 3, pp. 992–995.

Schlapbach, A., Kilchherr, V. and Bunke, H. (2005). Improving writer identification by means of feature selection and extraction, in *Proc. 8th Int. Conf. on Document Analysis and Recognition*, pp. 131–135.

Schlapbach, A., Liwicki, M. and Bunke, H. (2008). A writer identification system for on-line whiteboard data, *Pattern Recognition* **41**, pp. 2381–2397.

Schomaker, L. (1993). Using stroke- or character-based self-organizing maps in the recognition of on-line, connected cursive script, *Pattern Recognition* **26**, 3, pp. 443–450.

Schomaker, L. (1998). From handwriting analysis to pen-computer applications, *IEE Electronics & Communication Engineering Journal* **10**, 2, pp. 93–102.

Schuster, M. and Paliwal, K. K. (1997). Bidirectional recurrent neural networks, *IEEE Trans. Signal Processing* **45**, pp. 2673–2681.

Senior, A. W. and Robinson, A. J. (1998). An off-line cursive handwriting recognition system, *IEEE Trans. Pattern Analysis and Machine Intelligence* **20**, 3, pp. 309–321.

Shi, Z. and Govindaraju, V. (2004). Historical document image enhancement using background light intensity normalization, in *Proc. 17th Int. Conf. on Pattern Recognition*, Vol. 1, pp. 473–476.

Shilman, M., Wei, Z., Raghupathy, S., Simard, P. and Jones, D. (2003). Discerning structure from freeform handwritten notes, in *Proc. 7th Int. Conf. on Document Analysis and Recognition*, Vol. 1, pp. 60–65.

S.Knerr and E.Augustin (1998). A neural network-hidden Markov model hybrid for cursive word recognition, in *Int. Conf. on Pattern Recognition*, Vol. 2, pp. 1518–1520.

Srihari, S. N. (2000). Handwritten address interpretation: a task of many pattern recognition problems, *Int. Journal of Pattern Recognition and Artificial Intelligence* **14**, 5, pp. 663–674.

Srihari, S. N. and Kim, G. (1997). PENMAN: a system for reading unconstrained handwritten page images, in *Symposium on Document Image Understanding Technology*, pp. 142–153.

Srihari, S. N. and Shi, Z. (2004). Forensic handwritten document retrieval system, in *Proc. 1st Int. Workshop on Document Image Analysis for Libraries*, pp. 188–194.

Starner, T., Makhoul, J., Schwartz, R. and Chou, G. (1994). Online cursive handwriting recognition using speech recognition techniques, in *Int. Conf. on Acoustics, Speech and Signal Processing*, Vol. 5, pp. 125–128.

Steinherz, T., Rivlin, E. and Intrator, N. (1999). Offline cursive script word recognition – a survey, *Int. Journal on Document Analysis and Recognition* **2**, 2–3, pp. 90–110.

Suen, C. Y., Kim, K., Xu, Q., Kim, J. and Lam, L. (2000). Handwriting recognition – the last frontiers, in *Proc. 15th Int. Conf. on Pattern Recognition*, Vol. 4, pp. 4001–4010.

Szummer, M. and Qi, Y. (2004). Contextual recognition of hand-drawn diagrams with conditional random fields, in *Proc. 9th Int. Workshop on Frontiers in Handwriting Recognition*, pp. 32–37.

Taira, E., Uchida, S. and Sakoe, H. (2004). Nonuniform slant correction for handwritten word recognition, *IEICE Trans. Information & Systems* **E87-D**, 5, pp. 1247–1253.

Tapia, E. and Rojas, R. (2003). Recognition of on-line handwritten mathematical formulas in the E-Chalk system, in *Proc. 7th Int. Conf. on Document Analysis and Recognition*, pp. 980–984.

Tappert, C. C., Suen, C. Y. and Wakahara, T. (1990). The state of the art in online handwriting recognition, *IEEE Trans. Pattern Analysis and Machine Intelligence* **12**, 8, pp. 787–808.

Tenwolde, H. (1934). More on sex differences in handwriting, *Journal of Applied Psychology* **18**, pp. 705–710.

Varga, T. and Bunke, H. (2005). Tree structure for word extraction from handwritten text lines, in *Proc. 8th Int. Conf. on Document Analysis and Recognition*, Vol. 1, pp. 352–356.

Velek, O., Jäger, S. and Nakagawa, M. (2003). Accumulated-recognition-rate normalization for combining multiple on/off-line Japanese character classifiers tested on a large database, in *Proc. 4th Workshop on Multiple Classifier Systems*, pp. 196–205.

Velek, O., Liu, C.-L., Jäger, S. and Nakagawa, M. (2002). An improved approach to generating realistic Kanji character images from on-line characters and its benefit to off-line recognition performance, in *Proc. 16th Int. Conf. on Pattern Recognition*, pp. 588–591.

Viard-Gaudin, C., Lallican, P. M., Binter, P. and Knerr, S. (1999). The IRESTE on/off (IRONOFF) dual handwriting database, in *Proc. 5th Int. Conf. on Document Analysis and Recognition*, pp. 455–458.

Vinciarelli, A. (2002). A survey on off-line cursive script recognition, *Pattern Recognition* **35**, 7, pp. 1433–1446.

Vinciarelli, A. and Bengio, S. (2002). Writer adaptation techniques in HMM based off-line cursive script recognition, *Pattern Recognition Letters* **23**, 8, pp. 905–916.

Vinciarelli, A. and Perrone, M. (2003). Combining online and offline handwriting recognition, in *Proc. 7th Int. Conf. on Document Analysis and Recognition*, pp. 844–848.

Vuurpijl, L., Niels, R., van Erp, M., Schomaker, L. and Ratzlaff, E. (2004). Verifying the UNIPEN devset, in *Proc. 9th Int. Workshop on Frontiers in Handwriting Recognition*, pp. 586–591.

Wagner, R. and Fischer, M. (1974). The string-to-string correction problem, *Journal of the ACM* **21**, pp. 168–173.

Waibel, A., Schultz, T., Bett, M., Malkin, R., Rogina, I., Stiefelhagen, R. and Yang, J. (2003). SMaRT: the smart meeting room task at ISL, in *Proc. IEEE ICASSP*, Vol. 4, pp. 752–755.

Wang, L. and Jiang, T. (1994). On the complexity of multiple sequence alignment, *Journal of Computational Biology* **1**, 4, pp. 337–348.

Wellner, P., Flynn, M. and Guillemot, M. (2004). Browsing recorded meetings with Ferret, in *Machine Learning for Multimodal Interaction*, pp. 12–21.

Wenyin, L. (2003). On-line graphics recognition: state-of-the-art, in *5th Int. Workshop on Graphics Recognition*, pp. 291–304.

Wilfong, G., Sinden, F. and Ruedisueli, L. (1996). On-line recognition of handwritten symbols, *IEEE Trans. Pattern Analysis and Machine Intelligence* **18**, 9, pp. 935–940.

Wilkinson, R., Geist, J., Janet, S., Grother, P., Burges, C., Creecy, R., Hammond, B., Hull, J., Larsen, N., Vogl, T. and Wilson, C. (eds.) (1992). *1st Census Optical Character Recognition Systems Conf.*

Williams, R. J. and Zipser, D. (1990). Gradient-based learning algorithms for recurrent connectionist networks, in Y. Chauvin and D. E. Rumelhart (eds.), *Backpropagation: Theory, Architectures, and Applications* (Erlbaum, Hillsdale, NJ), pp. 433–486.

Wiskott, L., Fellous, J.-M., Krüger, N. and von der Malsburg, C. (1995). Face recognition and gender determination, in *Proc. Int. Workshop on Automatic Face- and Gesture-Recognition*, pp. 92–97.

Wu, B., Ai, H. and Huang, C. (2003). *Audio- and Video-Based Biometric Person Authentication, LNCS*, Vol. 2688, chap. *LUT-Based Adaboost for Gender Classification* (Springer), pp. 104–110.

Ye, M., Sutanto, H., Raghupathy, S., Li, C. and Shilman, M. (2005). Grouping text lines in freeform handwritten notes, in *Proc. 8th Int. Conf. on Document Analysis and Recognition*, pp. 367–373.

Ye, X., Cheriet, M. and Suen, C. Y. (2001). A generic method of cleaning and enhancing handwritten data from business forms, *Int. Journal on Document Analysis and Recognition* **4**, 2, pp. 84–96.

Ye, X., Cheriet, M. and Suen, C. Y. (2002). StrCombo: combination of string recognizers, *Pattern Recognition Letters* **23**, pp. 381–394.

Young, S., Russel, N. and JHS, T. (1989). Token passing: a simple conceptual model for connected speech recognition systems, Tech. rep., Cambridge University Engineering Dept.

Yu, B. and Jain, A. K. (1996). A robust and fast skew detection of algorithm for generic documents, *Pattern Recognition* **29**, 10, pp. 1599–1629.

Zanibbi, R., Blostein, D. and Cordy, J. R. (2004). A survey of table recognition: Models, observations, transformations and inferences, *Int. Journal on Document Analysis and Recognition* **7**, 1, pp. 1–16.

Zimmermann, M. and Bunke, H. (2002a). Automatic segmentation of the IAM off-line database for handwritten English text, in *Proc. 16th Int. Conf. on Pattern Recognition*, Vol. 4, pp. 35–39.

Zimmermann, M. and Bunke, H. (2002b). Hidden Markov model length optimization for handwriting recognition systems, in *Proc. 8th Int. Workshop on Frontiers in Handwriting Recognition*, pp. 369–374.

Zimmermann, M. and Bunke, H. (2004). Optimizing the integration of a statistical language model in HMM-based offline handwritten text recognition, in *Proc. 17th Int. Conf. on Pattern Recognition*, pp. 541–544.

Zimmermann, M., Chappelier, J.-C. and Bunke, H. (2003). Parsing *n*-best lists of handwritten sentences, in *Proc. 7th Int. Conf. on Document Analysis and Recognition*, pp. 572–576.

Index